BEST of the BEST
from the
Great Plains

Selected Recipes from the
FAVORITE COOKBOOKS
of North Dakota, South Dakota,
Nebraska and Kansas

BEST
of the BEST
from the

Great Plains

Selected Recipes from the
FAVORITE COOKBOOKS
of North Dakota, South Dakota
Nebraska and Kansas

EDITED BY
Gwen McKee
AND
Barbara Moseley

Illustrated by Tupper England

QUAIL RIDGE PRESS
Preserving America's Food Heritage

Recipe Collection © 1999 Quail Ridge Press, Inc.

All About Bar-B-Q Kansas City Style © 1997 Pig Out Publication; *The Best Little Cookbook in the West* © 1996 Loaun Werner Vaad; *A Cooking Affaire I & II* © 1984 and 1991 Jan Bertoglio and JoLe Hudson; *Easy Livin' Microwave Cooking* © 1989 Karen Kangas Dwyer; *Easy Livin' Microwave Cooking for the Holidays* © 1989 Karen Kangas Dwyer; *Easy Livin' Low-Calorie Microwave Cooking* © 1990 Karen Kangas Dwyer; *Egg Gravy* © 1994 Linda K. Hubalek; *Give Mom a Rest Cookbook* ©1998 Rita Hewson; *Hall's Potato Harvest Cookbook* ©1993 by the Hall Family; *Heart of the Home Recipes* © 1980 Capper Press, Inc.; *If It Tastes Good, Who Cares?* © 1992 Spiritseekers Publishing; *If It Tastes Good, Who Cares? II* © 1992 Spiritseekers Publishing; *In the Kitchen with Kate* © 1995 Capper Press, Inc.; *Kansas City Barbeque Society Cookbook* © 1998 Kansas City Barbeque Society; *The Kearney 125ᵗʰ Anniversary Community Cookbook* © 1998 Cookbooks by Morris Press; *License to Cook Kansas Style* © 1994 Linda Hubalek; *More Heart of the Home Recipes* © 1982 Capper Press, Inc.; *The Mormon Trail Cookbook* © 1997 Cookbooks by Morris Press; *North Dakota...Where Food is Love* © 1994 Marcella Richman; *The Oregon Trail* © 1993 Cookbooks Morris Press; *Presentations* ©1993 Friends of Lied; *Pumpkin, Winter Squash and Carrot Cookbook* © 1994 Litchville Committee 2000; *Pure Prairie* © 1995 Pig Out Publications; *Que Queens: Easy Grilling and Simple Smoking* © 1997 Pig Out Publications; *Readers' Favorite Recipes* © 1995 Capper Press, Inc.; *REC Family Cookbook* ©1987 North Dakota Association of Rural Electric Cooperatives; *Recipes Worth Sharing* © 1997 Janet Majure; *Ritzy Rhubarb Secrets Cookbook* © 1992 Litchville Committee 2000; *Savor the Inns of Kansas* © 1994 Tracy M. Winters and Phyllis Y. Winters; *South Dakota Sunrise* © 1997 Tracy Winters; *A Taste of Prairie Life* © 1996 Loaun Werner Vaad; *Taste the Good Life! Nebraska Cookbook* © Cookbooks by Morris Press; *Treasures of the Great Midwest* © 1995 Junior League of Wyandotte & Johnson Counties; *Y Cook?* © 1994 The Fargo-Moorhead YWCA.

Library of Congress Cataloging-in-Publication Data

Best of the best from the Great Plains: selected recipes from the favorite
cookbooks of North Dakota, South Dakota, Nebraska and Kansas /
edited by Gwen McKee and Barbara Moseley.
    p. cm.
Includes index.
ISBN 0-937552-85-2
1. Cookery, American. 2. Cookery—Great Plains. I. McKee, Gwen.
II. Moseley, Barbara.
TX715.B485647 1999
641.5973—dc21   99-17195
                                              CIP

QUAIL RIDGE PRESS
1-800-343-1583 • Email: info@quailridge.com • Website: www.quailridge.com

CONTENTS

Chimney Rock, the slender spire soaring some 500 feet up from the valley floor, signaled to Oregon Trail travelers the end of the prairie and the beginning of the rugged high plains. Bayard, Nebraska.

PREFACE

Follow the Missouri River just as Lewis and Clark did some 200 years ago through the wild and splendid lands of North Dakota, cutting through the middle of South Dakota, then outlining the eastern borders of Nebraska and Kansas, and you will have touched on the lands that helped produce some of the most outstanding foods of the Great Plains.

We welcome you to take a tasting journey through the Badlands and the Black Hills, around Mount Rushmore and along the Oregon Trail. Venture with us into the grassland prairies, and walk in the footsteps of Old West legends. The people of these lands are duly proud of their heritage and love sharing it through the recipes that have come down for generations.

In our search for the classic traditional recipes of this region, we have reviewed hundreds of cookbooks from these Great Plains States. We learned not only of the handed-down recipes, but of new and innovative ones that have been created in more recent years to speed preparation and utilize the growing number of new products available. The end result is over 400 of the best recipes from leading cookbooks all over Kansas, Nebraska, North Dakota and South Dakota. And what a delicious variety!

When you say Kansas to somebody and ask about food, they are likely to say barbecue. And well they might. We are amazed at how seriously these Sunflower State folks take their barbecue. There are restaurants, organizations, associations and individuals all boasting their excellent barbecue recipes. Try the Indoor/Outdoor Ribs or the Blue Ribbon Barbecued Country Back Ribs and you'll see why they brag!

Nebraska has been called a 77,000-square-mile museum without walls. Since campfire cooking at authentic covered wagon treks are just as likely to occur in the Cornhusker State as fine dining after the theatre, you can understand why they have such delicious ranges of recipes from Peppery T-Bone Steaks & Chili Corn to God's Country White Chocolate Cheesecake with Raspberry Sauce.

North Dakota also has an abundance of beef and dairy cattle, hogs, and sheep, and so much grain that they lead the nation in the production of durum and other spring wheat. Fishing and hunting are big in the Peace Garden State, too, with abundant game birds such as duck, grouse, pheasant and goose. Try the Creamed Pheasant, and also the Beef Potato Cakes, Toffee Delight Muffins, Rave Reviews Coconut Cake . . . yum!

South Dakota leads the nation in the production of oats and rye. Its fertile soils and extensive grazing lands yield bountiful farm and cattle crops. Recipes from the Coyote State couple the bounty of the land with the creativity of its people through innovative recipes like Popcorn Salad, Cow Punching Chili and Dumplings, and Lollipop Cookies.

We are always delighted to make friends with so many people from across the states, the many cookbook chairmen, food editors, book store managers, chamber of commerce personnel, as well as interested cookbook enthusiasts. The efforts of our staff members, Sheila, Annette, Shonda, and Cyndi are invaluable in helping us locate the many cookbooks that are represented here and then to stylize them into this lovely book. Our "Best" illustrator Tupper England always provides that special touch that makes each state book individual. All of the people involved with the contributing cookbooks from each state were so pleasant to work with and we thank them sincerely. Please turn to page 253 to find out more about these books and how you can order them directly.

There's an ingredient we tucked inside these pages called enjoyment, and we hope you find it in every recipe. We also hope this cookbook reflects the many outstanding things we learned about The Great Plains.

Enjoy America's bounty, enjoy the best.

Gwen McKee and Barbara Moseley

CONTRIBUTING COOKBOOKS

All About Bar-B-Q Kansas City Style
Amana Lutheran 125th Anniversary Cookbook
The Best Little Cookbook in the West
Blew Centennial Bon-Appetit
Centerville Community Centennial Cookbook
A Century in His Footsteps
A Cooking Affaire I and II
Cooking with Iola
Cookin' with Farmers Union Friends
Eastman Family Cookbook
Easy Livin' Low-Calorie Microwave Cooking
Easy Livin' Microwave Cooking
Easy Livin' Microwave Cooking for the Holidays
Egg Gravy
Favorite Recipes of Rainbow Valley Lutheran Church
Feed My Lambs
The Give Mom a Rest (She's on Vacation) Cookbook
The Hagen Family Cookbook
Hall's Potato Harvest Cookbook
Heart of the Home Recipes
Heavenly Delights
Heavenly Recipes
Home at the Range I, II, III, and IV
Homemade Memories
If It Tastes Good, Who Cares? I and II
I Love Recipes
Incredible Edibles
In the Kitchen with Kate
Iola's Gourmet Recipes in Rhapsody
The Joy of Sharing
The Kansas City Barbeque Society Cookbook
The Kearney 125th Anniversary Community Cookbook
Kelvin Homemakers 50th Anniversary Cookbook
Lakota Lutheran Church Centennial Cookbook
License to Cook Kansas Style
Measure for Pleasure
More Heart of the Home Recipes
The Mormon Trail Cookbook
90th Anniversary Trinity Lutheran Church Cookbook
Norman Lutheran Church 125th Anniversary Cookbook
North Dakota American Mothers, Inc. Cookbook

CONTRIBUTING COOKBOOKS

North Dakota...Where Food is Love
125 Years of Cookin' with the Lord
The Oregon Trail Cookbook
Our Daily Bread
Our Heritage
Pioneer Daughters of Towner Cookbook
Presentations
Pumpkin, Winter Squash and Carrot Cookbook
Pure Prairie
Que Queens: Easy Grilling & Simple Smoking
Rainbow's Roundup of Recipes
Readers' Favorite Recipes
REC Family Cookbook
Recipes & Remembrances / Buffalo Lake Lutheran Church
Recipes & Remembrances / Courtland Covenant Church
Recipes from the Heart / Epsilon Omega Sorority
Recipes from the Heart / 100 Years of Recipes and Folklore
Recipes: 1978-1998
Recipes Worth Sharing
Red River Valley Potato Growers Auxiliary Cookbook
Regent Alumni Association Cookbook
Ritzy Rhubarb Secrets Cookbook
Savor the Inns of Kansas
Sharing God's Bounty
Sharing Our "Beary" Best II
Silver Celebration Cookbook
Sister's Two II
South Dakota Sunrise
St. Joseph's Table
Taste of Coffeyville
Taste the Good Life! Nebraska Cookbook
A Taste of Prairie Life
To Tayla with TLC
Treasures of the Great Midwest
Tried & True II
We Love Country Cookin'
Whole Wheat Cookery
Wyndmere Community Alumni Cookbook
Y Cook?
Y Winners: Cookbook of Champions
Years and Years of Goodwill Cooking
Yesterday and Today Friendly Circle Cookbook

BEVERAGES
and
APPETIZERS

PHOTO BY CHAD COPPESS, SOUTH DAKOTA DEPARTMENT OF TOURISM

South Dakota's Black Hills provide the backdrop for Mount Rushmore. Washington, Jefferson, Teddy Roosevelt, and Lincoln are the most famous men in rock.

French Iced Coffee

3 cups very strong brewed
  coffee
2 cups sugar

1 pint cream (or half-and-half)
1 quart milk
3 teaspoons vanilla

Dissolve sugar in hot coffee. Cool. Add cream, milk, and vanilla. Pour into milk cartons or ice cream buckets. Freeze. Remove from freezer several hours before serving. Remove carton. Chop up with knife until slushy. Serve very icy.

Cooking with Iola

Angel Frost

1 (6-ounce) can frozen pink
  lemonade, thawed
1 cup milk
1 (10-ounce) package frozen
  strawberries in syrup, partially thawed

1 pint vanilla ice cream
Fresh strawberries (optional)

In a blender, place first 4 ingredients in the order given; blend until smooth. Pour into glasses. Garnish with fresh strawberries, if desired. Yields approximately 4-6 servings.

Sharing God's Bounty

Mint Punch

14 sprigs fresh mint, washed
1 cup sugar
Juice of 6 lemons
5 cups water

Juice of 6 oranges or 1 (6-ounce)
  can frozen orange juice, prepared
1 large can pineapple juice
2 quarts chilled ginger ale

Leave overnight (or at least 8 hours) mint sprigs, sugar, lemon juice, and water in glass jar (or pitcher) in refrigerator. In morning, add orange juice and pineapple juice to mint mixture. Continue soaking another 8 hours in refrigerator. When ready to serve, strain out mint leaves and add ginger ale. Pretty served with a fresh sprig of mint and cherry in each cup or glass.

Eastman Family Cookbook

Homemade Orange Julius

This is nice to serve as a refresher on a busy day in glasses that have been turned upside-down in orange juice, then dipped into granulated sugar and let dry for one hour. Top with slice of orange, twisted.

1 (6-ounce) can frozen orange
 concentrate, thawed
¼ cup sugar
½ cup half-and-half

1 teaspoon vanilla
6 ounces cold water
12 ice cubes

Put first 4 ingredients in blender and blend on low speed. Gradually add cold water and 12 ice cubes. Blend at high speed until slushy. Serve immediately to 4 guests.

For a low-calorie drink use:

1 (6-ounce) can frozen orange
 juice concentrate, thawed
1 teaspoon low calorie
 sweetener

⅓ cup nonfat dry milk
2 teaspoons vanilla
6 ounces cold water
12 ice cubes

Cooking with Iola

Fruit Slush

An excellent fruit dish to serve for breakfast or with a wafer for dessert.

1 (10-ounce) package frozen
 strawberries, quartered
1 (6-ounce) can frozen pink
 lemonade concentrate
1 (6-ounce) can frozen orange
 juice concentrate

1 (20-ounce) can crushed
 pineapple with juice
6 bananas, sliced or mashed
2 (12-ounce) cans 7-Up

Cut strawberries when slightly thawed. Defrost lemonade and orange juice; stir together. Add other ingredients, including strawberries; mix well and dip into plastic punch cups. Cover with Saran Wrap or foil, and freeze. To serve, remove from freezer to refrigerator the night before serving, or leave at room temperature for approximately 3 hours. Makes 16 servings.

Recipe from Fort's Cedar View, Ulysses, Kansas.

Savor the Inns of Kansas

Summer Slush

9 cups water
2 cups sugar
1 (12-ounce) can frozen
  orange juice
1 (12-ounce) can frozen
  lemonade

2 tea bags
2 cups hot water
1½ cups vodka

Bring 9 cups water and sugar to boil until sugar is melted. Cool completely. Add frozen orange juice and lemonade. Steep 2 bags of tea in 2 cups hot water. Add to mixture when cool. Add vodka. Stir together and put into freezer.

Taste of Coffeyville

Harvest Day Drink

This drink was served on farms when harvesting was done. It's a real thirst quencher.

1⅓ cups molasses
2 teaspoons ginger

⅔ cup vinegar
7 pints cold water

Mix ingredients together in order given. Serve on hot days. Makes 1 gallon.

The Mormon Trail Cookbook

Hot Buttered Rum
(Non-alcoholic)

This is an elegant drink—but so easy.

½ cup (1 stick) butter
½ cup brown sugar

1 cup vanilla ice cream, softened
4 teaspoons rum extract

Melt butter. Stir in brown sugar until heated. Pour hot mixture over ice cream. Beat by hand until smooth. Add rum extract.

To serve, put ¼ cup mixture in a cup and add ¾ cup boiling water. Sprinkle with nutmeg. Yields 1¾ cups mix or 7 cups hot buttered rum.

The Give Mom a Rest (She's on Vacation) Cookbook

Cappuccino Mix

1 cup instant coffee creamer	½ cup powdered sugar
1 cup instant Quik Chocolate	¼ teaspoon cinnamon
⅔ cup instant coffee	¼ teaspoon nutmeg

Combine all ingredients in blender until very fine. Store in air-tight container. Use 3 tablespoons mix to 8 ounces hot water. Makes about 3 cups dry mix.

Iola's Gourmet Recipes in Rhapsody

Appetizer Dip

1 (2-pound) box Velveeta cheese	1 onion, finely chopped
1 can evaporated milk	½ pound Monterey Jack cheese, grated
3 small cans green chile peppers, diced	½ pound Colby cheese, grated
3 tomatoes, chopped	1½ pounds ground beef

Mix together Velveeta cheese and evaporated milk. Melt over low heat, stirring occasionally. Add peppers, tomatoes, onion, Monterey Jack cheese and Colby cheese. Simmer over low heat about one hour. Fry beef; drain and mix into cheese mixture. Serve warm with tortilla chips. May be frozen. Can also be made without beef.

Recipes from the Heart / Epsilon Omega Sorority

Tonia's Spinach Dip Supreme

2 large green onions with tops, minced
1 pint sour cream
1 (8-ounce) package cream cheese, softened
1 cup Cheddar cheese, shredded
1 cup chopped pecans
½ teaspoon lemon juice

1 teaspoon Worcestershire sauce
1 package (dry) Hidden Valley Original Salad Dressing mix
1 (10-ounce) package frozen, chopped spinach, thawed, drained well and squeezed dry
1 can water chestnuts, chopped fine

Mix all ingredients and chill thoroughly several hours, preferably overnight. Serve in hollowed loaf of rye or pumpernickel bread, with cubes of bread in basket to the side. It is also very pretty in a red cabbage shell.

A Cooking Affaire II

Radish Dip

1 (8-ounce) package cream cheese, softened
¼ cup butter or margarine, softened
½ teaspoon celery salt
Dash of paprika

½ teaspoon Worcestershire sauce
1 cup finely chopped radishes
¼ cup finely chopped green onion

Mix cheese, butter, celery salt, paprika, and Worcestershire sauce together until smooth. Stir in radishes and onion. Chill spread several hours to blend flavors.

Silver Celebration Cookbook

Shrimp Dip

1 (8-ounce) package cream
  cheese, softened
1 can cream of shrimp frozen
  soup, defrosted
1 teaspoon Worcestershire sauce

1 teaspoon onion flakes
1 can drained cooked shrimp
1/2 cup chopped ripe olives

Mix first 4 ingredients together well. Add shrimp and olives.

Pioneer Daughters Cookbook

Apple Dip

A very delicious dip or ball that may be served with apples for a wonderful appetizer. Especially good for those health-conscious souls.

2 (8-ounce) packages cream
  cheese, softened
3/4 cup sugar, scant
1/2 cup pecans, chopped
1/2 cup raisins, chopped
1/2 cup coconut
1/2 cup maraschino cherries,
  diced and drained

1/2 cup crushed pineapple,
  well drained
1/4 teaspoon lemon juice
2 teaspoons vanilla
1/8 teaspoon nutmeg
1/8 teaspoon ground allspice
1/8 teaspoon mace (optional)

Mix all ingredients together until spreadable. Cool slightly in refrigerator, then roll into a ball. Makes about 4 cups.

A Cooking Affaire II

Nacho Cheese Dip

2 pounds ground beef, browned
  and drained
2 pounds Velveeta cheese,
  melted

1 can cream of mushroom
  soup
1 (8-ounce) jar picante sauce

Combine ingredients and serve hot with tortilla chips. Crock pot works well.

The Joy of Sharing

Tortilla Torte

1 (8-ounce) package cream
  cheese, softened
3 tablespoons canned green
  chili peppers, drained
1 (4½-ounce) can deviled ham

½ cup dairy sour cream
¼ cup taco sauce
10 (10-inch) flour tortillas
Chopped, pitted ripe olives
Shredded Cheddar cheese

Beat cream cheese with electric mixer for 30 seconds; set aside one tablespoon chopped chilies. Add remaining chilies, deviled ham, sour cream and 2 tablespoons taco sauce to cream cheese. Beat until well combined. Place one tortilla on serving platter; spread with 3 tablespoons of cheese mixture. Repeat with remaining tortillas and cheese. Cover and chill 4 hours or overnight. Before serving, spread remaining 2 tablespoons taco sauce on top layer. Garnish with remaining chilies, cheese and olives. Cut into small wedges.

Amana Lutheran Church 125th Anniversary Cookbook

Mini Pizzas

1 package English muffins
1 small jar Ragu sauce
¼ pound sliced pepperoni

Onions, olives, etc. (optional)
8 ounces shredded mozzarella
  cheese

Cut muffins in half. Spread sauce on muffins. Layer pepperoni and whatever you like and top with the cheese. Place on cookie sheet and bake at 350° for 10-12 minutes.

The Hagen Family Cookbook

Artichoke-Tomato Tart

1 refrigerated unbaked pie
  crust
1 (8-ounce) package shredded
  mozzarella cheese
8 Roma tomatoes
1 (14-ounce) can artichoke
  hearts, drained and chopped

1 cup loosely packed fresh
  basil leaves
4 cloves garlic
1/2 cup Hellmann's
  mayonnaise
1/4 cup grated Parmesan
  cheese

Bake pie crust according to package directions in a 9-inch quiche dish. Remove from oven. Sprinkle 3/4 cup of the mozzarella cheese over the baked pie shell. Cut Roma tomatoes into wedges; drain on paper towels. Arrange tomato wedges atop the cheese in the baked pie shell. Sprinkle artichoke hearts over the tomato wedges. In a blender, combine basil leaves and garlic and process till coarsely chopped, and sprinkle over the tomatoes. Combine remaining mozzarella cheese, mayonnaise, and Parmesan cheese and spoon over basil mixture, spreading evenly to cover the top. Bake in a 375° oven for 35 minutes or till top is golden and bubbly. Serves 8.

Recipes & Remembrances / Buffalo Lake

Holiday Pinwheels

2 (8-ounce) packages cream
  cheese, softened
1 (1-ounce) package Hidden
  Valley Ranch Salad Dressing
  Mix
3 green onions, minced fine
1 (4-ounce) jar pimento, diced

1 (4-ounce) can green chilies,
  diced
1 (2 1/4-ounce) can black olives,
  diced
1 (3-ounce) package dried beef,
  cut fine
4 (12-inch) flour tortillas

Mix all ingredients together (except tortillas) and spread on flour tortillas. Roll tightly and wrap in Saran Wrap. Chill for at least 2 hours. Slice and place on serving tray.

Cooking with Iola

Crab Canapés

1 (7½-ounce) can crab meat, drained
1 tablespoon chopped green onion
1 cup shredded Swiss cheese (4 ounces)
½ cup mayonnaise
¼ teaspoon curry powder
½ teaspoon salt
1 teaspoon lemon juice
1 (8-ounce) package butterflake dinner rolls
Slivered almonds
Sliced water chestnuts

Preheat oven to 400°. Grease a baking sheet; set aside. In medium bowl, combine crab meat, onion, cheese, mayonnaise, curry powder, salt, and lemon juice. Mix well. Separate each roll into 3 layers, making 36 pieces. Place pieces on baking sheet. Spoon a small amount of crab meat mixture on each piece. Top with almond or water chestnut slice. Bake 12 minutes or until puffed and browned. Serve hot. Makes 36.

Heavenly Recipes

Crab Rolls

20 slices white bread
8 ounces Velveeta cheese
1 cup butter
2 (7-ounce) cans crab meat
1 cup melted butter
2 cups sesame seeds, toasted

Trim crusts from bread; roll to flatten. Combine Velveeta cheese and one cup butter in double boiler. Cook over hot water until melted, stirring frequently. Stir in crab meat. Spread crab mixture on bread slices; roll to enclose filling. Dip in one cup melted butter; roll in sesame seeds. Place seam-side-down in dish. Freeze, covered, until firm. Thaw slightly; cut rolls into thirds. Place on nonstick baking sheet. Broil for 3-5 minutes or until golden brown. Yields 60 servings.

Y Cook?

Smoked Salmon Spread

1 (6-ounce) can smoked
  salmon
1 (3-ounce) package cream
  cheese, softened
1 tablespoon plus 2 teaspoons
  cream-style horseradish

1 tablespoon lemon juice
2 tablespoons minced onion
  (optional)
³/₄-1 cup chopped nuts

Drain off excess oil from salmon. In a food processor, grind salmon until fine. Transfer to mixing bowl. With a mixer on medium speed, add cream cheese, horseradish, lemon juice, and onion. Shape into ball and roll in nuts.

Incredible Edibles

Sausage Squares

1 pound sausage
¹/₂ cup onion, chopped
¹/₄ cup grated Parmesan
  cheese
¹/₂ cup grated Swiss cheese
1 egg, beaten
¹/₄ teaspoon Tabasco

1¹/₂ teaspoons salt
2 tablespoons parsley,
  chopped
2 cups Bisquick
²/₃ cup milk
¹/₄ cup mayonnaise
1 egg yolk

Cook sausage and onion over low heat until brown. Drain off fat. Add cheeses, whole egg, Tabasco, salt, and parsley. Make Bisquick dough by mixing with milk and mayonnaise. Spread half of dough over bottom of greased 8-inch square pan. Cover with sausage mixture and top with remaining dough mixture. Brush with beaten egg yolk. Bake 25-30 minutes at 400°. Cut in squares. May be served for a brunch, or coffee, or as appetizers. Makes 16 squares.

Home at the Range I

Lawrence Welk was born in a sod house on North Dakota's prairie near Strasburg.

Beef in a Bread Bowl

½ cup chopped onion
2 tablespoons butter
1 tablespoon cornstarch
1 cup Carnation evaporated
  milk, undiluted
½ cup water
1 (3-ounce) package cream
  cheese

1 (5-ounce) package dried beef,
  rinsed and diced
¼ cup chopped green
  pepper
8-10 drops of Tabasco sauce
1 teaspoon prepared mustard
1 large or 2 small uncut loaves
  round crusty bread

Sauté onion in butter over medium heat. Stir in cornstarch and mix thoroughly. Gradually add milk and water. Cook mixture over medium heat, stirring constantly until the mixture just comes to a boil and thickens. Stir in cream cheese, dried beef, green pepper, Tabasco sauce, and mustard. Continue to cook and stir until the cheese is melted. Cut the top off the crusty bread and pull the center of the bread out to form a bread bowl. Tear the bread top and center pieces up to use as dippers. Just before serving, spoon the hot beef mixture into the hollowed bread and serve. Makes 2⅔ cups.

Recipes & Remembrance / Buffalo Lake

Teriyaki Tidbits

1 (10-ounce) jar apricot jam
½ cup barbecue sauce
1-2 tablespoons teriyaki
  sauce
1 pound wieners, cut into 1-inch
  pieces, or 1 pound cocktail franks

1 (15¼-ounce) can pineapple
  chunks, drained
1 large green pepper, cut into
  ¾-inch squares

In large saucepan over medium heat, combine preserves, barbecue sauce, and teriyaki sauce. Heat until hot and bubbly, stirring constantly. Stir in wieners, pineapple, and green pepper. Heat thoroughly. Transfer mixture to chafing dish, keeping warm over low heat. Serve with toothpicks. (Stick pretzels can be used instead.)

We Love Country Cookin'

"Devil" Eggs

6 eggs
2 tablespoons mayonnaise
1 tablespoon prepared
  horseradish
1 tablespoon vinegar
1 teaspoon mustard
1 teaspoon dill relish

½ teaspoon salt
½ teaspoon pepper
1 teaspoon sugar
Salsa (optional)
Sliced canned jalapeño peppers
  (optional)

Put eggs in medium saucepan and cover with cold water. Bring to a boil. Remove from heat and let stand, covered, 10 minutes. Drain. Peel shells from eggs while holding them under cold running water. Cut eggs in half lengthwise. Remove yolks and mix with mayonnaise, horseradish, vinegar, mustard, dill relish, salt, pepper, and sugar. Use mixture to fill egg whites. Garnish with a dab of your favorite salsa and top with a slice of jalapeño on each. Makes 6 servings.

Note: These are hot! The faint-hearted might want to start with one teaspoon horseradish, then add more to taste.

Recipes Worth Sharing

Pickled Eggs

Remove the shells from 3-4 dozen hard-boiled eggs. Carefully arrange in jars. Boil one pint vinegar with allspice, ginger, and a couple of cloves of garlic. Add another pint of vinegar, bring to a boil again. Pour scalding hot mixture over eggs. When cold, seal up jars for a month before using eggs.

Egg Gravy

Perfect Cheese Ball

Tie with a bow for gifts.

4 (8-ounce) package cream
  cheese
1 pound margarine
8-10 green onions, chopped
  fine, (green also)

1 can black olives, chopped
  fine
1 small jar pimentos, diced
4 ounces blue cheese

Put cream cheese and margarine in large bowl; let soften, then add onions, olives, pimentos, and blue cheese. Mix real well. Shape into 4 or 5 balls. Wrap in plastic wrap.

Recipes from the Heart: 100 Years of Recipes and Folklore

Favorite Cheese Ball or Dip

2 (8-ounce) packages cream
  cheese
1 (8½-ounce) can crushed
  pineapple, drained
¼ cup chopped green pepper

1-2 tablespoons chopped
  onion
1 tablespoon seasoned salt
1 cup chopped pecans

Mix all ingredients well; chill, then make into balls. Roll in more pecans. Keep refrigerated till serving with assorted crackers. Delicious with celery.

Eastman Family Cookbook

Sweet and Hot Marmalade Chutney

2 cups chopped red onions
½ cup chopped dried
   apricots
½ cup orange marmalade
2 tablespoons white wine
   vinegar

2 tablespoons white wine
¼ teaspoon ground white
   pepper
⅛ teaspoon dried red pepper
   flakes

Combine all ingredients in a glass bowl. Refrigerate overnight.
Makes about 3 cups.

Que Queens: Easy Grilling & Simple Smoking

Chutney Cheese Paté

1 (8-ounce) package cream
   cheese
4 ounces Cheddar cheese,
   grated
¼ cup dry sherry

½-1 teaspoon curry powder
1 bottle chutney
1 bunch green onions,
   minced

Cream cheeses. Add sherry and curry powder and thoroughly
blend. Form into oval on serving platter, about ½-inch thick.
Cover and refrigerate. At serving time, pour chutney over cheese
and sprinkle onions generously over chutney. Serve with Triscuits
or wheat crackers. Serves 10-12.

A Cooking Affaire I

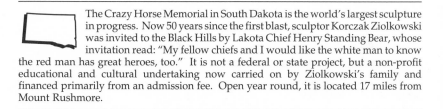

The Crazy Horse Memorial in South Dakota is the world's largest sculpture
in progress. Now 50 years since the first blast, sculptor Korczak Ziolkowski
was invited to the Black Hills by Lakota Chief Henry Standing Bear, whose
invitation read: "My fellow chiefs and I would like the white man to know
the red man has great heroes, too." It is not a federal or state project, but a non-profit
educational and cultural undertaking now carried on by Ziolkowski's family and
financed primarily from an admission fee. Open year round, it is located 17 miles from
Mount Rushmore.

Brie with Cranberry Glaze

". . . a special treat at our Christmas Eve open house . . ." This makes an
especially pretty platter when garnished with fresh holly and surrounded
with heart-shaped crackers, red and green apple slices and fresh pears.

CRANBERRY GLAZE:

3 cups cranberries (12-ounce
   package)
³/₄ cup brown sugar
¹/₃ cup dried currants or
   raisins
¹/₃ cup water
²/₃ teaspoon dry mustard

²/₃ teaspoon ground allspice
²/₃ teaspoon cardamom
²/₃ teaspoon ground cloves
²/₃ teaspoon ground ginger
¹/₄ cup coarsely ground walnuts
   (optional)

Combine all ingredients except nuts in heavy non-aluminum
saucepan. Cook over medium heat until berries pop (5 minutes).
Cool to room temperature. (May refrigerate for 3 days.)

CHEESE:

1 (8-inch) wheel Brie cheese
Crackers

Apple slices
Pear slices

Use sharp knife, cut circle in top of Brie, leaving ½-inch border
on rind. Carefully remove top rind and do not cut through side
rind. Place cheese on dish or a foil-lined cookie sheet. Spread
Cranberry Glaze over, and nuts, if desired. You can prepare to
this point 6 hours ahead. Place in 300° oven for 12 minutes. Serve
surrounded with crackers and fruit slices.

Presentations

Antipasto

1 (12-ounce) jar ketchup
1 (12-ounce) jar chili sauce
½ cup French dressing
2 small cans small shrimp,
   drained

1 can water packed tuna, drained
1 can water chestnuts, drained
   and cut up
½ cup ripe olives, drained and
   chopped

Mix all the ingredients together at least 24 hours in advance; keep
refrigerated. Serve this on club or any other crackers. This freezes
and refreezes beautifully.

St. Joseph's Table

Dr. Quales' Salsa

10 jalapeño peppers
15 serrano peppers
1 bunch green onions
1 yellow onion
1 bunch cilantro

1-1½ tablespoons salt
4 cans stewed tomatoes,
  chopped
Juice of 1½ or 2 lemons
1 teaspoon garlic powder

Chop peppers (see note), onions, and cilantro. Mix with the salt. Let sit for 20 minutes. Add stewed tomatoes, lemon juice, and garlic powder. Mix and eat. (If it's too hot, add more tomatoes, wimp!)

Note: Control hotness with veins in peppers and amount of seeds you leave in. For milder sauce, take out the veins and all seeds.

To Tayla with TLC

Hot Potato Skins

Bake potatoes until tender. Cool, cut in quarters lengthwise, then in half crosswise, to form 8 sections. Scoop out potato pulp, leaving about ¼ inch. Brush skins on both sides with melted butter and a little soy sauce. Bake at 500° until crisp, about 10-12 minutes. Serve with assorted dips or add shredded cheese and crumbled, cooked bacon, then heat until cheese melts.

Red River Valley Potato Growers Auxiliary Cookbook

Spinach Balls

2 boxes chopped spinach,
  cooked and drained
2 cups Pepperidge Farm
  Stuffing (herb), more if
  needed
2 large onions, chopped well
6 eggs, beaten

³/₄ cup melted butter
¹/₂ cup Parmesan cheese
1 tablespoon garlic salt
¹/₂ teaspoon thyme
1 tablespoon pepper or less to
  suit taste
1 tablespoon Accent

Be sure all water is out of spinach. In a bowl, mix all ingredients together well. Form into balls by hand or use a cookie dropper. Place in freezer in covered container or on cookie sheet covered until firm. Bake at 350° for about 30 minutes.

Note: Half a recipe makes about 3 dozen. Formed balls may be stored in freezer indefinitely. Remove from freezer and allow to thaw for at least one hour before baking.

Silver Celebration Cookbook

One of a very few women hanged in the days of the Old West was named Elizabeth Taylor. The graves of her and her twin brother, Tom Jones, lie in a cemetery just a stone's throw from the ghost town of Spring Ranche, Nebraska.

Nibblin & Fish

10 cups Cheerios
6 cups pretzel sticks
4 cups small fish-shaped
  crackers

1⅓ cups cooking oil
3 tablespoons Worcestershire
  sauce

Mix and bake in baking pans or cookie sheets at 300° for 30 minutes. Stir every 10 minutes.

Heavenly Delights

Homemade Fiddle Faddle

2 cups brown sugar
2 sticks margarine
½ cup white corn syrup
1 teaspoon salt
1 teaspoon butter flavoring

1 teaspoon maple flavoring
¼ teaspoon cream of tartar
1 teaspoon baking soda
7 quarts popped corn
2 cups mixed nuts

In saucepan, combine brown sugar, margarine, corn syrup, and salt. Boil for 6 minutes, stirring constantly. Add flavorings, cream of tartar, and soda. Pour over popped corn and nuts, mixing thoroughly. Bake in 200° oven for one hour.

Cooking with Iola

Cinnamon Trail Mix

2 cups toasted oat cereal
2 cups hexagon-shaped corn cereal
2 cups pretzel bits
³/₄ cup raisins
¹/₂ cup sunflower seeds
2 tablespoons reduced fat margarine
2 tablespoons brown sugar
1 tablespoon cinnamon

In a large bowl combine the cereals, pretzel bits, raisins, and sunflower seeds. Toss gently. Melt margarine in a microwave or saucepan and stir in brown sugar and cinnamon. Pour over the cereal mixture. Toss to coat. Bake 8-10 minutes in a 350° oven.

Sisters Two II

BREAD
and
BREAKFAST

America's bread fields. Wheat . . . as far as the eye can see. North Dakota

Mrs. Eisenhower's Bread

Ida Elizabeth Stover Eisenhower was Ike's mother.

1 cake compressed yeast or
   1 package active dry yeast
½ cup lukewarm water
   (105°-115°)
½ teaspoon sugar
½ cup shortening
½ cup sugar

1 egg, beaten
1½ teaspoons salt
2 cups milk, scalded and cooled
   to 105°-115°
8 cups sifted flour** (the less
   flour used, the better the bread)

Dissolve yeast in lukewarm water, stirring in the ½ teaspoon sugar. Let stand 45 minutes (5 minutes for active dry yeast). Cream shortening with ½ cup sugar; add egg, salt, milk, and yeast. Stir in flour a little at a time until dough is stiff enough to knead. Knead for 10-15 minutes until elastic. Place in greased bowl and let rise until double. Knead and let rise until double again. Divide and shape dough in 2 or 3 greased 9x5-inch loaf pans. Cover with clean, damp towel. When double again, bake at 375° for 35-40 minutes.

Note: For whole wheat bread, use just enough white flour to handle when kneading.

**Sifting flour was common practice in Ida's day. Today, stir flour, spoon into measuring cup, and level off.

License to Cook Kansas Style

Almost Grandma Larson's Rye Bread

For bread machine.

½ cup rye flour
2½ cups white bread flour
1 cup water (very warm)
3 tablespoons molasses

2 tablespoons margarine
1 teaspoon salt
2 teaspoons yeast
3 tablespoons brown sugar

Mix both flours together in a bowl before beginning. (A fine ground rye flour works best. If only a stone ground flour is available, place the rye flour in a food processor for a few minutes.) Place all the ingredients in the bread machine container, beginning with the water. Process as directed on the bread machine.

Amana Lutheran Church 125th Anniversary Cookbook

Cheezy Hot French Bread

1 long loaf French bread
1/2 cup oleo, softened
1 tablespoon prepared
    mustard
1/4 cup minced onion

2 tablespoon poppy seeds
1 (8-ounce) package sliced
    Swiss cheese, cut in thirds
2 slices bacon, cooked and
    crumbled

Slice loaf horizontally into two large pieces. Combine oleo, mustard, onion, and poppy seeds. Spread on bread and top with cheese. Place slices in a foil "boat" and sprinkle bacon on top. Bake 15 minutes in 375° oven; cut in serving pieces. Serves 8-12.

Home at the Range IV

Kathy's Cream Cheese Braid

2 packages dry yeast
1/2 cup warm water
1 cup sour cream
1/2 cup sugar

1 teaspoon salt
1/2 cup melted butter
2 eggs, beaten
4 cups flour

Mix yeast and warm water; set aside. Slowly heat sour cream; stir in sugar, salt, and melted butter. Cool to lukewarm and mix with yeast. Add eggs and flour. Cover and refrigerate overnight.

FILLING:

2 (8-ounce) packages cream
    cheese
3/4 cup sugar

1 egg
1/8 teaspoon salt
2 teaspoons vanilla

Prepare filling by combining all ingredients. Divide dough into 4 parts; roll each into 12x8-inch rectangles. Spread cream cheese mixture on dough and roll up like a jellyroll. Place seam-side-down on a baking sheet. Slit each roll at 2-inch intervals about 1/3 of the way through to resemble a braid. Cover lightly and let rise until double. Bake in preheated 375° oven.

GLAZE:

2 cups confectioners' sugar
4 tablespoons milk

2 teaspoons vanilla

Prepare glaze and spread on baked braid.

A Cooking Affaire II

Easy Refrigerator Rolls

2 packages active dry yeast
2 cups warm water
  (110°-115°)
½ cup sugar

2 teaspoons salt
¼ cup soft shortening
1 egg
6½-7 cups flour

Mix yeast with warm water. Stir in sugar, salt, shortening, and egg. Add flour, stirring in enough to form soft dough. Cover and place in refrigeratgor. About 2 hours before baking, shape dough into rolls, coffee cake, etc. Cover; let rise until double. Bake at 400° for 12-15 minutes. Can be made into rolls as soon as mixed.

Centerville Community Centennial Cookbook

No-Knead Whole-Wheat Rolls

1 package yeast
¼ cup lukewarm water
1 cup milk, scalded
½ cup butter or margarine
¼ cup sugar

1 teaspoon salt
1¾ cups stone ground whole
  wheat flour
1 egg, well beaten
1¾ cups all-purpose flour

Dissolve yeast in water. Pour hot milk over margarine, sugar, and salt. Let cool. Add whole wheat flour. Beat about 7 minutes. Add yeast and egg. Beat with mixer until smooth. Add approximately 1¾ cups all-purpose flour. (Add more flour if dough is too soft, although dough should be somewhat soft). Let rise until bubbly. Stir down, and let rise again. Stir down, and shape into rolls. Use for sweet or dinner rolls.

Note: If using dry milk in place of whole milk, add dry milk to sugar and be sure to add another cup of water.

Whole Wheat Cookery

Nebraska was the home and/or birthplace of William Jennings Bryan, Henry Fonda, Marlon Brando, Johnny Carson, Dick Cavett, Mari Sandoz, John J. Pershing, Willa Cather, Daryl F. Zanuck, Fred Astaire, and Gerald Ford, among others.

Fool-Proof Popovers

2 eggs
1 cup milk

1 cup flour
Scant teaspoon salt

Break eggs into bowl. Add milk, flour, and salt. Mix well. Grease an 8-cup muffin tin. Divide mixture into 8 parts, and fill tin. Turn oven heat to 425°. Put popovers into COLD OVEN. Bake 37 minutes. Do not peek!

North Dakota...Where Food is Love

Garlic Bubble Loaf

1 loaf frozen bread dough
¼ cup melted butter
1 egg
½ teaspoon garlic powder

1 teaspoon parsley powder (or parsley flakes)
¼ teaspoon salt

Thaw and soften dough; thoroughly blend remaining ingredients. Cut off pieces of softened dough the size of small walnuts. Dip into mixture; place into well-greased loaf pan. Use all the dough. If there is mixture left over, pour it over the top. Let rise until double in size. Bake at 375° for 30 minutes. (If top browns too rapidly, cover with foil during baking.) Yields 16 servings.

Nurtitional analysis: Cal 92; Carbo 12g; Prot 2g; Fat 2g; Chol 25mg; Sod 184mg.

REC Family Cookbook

Patio Bread

½ cup grated mozzarella
  cheese
½ cup margarine
½ cup mayonnaise
¼ teaspoon dill weed
¼ cup black olives

¼ cup green olives
¼ cup pimento
½ teaspoon garlic salt
¼ cup onion
French bread

Spread mixture on French bread sliced to desired thickness. Can top with pepperoni. Bake uncovered 20 minutes at 350°.

Sharing Our "Beary" Best II

Skorpor
(Swedish Rusks)

These should be eaten with coffee, milk or other beverage. They are quite hard.

1¼ cups sugar
½ cup shortening
1 egg, beaten
1 cup sour milk or 1 cup
  buttermilk

3½ cups flour
½ teaspoon salt
½ teaspoon soda
1 teaspoon baking powder
1 cup chopped nuts

Cream sugar and shortening; add egg and sour milk and stir. Sift flour, salt, soda, and baking powder together. Add to first mixture. Add nuts, if desired. In a 9x13-inch pan, bake one hour at 350°. Cut into 1½ x 3-inch strips and dry in slow oven, 300°, until crispy.

Measure for Pleasure

Almond Rusks

3 eggs
1 cup sugar
1 cup vegetable oil
3½ cups all-purpose flour

1 cup finely chopped almonds
1½ teaspoons baking powder
1 teaspoon salt

In a mixing bowl, beat eggs. Add sugar and oil; mix well. Combine flour, almonds, baking powder, and salt. Gradually beat into the sugar mixture. Chill the dough until firm. Divide into three pieces. Roll each piece into an 8x2-inch rectangle. Place on a greased baking sheet. Bake at 350° for 15-20 minutes or until firm to the touch. Cool on a wire rack for 15 minutes. Reduce heat to 300°. Carefully cut rectangle into ½-inch slices. Place slices with cut-side-down on baking sheet. Bake 8-10 minutes longer. Yields 4 dozen.

Sharing God's Bounty

Dandelion Jelly

Taste resembles honey.

1 quart of dandelion blossoms (pick early in the morning— without any of the stem)
1 quart water

1 package pectin
1 teaspoon lemon or orange extract
4¹/₂ cups sugar

Boil blossoms in water for 3 minutes. Drain off 3 cups liquid; add pectin, extract and sugar. Boil about 3 minutes. Pour into jars.

Heart of the Home Recipes

Monkey Bread

3 cans buttermilk biscuits
1 teaspoon cinnamon
²/₃ cup sugar

1¹/₂ sticks oleo, melted
1 teaspoon cinnamon
1 cup brown sugar

Cut buttermilk biscuits in fourths. Combine cinnamon and sugar with biscuits (place in a sack and shake well). Drop biscuits in a bundt pan. Mix together oleo, cinnamon and brown sugar, then pour over biscuits. Bake at 350° for 30 minutes.

Home at the Range III

Lemon Poppy Seed Bread

1 package lemon cake mix
¹/₂ cup oil
¹/₄ cup poppy seed
4 eggs

1 cup water
1 package instant lemon pudding

Mix. Bake in 2 greased bread pans for 40 minutes at 350°.

North Dakota American Mothers Cookbook

High-Energy Banana Bread

2¼ cups all-purpose flour
⅔ cup honey-crunch wheat
  germ
½ cup oats, uncooked
¼ cup packed brown sugar
1 tablespoon baking powder
½ teaspoon salt
¼ teaspoon baking soda
10 tablespoons light corn oil
  spread

1½ cups mashed bananas
  (about 3 medium)
1 (6-ounced) can frozen apple
  juice concentrate
½ cup thawed egg substitute
⅓ cup walnuts (optional)
1 teaspoon vanilla extract

Mix first 7 ingredients in a large bowl. With pastry blender, cut in corn oil spread until mixture resembles coarse crumbs. Add bananas, undiluted apple juice concentrate, egg substitute, walnuts, and vanilla, stirring just until flour is moistened. Spoon batter into pan. Bake at 350° for 60 minutes, or until toothpick inserted into center of bread comes out clean. Cool bread in pan on wire rack for 10 minutes. Remove from pan and cool slightly before cutting. Makes one loaf.

Y Winners...Cookbook of Champions

Toffee Delight Muffins

2 cups flour
1 cup sugar
1 cup water
4 eggs
1 small package instant vanilla
  pudding

1 small package instant
  butterscotch pudding
2 teaspoons baking powder
1 teaspoon salt
¾ cup vegetable oil
1 teaspoon vanilla

TOPPING:
1 cup firmly packed brown
  sugar

¾ cup chopped pecans
1 teaspoon cinnamon

Mix together all except topping. Beat 2 minutes. Using ½ of batter, pour and fill each muffin cup ⅓ full. Mix together topping. Sprinkle ½ of topping on muffins. Add remaining batter to fill each muffin cup ⅔ full, then put rest of topping on. Bake 15-20 minutes at 350°.

Heavenly Recipes

Pumpkin Chip Muffins

4 eggs
2 cups sugar
1 (16-ounce) can pumpkin
1½ cups vegetable oil
3 cups flour
2 teaspoons baking soda

2 teaspoons baking powder
1 teaspoon ground cinnamon
1 teaspoon salt
2 cups (12 ounces) chocolate
  chips

In a large mixing bowl, beat eggs, sugar, pumpkin, and oil until smooth. Combine flour, baking soda, baking powder, cinnamon, and salt. Add to pumpkin mixture and mix well. Fold in chocolate chips. Fill greased or paper-lined muffin cups ¾ full. Bake at 400° for 16-20 minutes or until muffins test done. Cool in pan 10 minutes before removing to a wire rack. Makes about 24 standard-size muffins.

Recipes from the Heart / Epsilon Omega Sorority

Bran Flakes Muffins

1½ cups flour	3 cups bran flakes
⅔ cup packed brown sugar	2 egg whites
1 teaspoon soda	1½ cups buttermilk
½ teaspoon cinnamon	⅓ cup oil
¼ teaspoon salt	⅓ cup raisins

Mix well flour, sugar, soda, cinnamon, and salt. Stir in cereal. Beat egg whites, buttermilk, and oil. Stir into flour mixture just until moistened. Mix in raisins. Spoon into 12 (or more) large muffin tins. Bake 20 minutes at 400°. Let stand 5 minutes. Remove from pan.

Centerville Community Centennial Cookbook

Cocoa-Raisin Muffins

Try icing these and serve as cupcakes.

¼ cup butter or margarine, melted	¾ teaspoon baking soda
¼ cup cocoa	½ teaspoon cinnamon
¾ cup applesauce	¼ teaspoon nutmeg
1¼ cups unsifted all-purpose flour	¼ teaspoon salt
	1 egg, slightly beaten
1 cup sugar	½ cup raisins

Blend butter and cocoa in a bowl; add applesauce. Set aside. In a large bowl combine dry ingredients. Add cocoa mixture and egg. Blend just until moistened. Fold in raisins. Spoon into greased medium-size muffin pans, filling each about half full. Bake at 350° for 20 minutes or until cake springs back when gently touched with finger. Turn out onto wire rack and cool. Makes 12 muffins.

License to Cook Kansas Style

Carhenge, in Alliance, Nebraska, is an exact replica of Stonehenge made with junked cars.

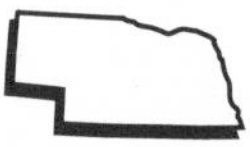

Peach Upside Down Muffins

2 cups flour
1½ cups sugar
1 tablespoon baking powder
½ teaspoon salt
¼ cup shortening, melted
2 eggs, lightly beaten
1 cup milk

6 tablespoons butter or
  margarine
1 cup plus 2 tablespoons packed
  brown sugar
3 cups sliced peeled ripe
  peaches

In a mixing bowl, combine flour, sugar, baking powder, and salt. Add shortening, eggs, and milk; mix until smooth. In bottom of 18 greased muffin cups, place one teaspoon butter and one tablespoon brown sugar. Place in a 375° oven for 5 minutes. Arrange peaches in the muffin cups. Fill each cup half full with batter. Bake at 375° for 25 minutes or until browned. Turn out of pans immediately.

Heavenly Recipes

Peach Coffee Cake

Delicious served warm or cold—offer whipped topping.

1 (18-ounce) package yellow
  cake mix
1 (21-ounce) can peach pie
  filling

3 eggs
3 tablespoons sugar
1 teaspoon cinnamon

Mix together by hand the cake mix, pie filling and eggs. Spread in a 9x13-inch pan that has been sprayed with vegetable oil. Stir together sugar and cinnamon. Sprinkle over cake batter. Bake, uncovered, at 350° for 30 minutes. Test with a toothpick. Yields 8 servings.

VARIATION:
For Apple Coffee Cake, substitute spice cake mix and apple pie filling. (You may want to cut up the apples a bit.)

The Give Mom a Rest (She's on Vacation) Cookbook

Raspberry Cream Coffee Cake

Freezes well. Everyone's favorite.

CREAM CHEESE MIXTURE:

1 (8-ounce) package cream cheese	1 egg
	1/4 cup sugar

Mix thoroughly, and set aside.

BATTER:

2 1/4 cups flour	1 egg
3/4 cup margarine	1/2 teaspoon almond extract
3/4 cup sugar	3/4 cup sour cream
1/2 teaspoon baking powder	2/3 cup raspberry jam
1/2 teaspoon baking soda	1/2 cup slivered almonds
1/4 teaspoon salt	

Cut together flour, margarine, and sugar with pastry blender until crumbly. Put aside one cup of mixture for topping. To the remaining mixture, add baking powder, baking soda, salt, egg, extract, and sour cream, and blend well. Grease and flour springform pan. Spread batter over bottom and up the sides. Spread the Cream Cheese Mixture over all.

Heat the jam in microwave and pour over cream cheese mixture. Mix the reserved one cup crumb mixture with almonds and spread over jam. Bake at 350° for 45-55 minutes. Cool 15 minutes before removing sides of springform pan.

If It Tastes Good, Who Cares? II

Night Before Coffee Cake

2/3 cup butter or margarine	1 teaspoon soda
1 cup sugar	1 teaspoon cinnamon
1/2 cup brown sugar	1/2 teaspoon salt
2 eggs	1 cup buttermilk
2 cups flour	1/2 cup raisins, nuts, dates, or
1 teaspoon baking powder	all three

Cream butter and sugars. Add eggs; mix. Mix together the dry ingredients. Alternately add flour and buttermilk to the creamed mixture. Add fruit and nuts. Pour into greased 9x13-inch pan.

TOPPING:

1/2 cup brown sugar	1/2 cup nuts
1 teaspoon cinnamon	1 teaspoon nutmeg

Mix topping ingredients together and sprinkle over cake. Cover tightly with foil and refrigerate overnight. Remove foil and bake at 350° for 35-40 minutes.

Home at the Range IV

Quick Caramel Rolls

1/2 cup butter	1/2 cup white sugar
1/2 cup vanilla ice cream	2 packs Big Country Biscuits
1/2 cup brown sugar	

Melt butter and vanilla ice cream; stir until well blended. Add brown sugar and white sugar. Mix together well and pour over biscuits in bundt pan. Bake at 350° for 25 minutes. They should be lightly browned. After removing from the oven, let set for a few minutes and tip pan upside down onto serving tray.

We Love Country Cookin'

Mount Rushmore is a national treasure. The 60-feet tall faces of Presidents Washington, Jefferson, Teddy Roosevelt, and Lincoln were originally carved at a cost $989,992.32. The sculptor, Gutzon Borglum, worked on the memorial 14 years, from 1927 until his death in 1941.

Cake Mix Sweet Rolls

4-5 cups flour
1 (9-ounce) white cake mix
  (Jiffy)
2 packages rapid-rise yeast
1 teaspoon salt

2 cups warm (120°-130°) water
Butter
Sugar
Cinnamon

In large mixing bowl, combine 2½ cups flour, cake mix, yeast, salt and warm water. Mix until smooth. Add enough of remaining flour to make a soft dough. Turn out on a floured surface and knead until smooth. Roll dough into a 9x18-inch rectangle. Spread with butter and sprinkle with sugar and cinnamon. Roll jellyroll-style, starting with long edge. Slice into 1-inch circles and place on greased cookie sheets. Cover and let rise until doubled, about 15 minutes. Bake at 350° for 15-18 minutes. Frost if desired. Makes 18 very large rolls.

Tried & True II

Cream Cheese Brunch Bars

2 tubes crescent rolls
2 (8-ounce) packages cream
  cheese, softened
1 cup sugar

1 egg, separated
½ cup sugar
1-2 teaspoons cinnamon

Spread one tube of crescent rolls in 9x13x2-inch pan, patting edges together to form crust. Meanwhile, whip softened cream cheese, one cup sugar, and egg yolk together. Spread on layer of rolls. Top with other tube of rolls. Glaze with beaten egg white. Mix together ½ cup sugar and cinnamon. Sprinkle over egg white. Bake at 350° for 20 minutes. Makes 24 bars. *Recipe from Candlelight Bed and Breakfast, Belle Fourche, South Dakota.*

South Dakota Sunrise

Cloud Biscuits

2 cups sifted all-purpose
  flour
1 tablespoon sugar
4 teaspoons baking powder
1/2 teaspoon salt

1/2 teaspoon cream of tartar
1/2 cup shortening
1 egg, beaten
2/3 cup milk

Sift together dry ingredients; cut in shortening till mixture resembles coarse crumbs. Combine egg and milk; add to flour mixture all at once. Stir till dough follows the fork around bowl. Turn out on lightly floured surface; knead gently with heel of hand about 20 strokes. Roll dough to 3/4-inch thickness. Cut straight down through dough (no twisting) with a 2-inch biscuit cutter dipped in flour. If desired, dough may be chilled 1-3 hours before cutting. Place on greased baking sheet. Bake in a very hot oven at 450° for 10 minutes or till lightly browned.

For drop biscuits: Increase milk to 3/4 cup; omit kneading. Drop from a tablespoon onto baking sheet; bake as above.

The Joy of Sharing

Cheese Puff

35 Ritz crackers, coarsely
  crushed
1 (8-ounce) package sharp
  Cheddar cheese, grated
1 (4-ounce) can sliced
  mushrooms, drained

4 eggs, slightly beaten
2 cups milk
1 tablespoon onion powder
1 tablespoon parsley flakes
1/4 tablespoon poultry
  seasoning

In greased 6-cup soufflé dish, combine crackers, cheese, and mushrooms. In medium bowl with electric mixer at medium speed, beat together eggs, milk, onion powder, parsley, and seasoning. Pour over mixture in soufflé dish. Bake at 350° for 1 hour and 10 minutes or until puffed and lightly browned. Serves 6.

I Love Recipes

Quick Apple Tarts

1 cooking apple, peeled and
  chopped
3 tablespoons sugar
2 tablespoons chopped walnuts
  (optional)
2 tablespoons raisins (optional)

¹/₄ teaspoon cinnamon
1 (8-ounce) can refrigerated
  crescent roll dough
3 tablespoons sugar mixed with
  1 teaspoon cinnamon

Stir together apple, sugar, nuts, raisins, and cinnamon in small bowl; set aside. Separate dough into 8 triangles, stretching slightly. Spoon one heaping tablespoon of apple mixture into center of each triangle. Fold corners over and pinch edges together to seal. Sprinkle with cinnamon/sugar mixture. Place tarts about one inch apart on ungreased baking sheet. Bake at 350° for 18-20 minutes. Cool tarts about 20 minutes on wire rack before serving. Best served same day. Makes 8.

Wyndmere Community Alumni Cookbook

Oven Baked French Toast

6 or 7 eggs
1¹/₂ cups milk
6 teaspoons sugar
Dash of salt
1 cup brown sugar

1¹/₂ teaspoons cinnamon
8 tablespoons butter or
  margarine, melted
14 slices French bread (³/₄-inch
  thick)

Beat eggs, milk, sugar, and salt slightly. Sprinkle brown sugar and cinnamon evenly in 9x13-inch pan. Drizzle butter over sugar and cinnamon. Dip bread slices into egg mixture. Arrange on top of sugar. Pour any remaining egg mixture over bread. Cover and refrigerate overnight. In the morning, bake at 350° for 35-45 minutes, uncovered. Cut in squares.

Kelvin Homemakers 50th Anniversary Cookbook

Baked Blueberry French Toast

12 slices day old white bread,
  cubed
2 (8-ounce) packages cream
  cheese
1 cup fresh or frozen blueberries

12 eggs
2 cups milk
1/3 cup honey or maple syrup

Cut bread in 1-inch cubes. Place in greased 9x13-inch pan. Cut cream cheese into 1-inch cubes and place over bread. Top with blueberries. In a large bowl beat eggs; add milk and syrup; pour over bread mixture. Cover and chill at least 8 hours. Remove from refrigerator, leave covered and bake at 350° for 30 minutes. Uncover and bake 30 minutes more.

SAUCE:

1 cup sugar
2 tablespoons cornstarch
2 cup water

1 cup fresh or frozen
  blueberries
1 tablespoon butter or oleo

In a saucepan combine sugar, cornstarch, and water. Boil for 3 minutes; add blueberries and simmer 8-10 minutes. Add butter. Serve over the baked toast.

Note: To make this recipe heart-healthy, use Eggbeaters, fat-free cream cheese, and skim milk. Also try other fresh or frozen fruits such as peaches, mixed fruit, cherries, etc.

Recipes 1978-1998

Pineapple Cream French Toast

3 eggs
³/₄ cup half-and-half
¹/₄ teaspoon ground nutmeg
1 (8-ounce) can crushed
   pineapple, with juice

¹/₂ cup brown sugar
²/₃ loaf French bread cut into
   ³/₄-inch slices
¹/₄ cup butter, for frying
Powdered sugar

In small bowl beat eggs, half-and-half, nutmeg, pineapple, and brown sugar. Place bread in single layer in 9x11-inch glass baking dish (may need an extra dish). Pour egg mixture over bread, lifting to let liquid run under bread. Refrigerate overnight.

In the morning melt 2 tablespoons butter in frying pan. Add 3 or 4 slices bread and cook over moderate heat until golden brown on each side. Melt 2 more tablespoons butter and cook remaining slices. Dust with powdered sugar; serve with syrup. Makes 3-4 servings. *Recipe from Creekside Cottage Bed and Breakfast, Hill City, South Dakota.*

South Dakota Sunrise

Supper Milk Toast

Lots of grandkids remember this treat at Grandma's house.

Toast homemade bread; butter it well. Sprinkle with sugar; cover with cream. Bake in oven until bubbly.

Blew Centennial Bon-Appetit

Egg Gravy

It has always been the staple meal, no matter how poor or rich we've been. No matter how low the staples were in the pantry or cellar—we always had eggs, milk and a little flour.

2 cups milk
2 eggs

2 tablespoons flour
Salt

Heat milk. Beat eggs, flour, and a little salt. When milk is hot, pour and stir the egg-flour mixture into the milk. Cook until thick. Put on toast or bread. Good served with bacon.

Egg Gravy

German Pancakes

1 cup flour
6 eggs
1 cup milk

4 tablespoons butter, melted
1/2 teaspoon salt

Place all ingredients in blender and blend until well mixed. Pour into greased 9x13-inch pan. Bake at 450° for 20 minutes. Serve with melted butter and powdered sugar.

Home at the Range II

Light-as-a-Feather Whole Wheat Pancakes

1 1/3 cups whole wheat flour
1 1/2 teaspoons baking
  powder
1/4 teaspoon salt
1/4 teaspoon baking soda

1 egg
1 1/3 cups buttermilk
1 tablespoon brown sugar
1 tablespoon oil

Stir dry ingredients together in a medium bowl. In a separate bowl beat egg, buttermilk, brown sugar, and oil together. Stir into dry ingredients just until moistened. Batter should be slightly lumpy. Pour 1/4 cup batter for each cake onto a well-seasoned hot griddle. Turn when bubbles appear on surface. Turn only once. Makes 12 (4-inch) pancakes. Try topping with hot, chunky, spiced applesauce.

License to Cook Kansas Style

Liberal, Kansas, hosts the International Pancake Race. On Shrove Tuesday (the day before Lent begins), women contestants run 415 yards through the main streets of town flipping pancakes in skillets.

Waffles Supreme

5¼ cups biscuit mix
1 cup oil
2 large eggs
3 cups club soda
1 teaspoon vanilla
½ cup chopped pecans

Put biscuit mix in large bowl. Add oil, eggs, and small amount of club soda. Mix. Add vanilla and pecans. Add rest of club soda in small amounts and mix. Heat waffle iron and cook as per instructions for your waffle iron. May freeze and reheat in toaster.

90th Anniversary Trinity Lutheran Church Cookbook

Turkey Sausage

2¼ pounds ground turkey
1¼ teaspoons pepper
¾ teaspoon ground ginger
1½ teaspoons salt
1 teaspoon sage
¼ teaspoon ground red
    pepper

Mix and freeze in patties. Use as breakfast sausage. Take out as many as you need and pan-fry.

Regent Alumni Association Cookbook

Sausage Bread

Great on Christmas morning. Can have ready to bake and stick in oven when opening gifts.

1 loaf fresh or frozen bread
    dough
1½ pounds sausage, cooked
    and drained
8 ounces skim mozzarella
    cheese, grated
¼ onion, diced small
1 tablespoon butter

Roll bread dough as to make cinnamon rolls. Layer dough with sausage, cheese, and onions. Roll like a cinnamon roll. Raise in greased pan. When double, bake at 350° until golden brown. Take a fork and run butter over baked loaf. Let cool before cutting.

Recipes from the Heart: 100 Years of Recipes and Folklore

Breakfast Pizza

1 pound sausage	5 eggs
1 package crescent rolls	½ cup milk
1 cup frozen hash browns, thawed	½ teaspoon salt
	⅛ teaspoon pepper
1 cup sharp Cheddar cheese, shredded	2 tablespoons grated Parmesan cheese

Cook sausage; drain off fat. Separate crescent rolls. Place in ungreased pizza pan with points toward center. Press over bottom and up sides to form crust. Seal edges. Spoon sausage over crust. Sprinkle with hash browns. Top with Cheddar cheese.

In bowl, beat eggs, milk, salt, and pepper. Pour over crust. Sprinkle with Parmesan cheese. Bake at 375° for 25-30 minutes. Yields 8-10 servings.

Centerville Community Centennial Cookbook

Overnight Omelet

1 pound sausage	1½ slices bread, torn
5 eggs	2 cups Cheddar cheese
1 (12-ounce) can evaporated milk	

Brown sausage and drain. Beat eggs and milk; add torn bread pieces, cheese, and sausage. Pour into 9x13x2-inch baking dish. Cover with foil and refrigerate overnight. Bake at 350° for 45 minutes. Makes 8 servings. *Recipe from The Cimarron, Elkhart, Kansas.*

Savor the Inns of Kansas

Deviled Egg Bake

8 hard-boiled eggs, peeled
¼ cup butter, melted
½ teaspoon Worcestershire
  sauce
1 teaspoon dried parsley

1 tablespoon grated onion
¼ teaspoon dry mustard
1 cup shredded Cheddar
  cheese

Cut hard-boiled eggs in half; remove yolks. To the yolks add melted butter, Worcestershire sauce, parsley, onion, and dry mustard. Mash and mix together. Fill egg whites and put into greased baking dish.

WHITE SAUCE:
2 tablespoons melted butter
¼ cup flour
1 cup hot water

Salt and pepper, to taste
¾ cup cream

Melt butter and blend in flour. Add hot water to flour mixture. Season with salt and pepper. Add cream. Mix well and cook over low heat until thick. Pour white sauce over eggs and sprinkle with cheese. Cover dish and bake at 350° for 25 minutes. Makes 4-6 servings. *Recipe from Willow Springs Cabins Bed & Breakfast, Rapid City, South Dakota.*

South Dakota Sunrise

Travis' Mexican Omelette

Chorizo or a spicy sausage
¼ cup green onions, sliced
1 cup sliced fresh mushrooms
1 tomato, chopped
4 eggs, beaten

¼ cup milk
Salt and pepper to taste
1 cup Cheddar cheese, shredded
Sour cream
Salsa

Sauté sausage, onions, mushrooms, and tomato. Add eggs, milk, salt and pepper, and scramble. Fold in the cheese. Serve topped with sour cream and salsa.

A Taste of Prairie Life

Scrumptious Eggs

1½ pounds Monterey Jack
   cheese, shredded
¾ pound fresh mushrooms,
   sliced (or 1 can)
½ onion, chopped
¼ cup margarine
1 or 2 cups cubed ham

7 eggs
1¾ cups milk
½ cup flour
1 tablespoon parsley or
   freeze-dried chives
1 teaspoon seasoned salt

Place half of cheese in buttered 9x13-inch pan. Sauté mushrooms and onions in margarine until tender. Spread ham over mushrooms and top with rest of cheese. Cover and refrigerate till ready to bake. When ready to bake, beat eggs, milk, flour, parsley, and seasoning. Pour evenly over casserole. Bake 45 minutes at 350°. Serves 7.

Home at the Range III

Ham and Swiss Melts

Make these ahead and refrigerate—they keep well for a couple of days.

6 hamburger buns
Butter
1 (6-ounce) package thin sliced
   deli ham

6 slices Swiss cheese
1 (7-ounce) can sliced
   mushrooms, drained

Split buns in half and butter lightly. Divide ham, cheese, and mushrooms and layer on bottom buns. Put on bun tops. Wrap in foil and bake at 350° for 10 minutes. Yields 6 sandwiches.

Note: When cold, add five minutes to the baking time. You may wrap them in paper towels and heat them in the microwave.

The Give Mom a Rest (She's on Vacation) Cookbook

Pioneer Mormons followed the north bank of the Platte River and the Oregon Trail; travelers took the south bank. The lucky ones who owned oxen-powered prairie schooners traveled at a rate of about 10 miles a day. As the journey lengthened, possessions were cast off to lighten the load. Today, explorers still find frontier souvenirs along the trails.

Poteca

1 package yeast	1 cup sugar
2/3 cup warm water	1/4 pound butter
3 eggs	3/4 teaspoon salt
1 cup scalded milk	About 6 cups flour

Mix together; knead well. May not need quite 6 cups flour (want soft dough). Let rise and knead down. Let rise again. While it is rising, make filling. In a warm room, sprinkle table with flour. Roll out dough as thin as you can. Then with warm butter on hands, slide hands under dough and carefully stretch dough out so it is like a tablecloth. Do not let it tear. Spread filling on dough and roll like a jellyroll. Grease a large cookie sheet and spiral on sheet. Let rise one hour. Bake at 350° for one hour. This can be served with ham sliced very thin or with butter.

FILLING:

1 cup milk	1½ cups honey
1 (10-ounce) package finely	1 cup sugar
ground walnuts	1/3 cup butter, at least

Heat ingredients. Cool on medium to medium-low heat so it doesn't burn, stirring constantly. When it turns dark, it is about done. It will thicken when it cools.

Our Heritage

Dog Ears

1 or more loaves, frozen or	Oil for frying
homemade bread dough	

Grease frozen loaves and let the dough rise on a cookie sheet according to the bread instructions. Once it has risen, heat oil in deep skillet. Carefully cut off chunks of dough ½-inch thick and stretch a little to make them flatter. Be careful not to work the dough, as it will sink. Place dough in the hot grease and brown on one side. You will be able to see the dough rising and cooking through. Then turn and brown on the other side. Place on a dish and let drain. Serve warm from stove with butter, jelly, jam, honey, etc. Leftovers may be microwaved to warm.

Kearney 125th Anniversary Community Cookbook

Duff's Bread Pudding

1 cup warm water	$1/4$ teaspoon salt
1 cup Coffee-mate	Several peach slices
$1/4$ cup margarine	Raisins
3 eggs	Cinnamon
$1/2$ cup sugar	4 slices white bread, cubed
1 teaspoon vanilla	

Combine warm water and Coffee-mate in small bowl until lump free. Add margarine and beat 30 seconds. Add eggs and beat one minute. Add sugar, vanilla, salt, and several peach slices; beat at high speed for 2 minutes. Set aside.

In an ungreased casserole, place $1\frac{1}{2}$ cups of mixture and sprinkle with raisins. Add bread and toss lightly and add the remaining mixture. Sprinkle with more raisins and cinnamon. Bake at 345° for 40-45 minutes. Remove and cool slightly. Top with Nutmeg Sauce.

NUTMEG SAUCE:

$1/2$ cup sugar	1 cup milk
1 tablespoon cornstarh	$1/4$ cup margarine
$1/2$ teaspoon nutmeg	1 teaspoon vanilla

Combine sugar, cornstarch, and nutmeg in a small pan. Stir in milk and margarine. Cook over medium heat until mixture starts to thicken slightly. Then add vanilla and stir constantly until mixture thickens, but do not boil. Remove from heat and pour over pudding. Serves 6.

Our Daily Bread

Auntie Em's Cheddar Biscuits

The lost recipe that could have bribed Miss Gulch, saved Toto, and spared Dorothy her concussion-induced hallucinations of talking scarecrows, friendly lions, and tin men. These are delicious served with country ham or as a topping to chicken pot pie.

10 cups unbleached all-purpose
   flour
4 tablespoons baking powder
½ cup sugar
1 teaspoon salt
2 cups heavy cream
2 cups buttermilk

1 pound (4 sticks) unsalted
   butter, melted
2 cups grated sharp Cheddar
   cheese
2 tablespoons chopped fresh
   chives

Preheat the oven to 375°. Cover a large baking sheet with parchment paper and set aside. Sift together the flour, baking powder, sugar, and salt. In a separate large bowl, mix together the cream, buttermilk, and unsalted butter. With a wooden spoon, blend together the dry ingredients with the buttermilk mixture. The dough should pull together, but still be crumbly. Fold in the cheese and chives. On a floured surface, roll out the dough to 1 inch in thickness. Cut with a 2-inch biscuit cutter, and place biscuits on the prepared baking sheet. Bake for 20 minutes, or until tops are golden brown. Makes 5 dozen.

Pure Prairie

The Wizard of Oz house, located in the Coronado Museum in Liberal, Kansas, is an exact replica of Auntie Em's house, complete with ruby slippers, and a stuffed replica of Toto.

Evelyn's Butterbean Soup

Serious, hearty soup. Can be a meal in itself.

1 pound dry butter beans
  (or 3-4 small cans)
¼ pound boiled ham, chopped
  (can use chorizo)
1 Spanish onion, chopped
1 carrot, chopped
2 stalks celery, chopped
¼ hot pepper, chopped
2 pieces crisp bacon, chopped

Salt and pepper
2 ounces olive oil
1 clove garlic, chopped
1 bay leaf
1 (28-ounce) can peeled
  tomatoes, chopped
Parsley
3 quarts water

Soak dry beans in water overnight. Drain and rinse. Cook 1-2 hours till tender. Cook ham or chorizo and chop. Add beans and rest of ingredients. Simmer one hour or until vegetables are tender. Works well in crockpot.

To Tayla with TLC

Baked Potato Soup

²/₃ cup butter or margarine
²/₃ cup flour
7 cups milk
4 large baking potatoes, baked,
  cooled, peeled and cubed
  (about 4 cups)
4 green onions, sliced

12 bacon strips, cooked and
  crumbled
1¼ cups Cheddar cheese
1 cup (8 ounces) sour cream
¾ teaspoon salt
½ teaspoon pepper

In a large soup kettle, melt the butter. Stir in flour; heat and stir until smooth. Gradually add milk, stirring constantly until thickened. Add potatoes and onions. Bring to a boil, stirring constantly. Reduce heat; simmer for 10 minutes. Add remaining ingredients. Stir until cheese is melted. Serve immediately. Yields 8-10 servings.

Amana Lutheran Church 125th Anniversary Cookbook

Broccoli Cheese Soup #3

2 tablespoons butter or
   margarine
3/4 cup onion, chopped finely
6 cups water
6 chicken bouillon cubes
1 (8-ounce) package fine egg
   noodles (4 cups)

1 teaspoon salt
1/8 teaspoon garlic powder
2 (10-ounce) packages frozen,
   chopped broccoli
6 cups milk
1 pound Velveeta cheese
Pepper to taste

Heat butter in large saucepan. Add onion and sauté over medium heat for 3 minutes. Add water and bouillon cubes. Heat to boiling, stirring occasionally until bouillon is dissolved. Gradually add noodles and salt so that bouillon mixture continues to boil. Cook, uncovered, for 3 minutes, stirring occasionally. Stir in garlic powder and broccoli. Cook one minute more. Add milk, cheese, and pepper, and continue cooking until cheese melts. Stir constantly and closely watch temperature of soup. As soon as it is hot, remove from heat, as this will curdle if it boils. Reheat leftovers in double boiler or low crockpot. Serves 12.

Home at the Range IV

Roasted Tomato Soup

4 pounds fresh Roma tomatoes,
   unpeeled
10 whole garlic cloves, peeled
1 1/2 tablespoons dried basil
1 1/2 tablespoons dried oregano

1/2 cup extra virgin olive oil
3 cups cream or milk
Salt and pepper to taste
2 tablespoons fresh basil leaves
(optional)

Preheat oven to 400°. Place tomatoes, garlic, dried herbs, and oil in pan and roast in oven for one hour. Remove and cool. Purée contents in blender until fairly smooth; transfer to soup pot. Add cream or milk, salt and pepper. Heat to just under boiling point and simmer 5 minutes. Garnish with fresh basil.

Norman Lutheran Church 125th Anniversary Cookbook

Zuppa Tortellini
(Tortellini Soup)

Freezes well—the taste of Italy.

1 smoked ham hock, split
4 cans chicken broth
1 quart water
2 tablespoons margarine
1 large onion, sliced
2 ribs celery, sliced
1 green pepper, diced
3 carrots, peeled and diced
1 clove garlic, minced

1 box fresh mushrooms, sliced
1 large can tomatoes
1 pound hot Italian sausage
1 package fresh tortellini (from deli section)
1 zucchini, sliced
Parmesan cheese
Parsley

Simmer ham hock in chicken broth and water until meat begins to fall off the bone. Remove, discarding fat and bone. Dice meat. In margarine, sauté onion, celery, green pepper, carrots, and garlic until onion begins to turn golden. Add vegetables to pot. Sauté mushrooms in remainder of margarine. Add to pot. Add tomatoes and simmer ¾ hour. Skim off fat. In the meantime, cook Italian sausage and slice when warm enough to handle. Add to pot. Ten minutes before serving, add tortellini. Five minutes before serving, add zucchini. Garnish with Parmesan cheese mixed with parsley.

If It Tastes Good, Who Cares? II

Tortellini Soup

1 (30-ounce) jar spaghetti sauce
1 jar water
1 (14½-ounce) can chopped tomatoes
1 tablespoon chicken base or bouillon

½ teaspoon basil
¼ teaspoon garlic powder
1 (8-ounce) package dry tortellini (cheese)
1 (4-ounce) package pepperoni (cut each one in half)

Combine all ingredients in a large stock pot. Bring to a boil; simmer for about 30 minutes until tortellini are soft.

Sharing God's Bounty

Chicken Tortilla Soup

1 can cream of chicken soup
1 can fiesta nacho cheese soup
2 soup cans milk
1 can green chili enchilada sauce
1 can chicken meat
Tortilla chips
Sour cream (optional)

In a saucepan, mix soups and milk. Heat till hot and add enchilada sauce and chicken. Heat and serve. Put crushed tortilla chips on top. Can garnish with sour cream, if you like.

Cookin' with Farmers Union Friends

Reuben Soup

$^1/_2$ cup chopped onion
$^1/_2$ cup diced celery
2 tablespoons butter
1 cup chicken broth
1 cup beef broth
$^1/_2$ teaspoon baking soda
2 tablespoons cornstarch
2 tablespoons water
2 cups light cream (half-and-half)
$^3/_4$ cup sauerkraut, rinsed and drained
Shredded carrots (optional)
2 cups corned beef, chopped
1 cup (4 ounces) shredded Swiss cheese
Salt and pepper to taste
Rye croutons (optional)

In a large saucepan, sauté onion and celery in butter until tender; add broths and baking soda. Combine cornstarch and water; add to pan. Bring to a boil; boil 2 minutes, stirring occasionally. Reduce heat; add cream, sauerkraut, carrots, and corned beef. Simmer and stir for 15 minutes. Add cheese; heat until melted. Add salt and pepper; garnish with croutons, if desired.

Favorite Recipes of Rainbow Valley Lutheran Church

Corn Chowder

3 tablespoons minced onions
4 cups sliced potatoes
2 tablespoons minced bacon or
  salt pork
2 cups whole or fresh corn

1 teaspoon salt
Pepper
2 tablespoons parsley
1 cup milk

Boil onions and potatoes in water about enough to cover. Brown bacon. Discard fat. Combine with rest of ingredients. Serve hot.

Our Heritage

Hamburger Soup

1 pound hamburger, browned
  and drained
2 (14-ounce) cans beef broth
1 (14-ounce) can tomatoes,
  diced
1 cup chopped onions

$^2/_3$-1 cup quick barley
2 cups frozen mixed vegetables
1 (4-ounce) can mushrooms
2 cans golden mushroom soup
1 cup chopped green pepper
Salt and pepper

Mix all ingredients in large saucepan. Bring to a slow boil. Simmer 15-20 minutes, or till barley is tender.

Cookin' with Farmers Union Friends

Swedish Fruit Soup
(Friskt Soppa)

$^1/_2$ pound seeded prunes
1 cup raisins
1 cup sugar
4 tablespoons minute tapioca
$^1/_4$ pound dried apricots

1 orange, sliced thin
1 lemon, sliced
1 (8-ounce) jar maraschino cherries
1 stick cinnamon
3 apples, diced (or dry apples)

Soak the fruits overnight (except apples) with tapioca, sugar, and cinnamon in enough water to cover. In the morning add diced apples and water and cook until fruit is soft. Add canned fruit last. May be served either hot or cold. This fruit soup is good as the first course or as dessert. Whipped cream or topping and slivered blanched almonds make a delicious topping.

Sharing God's Bounty

Butch's Dumplings

1¼ cups flour
2 teaspoons baking powder
½ teaspoon salt

1 egg
2 tablespoons melted butter
⅔ cup milk

In medium bowl combine flour, baking powder, and salt. Mix well. Stir in egg, melted butter, and milk. Drop dough by spoonfuls into gently boiling soup. Cover. Cook 5 minutes.

The Hagen Family Cookbook

Chili for a Crowd

1 large onion, chopped
1 green pepper, chopped
2 garlic cloves, minced
2 tablespoons butter or
  margarine
2 pounds lean ground beef
½-1 pound bacon, cut into
  ½-inch pieces
½ pound pinto beans, cooked
  till tender
1 (16 to 20-ounce) can chopped
  tomatoes

1 pint tomato juice
1½ tablespoons salt
1 teaspoon cumin
½ tablespoon sugar
2 quarts water from beans
2 tablespoons flour
2 tablespoons chili powder
1 tablespoon Worcestershire
  sauce
¼ cup water

Sauté onion, green pepper, and garlic cloves in butter. Add ground beef and bacon pieces and sauté till cooked thoroughly. Add beans, chopped tomatoes, tomato juice, salt, cumin, sugar, and water from beans. Cook ingredients together on medium heat till hot; reduce heat; cook for at least 2 hours. Mix together flour, chili powder, and Worcestershire sauce with water; add to chili; stir well. Simmer till ready to serve. Serves 10-12.

The Joy of Sharing

"Thar's gold in them thar hills." The Homestake Mine, at Lead in the Black Hills, South Dakota, is one of North America's principal gold mines.

Ron's Chili

Best chili, and comes out good every time.

4 (16-ounce) cans hot chili
  beans
1 (12-ounce) can tomato paste
2 (15-ounce) cans tomato sauce
2 (15-ounce) cans peeled
  tomatoes
2 (1-ounce) packages Williams
  Chili Mix

2 pounds hamburger, browned
  with black pepper and salt,
  drained
Jalapeño pepper (optional)
1 clove of garlic, chopped
1 onion, chopped
1/4 teaspoon cayenne pepper
  (optional)

Combine all of above in a large pot. Add cayenne, if desired. Cook for 30 minutes or so. Simmer until ready to serve. Can top with chopped onions and grated cheese, if desired.

Recipes from the Heart: 100 Years of Recipes and Folklore

Quick Microwave Chili

Super easy; super delicious!

1 1/2-2 pounds lean ground
  beef, crumbled
1 clove garlic, minced, or
  1/4 teaspoon garlic powder
1 large onion, chopped
1 (16-ounce) can stewed
  tomatoes

2 (16-ounce) cans kidney beans
1/2 cup water
2 tablespoons chili powder
1 tablespoon cumin
Dash of cayenne (optional)
Dash of sugar (or sugar
  substitute)

Combine beef, garlic, and onion in a 3-quart casserole. Cover with a paper towel. Microwave for 7-9 minutes at HIGH (100%) until beef is no longer pink, stirring twice. Drain. Stir in remaining ingredients. Cover. Microwave for 20-25 minutes at MEDIUM (50%) or 180°. Stir. Or, you may simmer chili for one hour at DEFROST (30%). Let stand 5 minutes. Serve garnished with grated Cheddar cheese. Yields 6-8 servings.

Easy Livin' Microwave Cooking

Cow Punching Chili and Dumplings

CHILI:

1 pound ground beef, browned
1 cup chopped onion
1 large can tomatoes
2 small cans tomato sauce
1 tablespoon chili powder
2 teaspoons salt
1 can beans (optional)

DUMPLINGS:

1 cup flour
1 cup mashed potato flakes
2 teaspoons baking powder
1/2 teaspoon salt
1 cup milk
1 egg
2 tablespoons oil

Make up chili (cook all in pot) and simmer until right before serving time. For dumplings, combine flour, flakes, baking powder, and salt. Mix milk with egg and oil and add to above. Stir to moisten. Let stand several minutes. Place spoonfuls on chili, cover tightly and cook 15 minutes.

The Best Little Cookbook in the West

Chili Blanco

1 large onion, chopped
1 tablespoon oil
2 (16-ounce) cans white beans
2 (14-ounce) cans chicken
  broth
1 teaspoon chicken soup base
2-3 cloves garlic, minced
2 (4-ounce) cans diced green
  chilies
1-2 teaspoons ground cumin
1 teaspoon dried oregano
  leaves
1/2 teaspoon pepper
4 cups cooked and diced
  chicken
1 cup sour cream
3 cups shredded Monterey Jack
  cheese

Sauté onion in oil. In crockpot, combine all ingredients except sour cream and cheese. Simmer several hours (at least 3) so flavors are blended. Just before serving, stir in sour cream and cheese, heating until cheese melts.

Years and Years of Goodwill Cooking

Jerry's Oyster-Oyster Stew

2 cups celery, chopped fine
1/2 cup chopped onions
Butter (about 4 tablespoons)
2 cans oysters
1 can smoked oysters

Milk (3 cups)
1 (12-ounce) can evaporated milk
   (or half-and-half)
Salt and pepper
Hot pepper sauce

Sauté celery and onions in butter. When tender, add regular oysters and bring to a boil. Let simmer several minutes. Drain smoked oysters and add with milks (3 cups or so), salt and pepper. Bring back to simmer. Let "stew" for at least 15 minutes just below simmering. Add a few drops hot pepper sauce in each bowl, if desired.

The Best Little Cookbook in the West

Catfish Gumbo

1 pound catfish fillets
1/2 cup chopped celery
1/2 cup chopped green
   pepper
1/2 cup chopped onion
1 clove garlic, minced
1/4 cup melted fat or oil
2 beef bouillon cubes
2 cups boiling water

1 (1-pound) can tomatoes
10 ounces frozen okra, sliced
2 teaspoons salt
1/4 teaspoon pepper
1/4 teaspoon thyme
1 whole bay leaf
Dash Tabasco
1 1/2 cups hot cooked rice

Cut fillets into cubes. Sauté celery, green pepper, onion, and garlic in fat until tender. Dissolve bouillon cubes in water. Add bouillon, tomatoes, okra, and seasonings. Cover and simmer for 30 minutes. Add fish. Cover and simmer for 15 minutes more or until fish flakes easily. Remove bay leaf. Place 1/4 cup rice in each of 6 soup bowls. Fill with gumbo.

Taste the Good Life! Nebraska Cookbook

SALADS

Stirring ceremonial dances follow the drum beat at Native American powwows in Nebraska.

Three P's Salad

1 cup mayonnaise
1/2 package (dry) Hidden Valley
  Ranch Mix
1 tablespoon lemon juice
Sugar to taste (optional)
4 hard-cooked eggs, chopped

1 (16-ounce) package uncooked
  frozen peas
1 cup diced celery
2 cut-up diced sweet pickles
1 cup peanuts (unsalted)

Combine mayonnaise, dry dressing, and lemon juice in large bowl. Blend well; add remaining ingredients except peanuts. Chill. Add peanuts just before serving. Serves 10.

Nutritional analysis: Cal 313; Carbo 9.7g; Prot 8.9g; Fat 27g; Chol 120mg; Dietary Fiber 6.7g; Vit A 473IU; Vit B1 .3mg; Vit B2 .13mg; Vit B6 .15mcg; Vit B12 .26mcg; Folacin 62mcg; Niacin 3.9mg; Vit C 7.7mg; Vit E 8.4mg; Sod 263mg; Iron 1.8mg; Zinc 1.1mg.

REC Family Cookbook

Cauliflower Salad

1 cauliflower, cut into small
  pieces
1 can sliced water chestnuts,
  drained
3/4 cup lite mayonnaise

1 package dry ranch dressing
1 cup sliced radishes
1/2 cup chopped onion
3/4 cup sour cream
Dill weed, to taste (optional)

Mix all except dill weed together. Add dill and taste. Better if left overnight.

Pioneer Daughters Cookbook

Cucumber Salad

1 (3-ounce) package lemon or
  lime Jell-O
1 1/2 cups hot water
1/2 cup crushed pineapple
2 teaspoons vinegar

Pinch salt
1/8 teaspoon onion juice or
  finely grated onion
1/2 cup salad dressing
1 medium cucumber, diced

Dissolve Jell-O in hot water. Let set until slightly thickened, then beat until thick and foamy. Add pineapple, vinegar, salt, onion, salad dressing and cucumber. Chill until set. Serves 6.

Home at the Range I

Summertime Corn
and Cracked Wheat Salad

1 cup cracked wheat or bulgur
2 cups warm water
1 (10-ounce) packaged frozen
  shoepeg corn, cooked and
  drained
2 tomatoes, finely chopped
4 green onions, finely chopped
  including some green

1 small cucumber, seeded and
  finely chopped
3 tablespoons chopped
  parsley
¼ cup olive oil
1 tablespoon lemon juice
Salt and freshly ground pepper
  to taste

Combine cracked wheat and warm water in a small bowl for one hour. Drain off any remaining water and squeeze wheat dry. Combine wheat, corn, tomatoes, onions, cucumber, and parsley in a medium-sized bowl. Whisk oil and lemon juice together and pour over the salad. Toss to combine. Serves 6-8.

Que Queens: Easy Grilling & Simple Smoking

Sweet-Sour Green Beans

3 pounds green beans
3 onions, thinly sliced and
   separated into rings
1¹/₃ cups vinegar
1²/₃ cups sugar

²/₃ cup water
3 tablespoons salad oil
1¹/₂ teaspoons salt
¹/₂ teaspoon pepper

Cut off tips of beans; leave whole. Cook in boiling salted water until tender; drain. Combine beans and onion rings in large bowl. Stir together remaining ingredients; pour over bean mixture. Refrigerate at least 24 hours, stirring occasionally. Makes about 3½ quarts.

Note: If fresh beans are not available, use 3 (1-pound) cans whole green beans.

Blew Centennial Bon-Appetit

Bean Salad

1 (20-ounce) can red beans
1 (20-ounce) can green beans
1 (20-ounce) can wax beans
1 (20-ounce) can garbanzo
   beans
1 medium onion, chopped

3 tablespoons olive oil
2 tablespoons Dijon mustard
2 teaspoons red wine vinegar
1 tablespoon lemon juice
1 teaspoon Louisiana hot sauce
1 clove of garlic, minced

Drain and rinse beans. Combine beans and onion in bowl; mix well. Pour mixture of olive oil, Dijon mustard, wine vinegar, lemon juice, hot sauce, and garlic over bean mixture, stirring to coat. Chill, covered, for 2-8 hours before serving. Yield: 12 servings.

The Kansas City Barbeque Society Cookbook

De Smet, South Dakota, is the location of "Little House on the Prairie," made famous by author Laura Ingalls Wilder's pioneer adventure books. Wilder moved to De Smet with her family when she was 12.

Marinated Salad

1 (17½-ounce) can garbanzos
1 (16-ounce) can pitted black
  olives
1 (8½-ounce) can artichoke
  hearts, packed in water
1 (8-ounce) can green beans
1 (4-ounce) jar diced pimientos

1 thinly sliced cucumber
1 teaspoon dill weed
1 teaspoon oregano
Black pepper
1 (16-ounce) bottle Italian
  dressing

Drain all ingredients. Cut artichoke hearts in fourths. Combine vegetables and add spices. Add enough dressing to moisten. Refrigerate at least 2 hours, longer if possible.

Incredible Edibles

The Ultimate Broccoli Salad

1 bunch broccoli
½ cup slivered almonds
1 cup chopped celery
½ cup chopped onion
½ cup chopped green pepper

1 cup green grapes, halved
1 cup red grapes, halved
8 slices bacon, fried crisp and
  crumbled

DRESSING:
1 cup mayonnaise
⅓ cup sugar

1 tablespoon vinegar

Break broccoli into bite-size pieces. Toast almonds at 350° until lightly browned. Mix dressing ingredients and chill. Right before serving, mix all ingredients and blend with dressing.

We Love Country Cookin'

Spinach Salad

2 (10-ounce) packages frozen
   chopped spinach
3 boiled eggs, chopped
$1/2$ cup chopped celery

$1/2$ cup chopped onion
1 cup Longhorn cheese,
   cubed

Squeeze moisture from thawed spinach. Add chopped eggs, celery, onion, and cheese. Add dressing. Best if stored overnight.

DRESSING:
1 cup Miracle Whip
$1/2$ teaspoon salt

$1/2$ teaspoon Tabasco
2 tablespoons vinegar

Eastman Family Cookbook

Strawberry & Romaine Salad

A wonderful salad. The combination of strawberries and onion is simply delicious—everyone's favorite.

Romaine, washed and torn
Red onion, sliced

Fresh strawberries, sliced
Slivered almonds for garnish

DRESSING:
2 cups mayonnaise
$2/3$ cup sugar
$1/3$ cup light cream

$1/3$ cup raspberry vinegar
2 tablespoons poppy seeds
2-3 tablespoons raspberry jam

Combine dressing ingredients. Toss romaine, onion, and strawberries. Just before serving, drizzle dressing over salad. Dressing can be kept at least a week in refrigerator. Good on fruit, too.

If It Tastes Good, Who Cares? I

The awesome spire of Chimney Rock (500 feet up from the valley floor) could be spotted by settlers four days before they reached it. Fanciful descriptions of it were created in thousands of pioneer diaries. Chimney Rock is located 25 miles southeast of Scottsbluff, Nebraska. Just west of Gering, Nebraska is the imposing 800-foot landmark known as Scotts Bluff, which some Pioneers described as a massive medieval city.

Seafood Salad in Mini Cream Puffs

1 package crab meat, flaked
2 tablespoons fine chopped
  onion
3 tablespoons sliced black
  olives

3 tablespoons chopped dill
  pickle
½ teaspoon lemon juice
½ cup mayonnaise or salad
  dressing

Thoroughly mix salad ingredients and chill.

CREAM PUFFS:
½ cup hot water
¼ cup margarine
½ cup flour

¼ teaspoon salt
2 eggs

Preheat oven to 425°. In medium saucepan, heat margarine and water to boiling; stir in flour and salt. Cook over medium heat, stirring vigorously until mixture leaves sides of pan in smooth compact ball, about 2 minutes. Remove from heat. Add eggs, one at a time, beating vigorously after each egg until smooth and glossy. Drop by teaspoon onto ungreased cookie sheet. Bake 13-17 minutes. Let cool. Stuff with salad mixture.

Norman Lutheran Church 125th Anniversary Cookbook

Potato Chip Taco Salad

1 head of lettuce or 1 large
  bowl of mixed greens
8 ounces fresh spinach
1 pound ground beef
1 (1¼-ounce) package taco
  seasoning mix
⅔ cup water
1 (15-ounce) can kidney beans

2 large tomatoes, chopped
½ cup finely chopped onion
5 cups crushed rippled potato
  chips
1 cup grated Cheddar cheese
½ cup peppercorn ranch
  dressing
¼ cup salsa

Wash lettuce and spinach. Tear into bite-size pieces and spin dry in a salad spinner. Refrigerate while browning ground beef. Drain fat from ground beef and add taco seasoning, water, and drained kidney beans. Heat to boiling, reduce heat, and simmer for 15 minutes, stirring occasionally. Cool 10 minutes. In a large bowl, mix greens, tomatoes, onion, chips, and cheese. Add ground beef mixture and toss. Combine salad dressing and salsa. Pour over salad and toss gently. Serve immediately.

Red River Valley Potato Growers Auxiliary Cookbook

Smoked Turkey Salad

Delicious served on fresh salad greens, in half a cantaloupe, or on good-quality bread as a sandwich filling, this recipe makes plain old chicken salad taste pretty tame.

2¼ cups bite-sized pieces of
  smoked turkey
1 cup chopped red onion
4 hard-boiled eggs, chopped
  fine
2 cups mayonnaise

2 tablespoons Dijon mustard
1 teaspoon celery salt
1 jalapeño pepper, diced
1 teaspoon white pepper
1 teaspoon black pepper
1 teaspoon ground cumin

Combine turkey, onion, and eggs. In a separate bowl, combine mayonnaise with remaining ingredients. Add mayonnaise mixture to turkey mixture and blend well. Refrigerate until ready to serve. Serves 6-8.

All About Bar-B-Q Kansas City Style

Crunchy Chicken Salad

5 cups cooked chicken, cut in
  pieces
8 ounces water chestnuts, sliced

1 cup celery, chopped
1 cup pineapple tidbits
1 cup seedless grapes, halved

DRESSING:
1 cup Miracle Whip
1 cup real sour cream

3 tablespoons sugar
3/4 teaspoon seasoned salt

Combine salad ingredients. Combine dressing ingredients and toss with salad. Chill and serve. Serves 8.

90th Anniversary Trinity Lutheran Church Cookbook

Garden Herb Pasta Salad

1 (8-ounce) bag or box curly
  pasta noodles
1/2 bunch broccoli, chopped
1 large or 2 small tomatoes,
  chopped
1 (8-ounce) can sliced water
  chestnuts
1/4 cup red onion, chopped

1/2 cup sliced black olives
1 teaspoon dill weed
1 teaspoon salt
1/4 teaspoon pepper
1/4 teaspoon sugar
1 (16-ounce) bottle ranch
  dressing

Cook noodles according to package directions; drain. Put noodles in a bowl, then add broccoli, tomatoes, water chestnuts, onion, and olives. In a bowl, blend dill weed, salt, pepper, and sugar with the dressing. Add to the noodle mixture; toss lightly. Makes 16 servings.

Y Winners...Cookbook of Champions

The Red River of the North divides North Dakota and Minnesota. It probably got its name from a Sioux word for bloody in reference to battles there. The place in legend called the Red River Valley is hard to recognize as a valley at all; it is more like a plateau, as one can stand at its brink and not register a hair of a slope. The rich black soil in this valley is so fertile that few places on earth compare to it.

Shrimp and Macaroni Salad

2 cups cleaned and cooked
  shrimp
4 cups cooked macaroni
½ cup sliced celery
½ cup stuffed olives
½ cup chopped green
  pepper
½ cup sliced pimento

½ cup diced onion
½ teaspoon salt
¼ teaspoon pepper
3 tablespoons mayonnaise or
  salad dressing
Crisp greens
½ cup French dressing
Lemon and tomato wedges

Split each shrimp lengthwise. In large bowl combine shrimp, macaroni, celery, olives, green pepper, pimento, and onion. Cover and chill. Just before serving, stir together salt, pepper, and mayonnaise, and toss with shrimp mixture. Spoon mixture onto crisp greens, garnish with tomato wedges, and if desired, whole shrimp. Serve with French dressing and lemon wedges.

Our Daily Bread

Cranberry Chicken Salad

1 (3-ounce) package lemon
  Jell-O
1½ cups hot water
2 cups cooked, diced chicken
2 hard-boiled eggs, chopped
2 teaspoons minced onion

¼ cups chopped, stuffed
  olives
½ cup diced celery
½ cup salad dressing
1 cup cranberry sauce
2 teaspoons orange juice

Dissolve Jell-O in hot water. Mix chicken, eggs, onion, olives, celery, and dressing. Add ½ of Jell-O mixture to chicken mixture. Put this chicken/Jell-O mixture in an 8x8-inch pan. Chill. Meanwhile, mix cranberry sauce until smooth. Add orange juice and remaining Jell-O. Chill before pouring over the chicken layer. Refrigerate until all has set. Cut in squares and serve on a lettuce leaf.

North Dakota...Where Food is Love

Flying Farmers Salad

5 cups cooked, chunked
  chicken
2 tablespoons salad oil
2 tablespoons orange juice
1 teaspoon salt
3 cups cooked rice
1½ cups green seedless
  grapes

1½ cups sliced celery
1 (13½-ounce) can pineapple
  tidbits, drained
1 (11-ounce) can mandarin
  oranges, drained
1 cup slivered almonds
1½ cups mayonnaise

Mix all together. Let stand several hours or overnight. Serves 15.

Lakota Lutheran Church Centennial Cookbook

Chicken Wedding Salad

1 (7½-ounce) package of
  macaroni rings, cooked
2 cups cooked chicken or
  turkey
1 cup green grapes, cut in half
1 (11-ounce) can mandarin
  oranges, cut in half

⅓ cup slivered almonds
1 cup diced celery
1 teaspoon salt
1 cup salad dressing
1 (8-ounce) carton frozen
  whipped topping

Cool the macaroni and chicken. Mix all, folding in whipped topping last. Chill and serve.

North Dakota American Mothers Cookbook

Wild Rice Salad

3 cups diced white chicken
  breast
4 cups wild rice (or ½ white
  and ½ wild rice) cooked
2 cups green grapes, cut
1 cup cashews, chopped

1 cup sliced water chestnuts
2 cups mayonnaise
1 teaspoon soy sauce
¼ teaspoon curry powder
½ teaspoon Lawry's salt

Mix first 5 ingredients. Add mayonnaise, soy sauce, and seasonings. Toss and chill.

North Dakota...Where Food is Love

Zesty New Potato Salad

A tangy, light, side dish. Serve either hot or cold. Especially complimentary to ham on the grill.

1 pound small new potatoes,
  preferably red
2 ribs celery
3 green onions

¼ cup prepared Good Seasons
  Salad Dressing
2 tablespoons chopped fresh
  parsley

Peel a ¼-inch ribbon around the middle of each potato. Steam or boil potatoes until barely tender when pierced with a fork (about 15 minutes); drain and quarter. Place in medium bowl. Chop celery and onions, and add to potatoes. Add salad dressing and toss lightly. (Add dressing while potatoes are still warm so the dressing flavor seeps into the potatoes.) Chop parsley and sprinkle on top. Serve warm or chilled. Serves 4-6.

VARIATION:

To add color, toss in other vegetables like yellow squash, red onions, peas, tomatoes, roasted red bell peppers, or pimentos. Or add capers and fresh mint.

Hall's Potato Harvest Cookbook

Creamy Dijon Potato Salad

9 medium potatoes
4 hard-cooked egg whites,
  chopped
⅔ cup finely chopped dill
  pickle
½ cup finely chopped celery
⅓ cup finely chopped onion
2 cups Hellman's reduced-fat
  mayonnaise

2 tablespoons Dijon mustard
2 teaspoons salt
1 teaspoon paprika
1 teaspoon finely ground black
  pepper
1 teaspoon Lawry's seasoned
  salt

Boil potatoes until tender, then peel and cube (yields about 9 cups). Combine potatoes with egg whites, dill pickle, celery, and onion. Combine remaining ingredients and add to potato mixture, tossing gently. Refrigerate until served. Serves 14-16.

All About Bar-B-Q Kansas City Style

Easy German Potato Salad

1 (24-ounce) package frozen
   hash brown potatoes
4 slices bacon
1 small onion, chopped
2 teaspoons sugar
1 teaspoon flour

1 teaspoon instant beef
   bouillon
1 teaspoon salt
¼ cup vinegar
½ cup water
1 teaspoon chopped chives

Thaw potatoes in a large skillet. Fry bacon until crisp; remove. Add onion to drippings. Cook until tender and golden. Stir in sugar, flour, bouillon, and salt. Cook over medium heat, stirring until bubbly. Remove from heat; stir in vinegar and water. Heat to boiling, stirring constantly. Crumble bacon; carefully stir bacon, potatoes, and chives into hot mixture. Heat thoroughly, stirring lightly to cover potatoes. Yields 5-6 servings.

Kearney 125th Anniversary Community Cookbook

Crispy Oriental Salad

DRESSING:
¾ cup canola oil
½ cup sugar

¼ cup red wine vinegar
2 tablespoons soy sauce

Ingredients can be made 3 days in advance and refrigerated.

SALAD:
½ cup margarine or liquid
   butter
1 (1-ounce) bottle sesame
   seeds
2 packages Ramen noodles,
   broken up (do not use
   seasoning)

1 (½-cup) package slivered
   almonds
2 tablespoons sugar
2 pounds bok choy (or Nappa
   cabbage)
5 green onions with tops,
   sliced

In a large skillet melt margarine over medium heat. Add sesame seeds, noodles, almonds, and sugar. Cook until lightly browned. Set aside, cool to room temperature. Meanwhile coarsely chop bok choy using both stalks and leaves. Combine with green onions and chill. Combine everything together just prior to serving. Serves 8-12.

The Hagen Family Cookbook

Country Coleslaw

1 medium head cabbage,
  shredded (8 cups)
1-2 medium onions, diced
  (2 cups)
3 tablespoons chopped canned
  pimento, drained
6 tablespoons chopped green
  bell pepper

¾ cup white vinegar
1 cup sugar
½ teaspoon celery salt
1 heaping tablespoon salt
1 teaspoon celery seed
Salt to taste

Combine all ingredients except salt, blend well, and barely cover with boiling water. Let stand for one hour. Pack into jars and refrigerate overnight. Drain and salt lightly before serving. Serves 6.

All About Bar-B-Q Kansas City Style

Onion Salad

8 onions, cut paper thin
½ cup water
½ cup vinegar
¾ cup sugar

1½ cups mayonnaise
Salt and pepper (optional)
1 tablespoon celery seed

Soak onions in water, vinegar, and sugar for at least 3 hours or overnight. Drain onions very well and mix with remaining ingredients. Purple onions work, too.

Pioneer Daughters Cookbook

Orange Jell-O Salad

2 cups water
1 small package orange Jell-O
1 small package tapioca
pudding

1 small can mandarin oranges
1 carton Cool Whip (any size)

Put water, Jell-O, and tapioca pudding in saucepan. Bring to boil. Let cool. Put in bowl. Drain mandarin oranges. Mix oranges and Cool Whip with Jell-O and pudding. Refrigerate one hour before serving.

Centerville Community Centennial Cookbook

Asparagus Salad

1 can asparagus soup
1/2 cup water
1 (3-ounce) package lemon or lime Jell-O
1 (8-ounce) package cream cheese, softened with a little milk

1/2 cup mayonnaise
3/4 cup chopped celery
1/2 cup green pepper
1/2 cup chopped nuts
1/2 cup or less finely chopped onion

Bring soup and water to a boil; add Jell-O, cream cheese, and mayonnaise. Set aside to cool. Add remaining ingredients and pour into mold and refrigerate.

A Century in His Footsteps

Eggnog Cranberry Salad

1 (3-ounce) package regular vanilla pudding
1 (3-ounce) package lemon Jell-O
3 cups water, divided
2 tablespoons lemon juice
1 (3-ounce) package raspberry Jell-O

1 (16-ounce) can whole cranberry or jellied cranberry sauce
1/2 cup chopped celery and nuts (optional)
1 (12-ounce) carton Cool Whip
Cinnamon or nutmeg

In saucepan, combine pudding mix, lemon Jell-O, and 2 cups of water. Cook and stir till mixture boils. Add lemon juice. Chill until partially set. Cook and stir till dissolved, the raspberry Jell-O and one cup water. Beat in cranberry sauce. Fold in celery and nuts, if desired. Chill until partially set. Fold Cool Whip into lemon mixture and put 1/2 on bottom, then red layer, and top with rest of lemon mixture. Sprinkle top with cinnamon or nutmeg.

We Love Country Cookin

Boys Town is internationally famous as a refuge for homeless boys. It began in Omaha, Nebraska, in 1917.

Festive Cranberry Salad

Also a quick and easy dessert.

1 can sweetened condensed
  milk
¼ cup lemon juice
1 (20-ounce) can crushed
  pineapple, drained

1 (16-ounce) can whole
  cranberry sauce
½ cup nuts, chopped
1 (9-ounce) carton whipped
  topping

Thoroughly mix all ingredients except topping. Fold in whipped topping. Freeze. Remove from freezer about 5 minutes before serving. Serves 12.

Note: Can be frozen in a large pan, or in individual servings.

Recipes 1978-1998

Cranberry Salad

2 packages raspberry gelatin
2 cups boiling water
1 can whole cranberry sauce

1 (13½-ounce) can crushed
  pineapple
½ cup nuts

Dissolve gelatin in boiling water. Fold in sauce, pineapple, and juice. Chill until thickened, stir in nuts. Pour into mold.

90th Anniversary Trinity Lutheran Church Cookbook

Cheese Jell-O Salad

You might as well double this recipe, as it is a winner in our family.

1 cup crushed pineapple
½ cup sugar
1 small package lemon Jell-O
1 cup water
Juice of 1 lemon

½ pound Cheddar or American
  cheese, grated
½ cup nuts
1 cup whipped topping

Heat pineapple and sugar until boiling; add Jell-O powder; stir until dissolved. Remove from heat; add cold water and lemon juice. Cool until partially set; add cheese, nuts, and whipped topping. Keep in refrigerator, if there is any left.

Blew Centennial Bon-Appetit

Our Necessary Salad

A real people pleaser.

1 (24-ounce) carton cottage
  cheese, large curd, if possible
1 carton non-dairy whipped
  topping
1 (15¼-ounce) can chunk
  pineapple, drained

1 (3-ounce) box pineapple Jell-O
  (dry)
1 (3-ounce) box orange Jell-O
  (dry)
Maraschino cherries, cut in half
  (optional)

Combine cheese, topping, and drained pineapple; mix together. Add dry Jell-Os and stir until all dry Jell-O is mixed well. Decorate top of salad with cherries. Add a few mint leaves. Makes 8 (1-cup) servings.

Recipes from the Heart: 100 Years of Recipes and Folklore

Apricot Salad

²/₃ cup sugar
1 (6-ounce) package apricot
  Jell-O
1 cup boiling water
1 (8-ounce) package cream
  cheese, softened

2 small jars strained apricot
  baby food
1 (15¼-ounce) can crushed
  pineapple, drained
1 (8-ounce) carton Cool Whip
½ cup chopped pecans

Add sugar to Jell-O; add boiling water. Stir warm Jell-O into softened cream cheese. Add strained apricots and pineapple; let cool. Fold in Cool Whip and nuts. Makes large bowl or 9x13-inch dish. Refrigerate.

Taste of Coffeyville

Pineapple Salad

1 (6-ounce) package apricot
  Jell-O
1 (15½-ounce) can crushed
  pineapple

2 cups buttermilk
1 (8-ounce) carton Cool Whip
1 cup chopped pecans (or less)
  (optional)

Boil together the Jell-O and crushed pineapple. Cool, and add
the buttermilk, Cool Whip, and pecans. Pour in 9x13-inch pan
and chill.

Home at the Range III

Hidden Pear Salad

1 (16-ounce) can pears (liquid
  drained and reserved)
1 (3-ounce) package lime
  flavored gelatin
1 (3-ounce) package cream
  cheese, softened

¼ teaspoon lemon juice
1 envelope whipped topping
  mix
Lettuce leaves

In a saucepan, bring pear liquid to a boil. Stir in gelatin until
dissolved. Remove from the heat and cool at room temperature
until syrupy. Meanwhile, purée pears in a blender. In a mixing
bowl, beat cream cheese and lemon juice until fluffy and smooth.
Add puréed pears and mix well. Prepare whipped topping according to package directions; fold into pear mixture. Fold in
cooled gelatin. Pour into an oiled 4½-cup mold. Chill overnight.
Just before serving, unmold salad onto a lettuce-lined platter.
Yield: 6-8 servings.

Rainbow's Roundup of Recipes

Raspberry Rice Jubilee Salad

3 cups milk
1½ cups instant rice
⅓-½ cup sugar
¼ teaspoon salt (optional)
1 teaspoon vanilla (preferably white)

1 (8-ounce) carton whipped topping
2 (10-ounce) packages frozen raspberries, thawed
2-3 tablespoons cornstarch

Over medium heat, boil milk, rice, sugar, and salt. Stir frequently so it doesn't scorch. Cool until milk is gone and rice is fluffy. Add vanilla and cool. Fold in whipped topping. While rice is cooking, cook raspberries and cornstarch together until thickened. Partially cool this before pouring on top of rice mixture which has been placed in large bowl. Garnish with raspberries and mint leaves. Can use fresh raspberries but then add sugar according to your taste. Also can vary amount of raspberries.

Wyndmere Community Alumni Cookbook

Cookies and Cream Salad

2 cups buttermilk
2 small package instant vanilla pudding
16 ounces Cool Whip
1 package crushed fudge stripe cookies

2 cans mandarin oranges, drained
1 small can crushed pineapple, drained

Mix together first 3 ingredients. Add remaining ingredients. Keeps well in fridge for 2-3 days.

Sharing Our "Beary" Best II

Centuries before cowboys tamed the West, dinosaurs ruled the former giant swamp that is now western North Dakota. There are many places to see dinosaur fossils in this area that offer impressive exhibits of North Dakota's pre-historic past.

Heart Healthy Fruit Salad

1 can no-sugar-added sliced
  peaches
1 can no-sugar-added chunk
  pineapple
1 can no-sugar-added sliced
  pears

1 package sugar-free instant
  vanilla pudding (dry)
2 tablespoons Tang or
  2 teaspoons sugar-free Tang
1 cup frozen whole strawberries
1-2 sliced bananas

Drain liquid from canned fruits. Keep one cup of this liquid. Mix pudding and Tang in bowl. Slowly stir in one cup fruit liquid. Add drained fruits, strawberries, bananas. Refrigerate until served.

125 Years of Cookin' with the Lord

Pear and Walnut Salad

½ cup oil
3 tablespoons vinegar
¼ cup sugar
½ teaspoon celery seeds
¼ teaspoon salt

¼ cup walnut halves
4 cups torn lettuce
1 pear, sliced or chopped
2 ounces bleu cheese,
  crumbled

Combine oil, vinegar, sugar, celery seeds, and salt in jar with tight-fitting lid; shake to dissolve sugar and mix well. Chill in refrigerator. Spread walnuts in baking dish. Bake at 375° for 3-5 minutes or microwave on HIGH for 3-4 minutes or until golden brown, stirring occasionally. Combine walnuts with lettuce, pear, and bleu cheese in salad bowl. Add dressing at serving time; toss lightly to coat well. Yields 4 servings.

Y Cook?

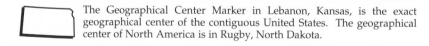

The Geographical Center Marker in Lebanon, Kansas, is the exact geographical center of the contiguous United States. The geographical center of North America is in Rugby, North Dakota.

Fall Fruit Salad

2 cups raw cranberries, ground   ½ cup seedless green grapes
3 cups tiny marshmallows   ½ cup broken walnuts
¾ cup sugar   Pinch of salt
2 cups diced unpared tart apples   1 cup cream, whipped

Combine cranberries, marshmallows, and sugar. Cover and chill overnight. Add apples, grapes, walnuts, and salt. Fold in whipped cream and chill.

Pioneer Daughters Cookbook

Carrot-Apple Salad

2 cups shredded carrots   ½ cup sunflower seeds
3 cups unpeeled, chopped   ½ cup Yogurt-Honey
   apples   Dressing
1 cup raisins   Alfalfa sprouts or lettuce

Combine carrots, apples, raisins, and sunflower seeds with dressing. Serve on alfalfa sprouts or lettuce. Serves 6.

YOGURT-HONEY DRESSING:
1 (8-ounce) container plain   2 tablespoons honey
   yogurt   ¼ cup sesame seeds

Blend and chill. Keep refrigerated. Makes one cup dressing.
Pumpkin, Winter Squash and Carrot Cookbook

Carrot Pickles

1 pound small, whole carrots   ½ teaspoon whole allspice
1 cup sugar   ½ teaspoon whole cloves
1 cup vinegar   1 stick cinnamon
1 cup water

Boil carrots until tender-crisp. Peel and put into sterilized pint jars. In a kettle, place the sugar, vinegar, water, and spices which have been tied in cheesecloth bag. Boil for 10 minutes. Remove spices. Pour over carrots. Seal. Put jars in hot water bath and boil for 10 minutes. Makes 4-6 pints.

Heavenly Recipes

Hot Bacon Dressing

4-5 slices bacon
1 large egg
1 tablespoon flour (heaping)
3 tablespoons granulated
   sugar

¹/₄ teaspoon salt
Dash black pepper
Cider vinegar to taste
1¹/₂ cups cold water

Cut bacon in pieces and fry until crisp. Remove from pan and drain. Mix egg, flour, granulated sugar, salt, pepper, vinegar (add by the tablespoon to taste) and water. Pour mixture into the frying pan. With heat set at medium, stir the mixture constantly until it thickens and begins to boil slowly.

Remove from heat when thick. Add drained bacon and ladle over salad greens; toss lightly. Makes 15 servings.

Per serving: 29 calories; 1.4g fat; 16mg cholesterol.

Reader's Favorite Recipes

Pretzel Salad

2²/₃ cup crushed pretzels
3 tablespoons sugar
1 cube oleo, melted
1 (8-ounce) package cream
   cheese
2 tablespoons milk
1 cup powdered sugar

1 cup Cool Whip
2 small packages strawberry
   Jell-O
2 cups boiling water
2 small packages frozen
   strawberries

Mix together crushed pretzels, sugar, and oleo. Pat into 9x13-inch pan. Bake 10 minutes at 375°. Cool. Mix together cream cheese and milk. Add powdered sugar and Cool Whip. Pour over crust. Mix together Jell-O and boiling water until well dissolved. Add frozen strawberries. Chill until just thickened. Pour over powdered sugar mixture. Chill until serving time.

Recipes from the Heart / Epsilon Omega Sorority

In search of adventure, Teddy Roosevelt returned to the Dakota Territory again and again to live the life of a cowboy, explore, invigorate his body, and renew his spirit. He later wrote: "I would not have been President had it not been for my experiences in North Dakota." Established as a Memorial Park in 1947, it became Theodore Roosevelt National Park in 1978.

VEGETABLES

Located in the Badlands of North Dakota, the 70,448-acre Theodore Roosevelt National Park was shaped by the Missouri River. Medora.

Roasted Potatoes

A must-try recipe! You can use this recipe as the base for many of your own creative variations.

4 pounds potatoes
8 cloves garlic
4 tablespoons chopped fresh
  parsley
2 teaspoons dried basil

2 teaspoons dried oregano
Ground black pepper to taste
8-12 tablespoons light olive or
  vegetable oil
Salt to taste

Preheat oven to 350°. Peel potatoes (or leave skins, if you wish), and cut each potato in 2-inch chunks. Mince garlic. In large bowl, combine all ingredients except salt, and toss so potatoes are covered with oil. Spread potatoes in single layer in 9x13-inch (or larger) pan. Bake uncovered for one hour—turning once—or until golden brown and cooked through. Season potatoes with salt before serving. Serves 4-6.

Hall's Potato Harvest Cookbook

Rustic Home-Fried Potatoes

2 tablespoons margarine
3 medium potatoes, thinly
  sliced
1 medium sweet onion, halved
  and thinly sliced
2 cloves garlic, minced
2 tablespoons parsley, dried

1 tablespoon rosemary, dried
  and crushed
1/4 teaspoon salt
1/8 teaspoon ground red
  pepper
1/8 teaspoon ground black
  pepper

In a large skillet melt margarine. Layer the sliced potatoes, onion, and garlic in the skillet. Sprinkle with parsley, rosemary, salt, ground red pepper, and ground black pepper. Cook potato mixture, covered, over medium heat for 8 minutes. Continue cooking, uncovered, for 8-10 minutes more or until potatoes are tender and brown, turning frequently.

The Mormon Trail Cookbook

Crusty New Potatoes

Wonderfully tender inside, and brown and crusty outside. Serve elegantly with chicken breasts or steak.

8 small new potatoes, preferably red	**¹/₂ teaspoon Lawry's or other seasoning salt**
¹/₄ cup butter	**1 cup crushed cornflakes**

Preheat oven to 400°. Boil unpeeled potatoes until tender when pierced with a fork (about 20 minutes); drain and peel. Melt butter, and add seasoning salt. Roll each potato in seasoned butter, then in crushed cornflakes; place in glass baking dish. Repeat with each potato. Bake potatoes 25 minutes. Serves 4.

Hall's Potato Harvest Cookbook

Ruth's Smashed Potato Bites

A perfect treat for unexpected guests because you can make them in advance, freeze them, and pop them in the oven when friends drop by.

1¹/₂ pounds potatoes, preferably red	**1 cup crushed barbecue potato chips**
2 slices bacon	**¹/₄ cup grated Parmesan Cheese**
1 small onion (¹/₄ cup finely chopped)	**1 egg, beaten**

Preheat oven to 400°. Peel potatoes, and cut in half. Boil until tender when pierced with a fork (about 20 minutes); drain. Cook bacon in microwave until crisp; crumble into fine pieces. Finely chop onion. Mash potatoes with bacon and onion. Form into 1-inch balls. Combine cheese and chips. Roll balls in egg, and then in cheese/chip mixture. Bake 8-10 minutes, or until hot throughout. Serves 24.

Note: If you are in a hurry, use instant dry potato flakes to make the mashed potatoes.

Hall's Potato Harvest Cookbook

North Dakota's cultural life owes much to the local Native American and immigrant Scandinavian, Russian, and German traditions.

Down Home Mashed Potatoes

6 boiling potatoes (2 pounds), peeled and cut into quarters
2 tablespoons olive oil
2 cloves of garlic, peeled and finely minced

1/2 cup sour cream
1/2 cup warm milk
1 tablespoon cider vinegar
Salt and fresh ground pepper, to taste

Place potatoes in saucepan, add enough cold water to cover. Bring to boil, reduce heat to simmer and cook for 25 minutes or until potatoes are tender. Drain. Meanwhile place olive oil in skillet. Add garlic and cook, stirring over low heat for 2 minutes or until garlic is golden. Place garlic in mixing bowl and add the drained potatoes. Mash potatoes and garlic together. Add sour cream. Slowly pour in the warm milk and continue to mash. Add vinegar and season with salt and pepper to taste. Serve immediately. Serves 4-6.

To Tayla with TLC

Refrigerator Mashed Potatoes

5 pounds potatoes (9 large)
2 (3-ounce) packages cream cheese
1 cup dairy sour cream
1 teaspoon onion salt

1 teaspoon salt
1/4 teaspoon pepper
2 tablespoons butter or margarine

Cook peeled potatoes in boiling salted water until tender. Drain. Mash until smooth, and no lumps. Add remaining ingredients and beat until light and fluffy. Cool.

Cover and place in refrigerator. May be used anytime within 2 weeks. To use, place desired amount in greased casserole, dot with butter and bake in moderate oven at 350° until heated, about 30 minutes.

Note: If you use the full amount, heat in a 2-quart casserole and dot with 2 tablespoons butter. It is also very good topped with shredded Cheddar cheese. Serves 12.

A Cooking Affaire I

Scalloped Potatoes

8 medium potatoes, peeled
   and sliced
3 tablespoons margarine
3 tablespoons flour

2 teaspoons salt
3 cups milk
1/4 cup chopped onion
Pepper to taste

Place sliced potatoes in casserole or roaster. Melt 3 tablespoons margarine in skillet. Gradually add flour and seasoning, then add milk to mixture to make a white sauce till heated and right thickness. Add onions and pour over potatoes. Chopped bacon or ham may also be added. Bake for 30-40 minutes at 350°. Uncover and bake for another 30 minutes. Serves 6-8.

Kelvin Homemakers 50th Anniversary Cookbook

Company Potatoes

6-8 potatoes, cooked, unpeeled
1 can cream of chicken soup
1 pint sour cream
1/4 cup butter
1/4 cup onion

1 1/2 cups grated American
   cheese
Salt and pepper to taste
2 cups crushed cornflakes
1/4 cup butter

Peel and grate potatoes. Combine with soup, sour cream, butter, onion, cheese, and seasonings. Put in casserole and top with the cornflakes and butter mixture. Bake, covered, 45 minutes at 350°.

We Love Country Cookin'

Potato and Ham Hot Dish

1 cup sour cream
1 cup mushroom soup
8 potatoes, sliced
1 cup chopped onions

6 slices ham, cut in pieces
1 cup Cheddar cheese
   shredded

Mix sour cream and soup together. Place sliced potatoes in casserole; add onions, ham, and cheese. Mix well. Bake for 2 hours at 325°.

Red River Valley Potato Growers Auxiliary Cookbook

Microwave Scalloped Potatoes

1 pound potatoes, peeled and
   cut in 1/4-inch slices
1/2 teaspoon salt
3/4 teaspoon Italian herb
   seasoning
1/8 teaspoon pepper
2 tablespoons butter

1/2 cup water
1/2 teaspoon instant beef bouillon
1/2 cup shredded Cheddar
   cheese
2 tablespoons grated Parmesan
   cheese
1/4 teaspoon paprika

Place all ingredients, except cheese and paprika into a 8-inch round baking dish. Cover loosely with plastic wrap. Microwave on HIGH 4 minutes, remove, stir, cover and cook 4 minutes more. Combine cheeses and paprika. Sprinkle over potatoes. Cook, uncovered for 2 minutes more. Let stand 5 minutes before serving. Makes 6 servings.

Silver Celebration Cookbook

Easy Au Gratin Potatoes

A nice compliment to ham or roast beef.

1 1/2 pounds (24 ounces) frozen
   hash browns (with onions
   and/or green pepper,
   optional)
1 (8-ounce) carton sour cream
1 can cream of potato soup,
   undiluted

1 to 2 cups (4 to 8 ounces)
   grated Cheddar cheese (either
   sharp or mild)
Dash of salt or pepper
2 tablespoons butter or
   margarine
Paprika (optional)

Microwave frozen potatoes in a 2-quart covered microwave-safe casserole for 5 minutes at HIGH (100%). Stir in sour cream, soup, cheese, salt, and pepper. Dot with butter. Microwave, covered, for 10 minutes at HIGH (100%). Stir. Sprinkle with paprika, if desired. Microwave, covered, again for 10-12 minutes at MEDIUM (50%). Let stand 5 minutes. Yields 4 servings.

Easy Livin' Microwave Cooking for the Holidays

Almost Pizza

STEP 1:

7 cups raw potatoes (sliced or diced)
1 pound ground beef
1 can nacho cheese soup

1 cup milk
Butter
Dash of salt
Dash of pepper

Place raw potatoes in greased 9x13-inch pan. Brown ground beef and cover potatoes. Heat nacho cheese soup and milk. Pour over hamburger. Dot with butter, sprinkle with salt and pepper.

STEP 2:

1 can tomato soup
$\frac{1}{2}$ teaspoon oregano
1 teaspoon sugar
$\frac{1}{2}$ cup chopped onion

2 cups sliced pepperoni
Parmesan cheese to sprinkle
1-2 cups shredded mozzarella cheese

Mix tomato soup, oregano, sugar, and onion. Pour this over nacho cheese soup. Place the pepperoni on top. Cover with foil and bake at 400° for 15 minutes. Turn oven down to 350° for one hour or until potatoes are done. Take out and sprinkle with Parmesan cheese and mozzarella cheese. Place in oven to melt cheese. Serves 8-10.

VARIATION:

Canadian bacon, green pepper, olives, or any other toppings may be added.

Red River Valley Potato Growers Auxiliary Cookbook

Yam 'N Cranberry Casserole

1 (12-ounce) package fresh,
  raw whole cranberries
  (about 3 cups)
1½ cups sugar (or less)
1 small unpeeled orange,
  sliced, seeded

½ cup pecan halves
¼ cup orange juice
¾ teaspoon cinnamon
¼ teaspoon nutmeg
⅛ teaspoon mace
1 (14-ounce) can yams, drained

Combine cranberries, sugar, orange slices, pecan halves, orange juice, and spices in a 2-quart casserole. Bake uncovered at 375° for 30 minutes. Stir yams into cranberry mixture; bake until hot throughout, about 15 minutes. Serves 8.

Recipes 1978-1998

Sweet Potato Casserole

3 cups mashed sweet potatoes
1 cup sugar
2 eggs
½ cup milk

1 teaspoon vanilla
Cinnamon cloves, nutmeg
  to taste

TOPPING:
1 cup brown sugar
1 cup chopped pecans or
  walnuts

½ cup flour
½ stick butter

Combine potatoes, sugar, eggs, milk, and vanilla. Add spices as desired (cinnamon, cloves and nutmeg). Mix well and pour into a greased pan. Combine Topping ingredients and spread over sweet potatoes. Bake at 400° for 30-40 minutes.

Rainbow's Roundup of Recipes

German Mennonite farmers from the Ukraine came to Kansas in 1874 with Turkey Red Wheat, laying the foundation for the thriving wheat industry Kansas enjoys today. Kansas is first in wheat production.

Corn Casserole

Good with Mexican meal.

1 cube butter (2 tablespoons)	1 can chopped green chilies
2 (3-ounce) packages cream cheese	Dash garlic salt
	2 cans white shoepeg corn

Melt butter and cream cheese. Add chilies, garlic salt, and corn. Bake in casserole at 350° until heated through, about 20 minutes.

Home at the Range III

Nebraska Corn Pie

6 strips bacon	1/4 teaspoon pepper
1 1/2 cups fine bread crumbs	1 teaspoon sugar
2 fresh tomatoes	3 cups fresh uncooked corn
1 green pepper, minced	2 tablespoons butter
1 teaspoon salt	

Place 3 strips of slightly cooked bacon in the bottom of a baking dish. Place the other strips around the sides. Add a layer of bread crumbs, and then a layer of peeled, sliced tomatoes and green pepper. Sprinkle with salt, pepper, and sugar. Over this, place a layer of corn, and continue with alternate layers until the dish is filled. Cover with bread crumbs and dot with butter. Bake at 375° for 35 minutes. Serves 6.

Taste the Good Life! Nebraska Cookbook

Baked Corn on the Cob

1 ear corn, fresh or frozen	1/4 teaspoon Knorr Swiss
1 tablespoon sour cream	Aromat Seasoning for meat
1 tablespoon margarine	1/8 teaspoon salt
1/2 slice bacon, chopped	1/8 teaspoon pepper

Shuck and wash the corn. Tear off a piece of aluminum foil large enough to wrap the ear of corn. Place corn in middle of foil. Combine all other ingredients and spread on corn. Tightly seal the corn in the foil. Bake at 350° for 30 minutes.

90th Anniversary Trinity Lutheran Church Cookbook

Best Ever Corn Casserole

Very good for potlucks. It's cleaned up fast.

1 can whole kernel corn,
   drained
1 can cream-style corn
1 (8-ounce) carton sour cream
1 egg

1 package corn muffin mix (Jiffy)
1 small onion, chopped, or
   dehydrated onion, if desired
Salt, pepper, dried parsley to
   taste

Combine all ingredients and stir together. Bake in a greased 8x8-inch casserole dish in 350° oven for 45 minutes. Serves 10.

More Heart of the Home Recipes

Crockpot Corn

2 (16-ounce) packages frozen
   corn
1 (8-ounce) package cream
   cheese

1 stick oleo
2 tablespoons sugar
2 tablespoons water

Place corn into regular-size crockpot. Cut cream cheese and oleo into small cubes. Add cheese, oleo, sugar, and water to corn. Cook on high for 45 minutes. Stir corn with wooden spoon. Turn to low and cook for 3 hours more. Stir occasionally.

Recipes & Remembrances / Courtland Covenant Church

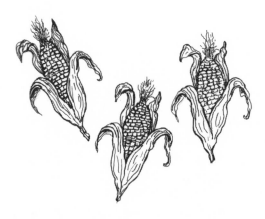

Broccoli-Corn Casserole

1 (10-ounce) package frozen, chopped broccoli
1 box Chicken-in-a-Biscuit crackers

½ cup butter, melted
1 can whole kernel corn
1 can cream-style corn

Cook broccoli as directed. Crumble crackers and mix with melted butter; reserve 1 cup. Mix broccoli, corns, and crackers; place in 2-quart dish; sprinkle reserved crackers over mixture; heat as 350° for 20 minutes or until hot.

Home at the Range III

Broccoli Casserole

¾ cup milk
1 (8-ounce) jar Cheez Whiz
1 can cream of chicken soup
½ cup diced onion

½-1 cup diced celery
½ cup diced water chestnuts
1 cup Minute Rice, uncooked
1 box frozen broccoli

Combine mixture of milk, Cheez Whiz, and soup and heat until cheese is melted. Mix onions, celery, water chestnuts, rice, and broccoli, and place in greased casserole. Pour heated mixture over other ingredients and bake at 350° for about 1¼ hours. Any bits of leftover ham may be added for variety. Serves 6.

Home at the Range I

The world's only Corn Palace is an a-*maize*-ing *ear*-chitecture. Built in Mitchell around 1892 to encourage settlement and prove the richness of eastern South Dakota soil, the palace is decorated inside and out with thousands of bushels of native corn, grain and grasses.

Tangy-Cheesy Cauliflower

Makes a beautiful accompaniment to any meat.

1 medium to large head
  cauliflower
¹/₄ cup mayonnaise, salad
  dressing, or yogurt (to save
  calories)

1 teaspoon prepared mustard
Dash of salt (optional)
¹/₂ cup shredded cheese (sharp
  Cheddar tastes great!)

Prepare cauliflower by removing stem end and greens. Rinse under water but do not shake to dry. Place in a microwave-safe dish. Cover or wrap loosely with plastic wrap. Microwave for 8-9 minutes at HIGH (100%). Combine mayonnaise, mustard, and salt while cauliflower cooks, to make the mustard sauce. Immediately spoon mustard sauce on top of cauliflower. Sprinkle with cheese. Let stand 5 minutes until cheese melts. Yields 6-8 servings.

Tip: For calorie watchers: You may brush the cooked cauliflower with as little as one teaspoon mayonnaise. Omit the mustard sauce. Sprinkle with grated cheese. (The mayonnaise helps the cheese cling to the cauliflower.)

Easy Livin' Microwave Cooking

Baked Cabbage

1 medium head cabbage,
  shredded or cut in ¹/₂-inch
  pieces
10 slices bacon
2 tablespoons flour

1 teaspoon salt
¹/₄ teaspoon pepper
2 teaspoons brown sugar
1 cup light cream

Preheat oven to 350°. Spray 2-quart casserole with vegetable spray. Place cabbage in casserole. Brown bacon until almost crisp; drain. Combine flour, salt, pepper, sugar, and cream. Stir and pour over cabbage. Sprinkle bacon over surface. Bake, covered, for 35 minutes. Remove cover and bake 10 minutes longer until bacon is browned.

Regent Alumni Association Cookbook

Zippy Glazed Carrots

No one will know that you did not take the time to peel, slice, and cook these delicious carrots.

1 tablespoon butter	¹/₄ teaspoon salt
1 tablespoon brown sugar	1 (15-ounce) can sliced carrots,
1 teaspoon mustard	drained

Combine butter, brown sugar, mustard, and salt in a 12-inch non-stick skillet. Cook until blended. Add carrots. Fry until carrots are heated and glazed. Yields 1¹/₂ cups or 4 servings.

The Give Mom a Rest (She's on Vacation) Cookbook

Copper Penny Carrots

Easy to make and attractive to serve.

1 pound carrots, sliced and cooked	¹/₄ cup vinegar
	³/₄ cup sugar
1 onion, chopped	1 teaspoon Worcestershire sauce
1 green pepper, diced	1 teaspoon prepared mustard
1 can tomato soup, undiluted	Dash hot pepper sauce
¹/₄ cup salad oil	Salt and pepper to taste

Prepare vegetables. In separate bowl, mix soup, oil, vinegar, sugar, and seasonings. Pour over vegetables and let stand in refrigerator overnight. Serve cold as a salad or as a hot vegetable.

Heart of the Home Recipes

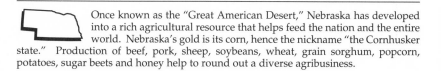

Once known as the "Great American Desert," Nebraska has developed into a rich agricultural resource that helps feed the nation and the entire world. Nebraska's gold is its corn, hence the nickname "the Cornhusker state." Production of beef, pork, sheep, soybeans, wheat, grain sorghum, popcorn, potatoes, sugar beets and honey help to round out a diverse agribusiness.

Raisin Sauced Beets

1 (1-pound) can sliced beets
  (reserve ⅓ cup liquid,
  drain the rest)
⅓ cup light or dark raisins

¼ cup sugar
1 teaspoon cornstarch
3 tablespoons lemon juice
2 tablespoons butter

In medium saucepan, combine reserved beet liquid and raisins. Cover; simmer until raisins are plumped, about 5 minutes. Combine sugar and cornstarch; stir into raisins. Add lemon juice and butter. Cook and stir over medium heat until slightly thickened. Stir in beets and simmer until mixture is heated through, about 5 minutes. If desired, garnish with a twist of lemon. Makes 5 servings.

Nutritional analysis: Cal 136; Carbo 24g; Vit E 2mg; Sod 208mg; Potas 198mg.

REC Family Cookbook

Pop's Pepper Poppers

Great as an appetizer, too!

Hot banana peppers or your
  choice
Cream cheese

Sharp Cheddar cheese
Bacon or bacon bits

Wash and cut stem end off peppers; remove seeds and cut in half lengthwise. Lay on foil-lined pan (for easy cleanup) and stuff with cream cheese or Cheddar cheese (or mixture). Put in 350° oven for 20 minutes. Meanwhile, fry bacon and crumble. Sprinkle on peppers and serve while hot.

Note: Because hot peppers contain oils that can burn your eyes, lips and skin, protect yourself when working with the peppers by covering one or both hands with plastic gloves or plastic bags. Be sure to wash your hands thoroughly before touching your eyes or face.

Sisters Two II

Fun Lady's Tomato Pie

Rich and delicious.

CRUST:
1 (9 or 10-inch) deep dish pie crust

Bake crust in preheated 350° oven for 10 minutes. Cool completely.

FILLING:

3 cups (10 ounces) shredded mozzarella cheese
1 pound cooked, crumbled bacon
1½ cups chopped green pepper
2 sliced avocados
2 large or 4 medium sliced, seeded tomatoes
Oregano
Basil
1 cup mayonnaise
1 cup freshly grated Parmesan cheese
⅛ teaspoon bottled hot pepper sauce
½ teaspoon Worcestershire sauce
¼ cup chopped fresh parsley

In pre-baked, cooled crust, layer in order: one cup mozzarella cheese and half each of the bacon, green pepper, avocados, and tomatoes. Sprinkle with oregano and basil. Repeat. Put the third cup of mozzarella cheese over the second layer.

Mix the mayonnaise, Parmesan, hot pepper sauce, and Worcestershire, and spread it over the top. Sprinkle with chopped parsley. Bake at 350° for 30 minutes or until golden. Let stand 10-15 minutes. Serve warm or cool. Store in refrigerator. Serves 6.

Presentations

Nationwide, North Dakota ranks as a top producer of barley, durum spring wheat, all dry edible beans, oats and sunflowers. It ranks second in production of all wheat and navy beans, and is one of four states leading the production of potatoes, sugar beets, and honey.

Fresh Vegetable Medley
with Parmesan-Lemon Sauce

VEGETABLE MEDLEY:

1 (1-pound) head cauliflower (about 1¹/₂ cups), cut into 1-inch pieces

1 pound fresh broccoli (about 2 cups), cut into 1-inch flowerets

1 large carrot, cleaned and cut into sticks

1 small zucchini and/or small yellow squash, peeled and thinly sliced

Using a 10-inch glass pie plate or microwave-safe serving dish, arrange cauliflower around the outer edge. Arrange broccoli inside the cauliflower ring, with the stems pointing toward outer edge of plate. Place carrot sticks between broccoli stems. Pile zucchini slices in the center.

PARMESAN-LEMON SAUCE:

¹/₂ stick (¹/₄ cup) reduced-calorie margarine, melted

2 teaspoons lemon juice

¹/₄ teaspoon garlic powder

¹/₄ teaspoon onion powder

1 teaspoon dried basil

¹/₄ cup grated Parmesan cheese

Mix ingredients except for the grated cheese in a small bowl. Pour over vegetables. Sprinkle with Parmesan cheese. Cover loosely with plastic wrap. Microwave for 8-10 minutes at HIGH (100%). Let stand 3 minutes. Yields 8 servings.

Nutritional analysis per serving (1/8 recipe): Cal 76; Carbo 5g; Prot 4g; Chol 5mg; Sod 131mg. Diabetic exchanges: Lean meat 0.25; Vegetable 1; Fat 0.5.

Easy Livin' Low-Calorie Microwave Cooking

Darrell's Baked Onions

Onions	Salt
Margarine	Pepper

Clean onions, remove top of center core with knife in a spiral "V". Place onions in a pan and fill center with margarine. Sprinkle generously with salt and pepper. Bake, covered, at 350° for 1½ hours or until tender.

Note: May substitute Lawry's seasoned salt for regular salt.

Recipes & Remembrances / Courtland Covenant Church

A Great Batter

Wonderful light bubbly batter.

³/₄ cup Argo Corn Starch	¼ teaspoon pepper
¼ cup flour	½ cup water
½ teaspoon salt	1 egg, slightly beaten

In a bowl, stir together first 4 ingredients. Add water and egg; stir till smooth. Dip veggies (zucchini, carrots, onion, mushrooms), chicken or fish (small pieces) into batter and fry.

Centennial Cookbook

Baked Pineapple

1 large can pineapple chunks, drained (reserve juice)	1 cup sugar
	2 tablespoons flour
1 cup semi-sharp cheese, grated	1 cup dry bread crumbs
	2 tablespoons butter

Put pineapple and cheese into a glass baking dish. Combine pineapple juice, sugar, and flour in a saucepan. Heat to near boiling. Pour over cheese and pineapple. Blend bread crumbs with butter; sprinkle on top. Bake in 350° oven for 20-25 minutes.

Blew Centennial Bon-Appetit

Bountiful Stuffed Squash

2 (1¼-pound) acorn squash
½ cup chopped onion
1 tablespoon or more
  vegetable oil
¾ cup ground turkey
1 cup finely chopped red
  cooking apple

1 tablespoon flour
1 tablespoon low sodium, light
  soy sauce
¼ cup raisins

Cut acorn squash in halves; remove fiber and seeds. Place cut-side-down in microwave dish and cover with plastic wrap. Microwave on HIGH 14 minutes or until tender yet firm. Turn dish once during baking.

Meanwhile, sauté onion in hot oil in large skillet over high heat until translucent. Add turkey and apple; cook and stir over medium heat, about 5 minutes, or until turkey is no longer pink. Sprinkle flour evenly over meat mixture; stir to blend. Gradually stir in light soy sauce; cook and stir until slightly thickened. Stir in raisins. Remove from heat. Fill each squash with the turkey mixture. Microwave on HIGH 1-2 minutes until heated through. Makes 4 servings.

Pumpkin, Winter Squash and Carrot Cookbook

Summer Squash Casserole

Even if your family doesn't like squash, they might like this!

2 pounds summer squash
  (yellow), unpeeled and sliced
¼ cup chopped onion
1 can cream of chicken soup
1 cup sour cream

1 cup raw shredded carrots
1 (8-ounce) package cornbread
  stuffing mix
1 stick oleo, melted

Combine squash and onion in saucepan; add salted water to cover. Boil 5 minutes. Drain thoroughly. Combine soup and sour cream. Add carrots, squash, and onion. Mix lightly. Combine stuffing mix and oleo. Spread half stuffing mixture in bottom of 9x13-inch pan. Spoon squash mixture on top. Sprinkle with remaining stuffing mix. Bake uncovered in 350° oven for 30 minutes.

Our Daily Bread

Italian Zucchini Crescent Pie

4 cups thinly sliced zucchini
1 cup chopped onions
2 tablespoons margarine or
  butter
2 tablespoons parsley flakes
1/2 teaspoon salt
1/2 teaspoon pepper
1/4 teaspoon garlic powder

1/4 teaspoon basil leaves
1/4 teaspoon oregano leaves
2 eggs, well beaten
2 cups shredded Muenster or
  mozzarella
1 (8-ounce) can refrigerated
  crescent rolls
2 teaspoons prepared mustard

Heat oven to 375°. In large skillet, cook zucchini and onions in margarine about 8 minutes until tender. Stir in parsley flakes, salt, pepper, garlic powder, basil, and oregano. In large bowl, combine eggs and cheese; mix well. Stir in cooked vegetable mixture.

Separate dough into 8 triangles. Place in ungreased 10-inch pie pan, 8x12-inch baking dish, or 11-inch quiche pan; press over bottom and up sides to form crust. Firmly press perforations to seal. Spread crust with mustard. Pour egg-vegetable mixture evenly into prepared crust. Bake at 375° for 18-22 minutes or until knife inserted near center comes out clean. (Cover edge of crust with strip of foil during last 10 minutes of baking, if necessary, to prevent excessive browning.) Let stand 10 minutes before serving. Makes 6 servings.

Taste of Coffeyville

Impossible Garden Pie

2 cups chopped or thinly sliced
  zucchini
1 cup chopped tomato
1/3 cup chopped onion
1 cup shredded Swiss or Jack
  cheese

2 cups milk
4 eggs, beaten
1 cup Bisquick
1/3 cup Parmesan cheese
1/4 teaspoon salt
1/8 teaspoon pepper

Grease a 10-inch pie plate, or 10x7-inch Pyrex casserole dish. Layer all vegetables in pan. Sprinkle cheese over vegetables. Beat milk, eggs, Bisquick, cheese, and spices. Pour over all and bake 35-40 minutes or until a knife inserted comes out clean. You may also add a layer of cooked ground beef and a few green pepper rings. (Use a slightly deeper casserole dish.) Garnish with zucchini and tomato slices, if desired.

Rainbow's Roundup of Recipes

Asparagus Casserole

2 pounds frozen asparagus
2 tablespoons margarine
3 tablespoons flour
1 teaspoon salt

1-1 1/2 cups milk
6 hard-boiled eggs
12 slices American cheese

Cook the asparagus in the microwave in the casserole dish you will bake it in until nearly done. In 4-cup glass mixing bowl, melt margarine in microwave. Stir in flour and salt; mix well. Add milk and cook in microwave until thick. Chop eggs and cheese, add to asparagus, and stir in white sauce. Bake in 350° oven for 30-40 minutes. You may add 2 cups chopped ham, if desired.

Amana Lutheran Church 125th Anniversary Cookbook

Smörgåsbord Casserole
(Vegetable Casserole)

1 (16-ounce) can French-style green beans	2 cups milk
1 (14½-ounce) can of asparagus spears or 3 cups fresh asparagus	¾ teaspoon salt
	⅛ teaspoon celery seed
	1½ tablespoons mustard
2 tablespoons butter	1 cup ham, chopped
¼ cup flour	2 hard-boiled eggs
	Buttered bread crumbs

Grease a 2-quart casserole. Arrange green beans and asparagus in bottom. In another pan, melt butter; add flour and blend. Stir in milk and cook until sauce is smooth and thick. Add salt, celery seed, mustard, and ham to sauce. Pour sauce over vegetables and top with finely chopped hard-boiled eggs. Cover with buttered bread crumbs. Bake uncovered at 350° for 25 minutes.

Measure for Pleasure

Zesty Green Bean Casserole

2 quarts green beans	4 ounces mild Mexican Cheez Whiz
¼ cup milk	¼ cup onion, chopped
1 (10¾-ounce) can cream of mushroom soup	Bacon bits

Drain beans and pour into large mixing bowl. Preheat oven to 350°. Heat milk, soup, Cheez Whiz, and onion in medium saucepan and stir until smooth, stirring often. Fold soup mixture into green beans. Place this into 2-quart casserole dish. Top with bacon bits and bake in oven 35-45 minutes or until slightly golden. Serve as a side dish.

Centerville Community Centennial Cookbook

In Meade, Kansas, the Dalton Gang Hideout is one of only several hideouts to be preserved, complete with secret passage tunnel. The museum in the barn shows more of their adventures.

Swiss Green Bean Casserole

2 tablespoons margarine
2 tablespoons flour
1 (8-ounce) carton French
  onion dip
2 tablespoons milk

2 (15½-16-ounce) cans whole
  green beans, drained (or cooked
  fresh)
¼ pound Swiss cheese, grated
Paprika

Melt margarine in a small heavy saucepan; add flour and stir until smooth. Add onion dip and milk, stirring until smooth. Layer beans and ⅔ of sauce in a 1½-quart, lightly buttered casserole. Top with cheese. Pour remaining sauce over all. Sprinkle with paprika. Cover and bake in 325° oven for 20 minutes or until cheese melts. Makes 8 servings.

In the Kitchen with Kate

Barbecued Green Beans

4 strips bacon
½ cup diced onion
½ cup catsup
½ cup brown sugar, packed

1 tablespoon Worcestershire
  sauce
3 cans French-style green
  beans, well-drained

Place bacon in baking dish, cover with waxed paper, and microwave on HIGH for 5 minutes or until crisp. Remove bacon and drain on paper towels. Sauté onion in bacon grease for 3 minutes. Add catsup, brown sugar, and Worcestershire sauce to the sautéed onions and mix. Add drained green beans and stir gently. Top with crumbled bacon. Cover. Bake at 325° for 2 hours. Makes 8 servings. *Recipe from Country Dreams, Marion, Kansas.*

Savor the Inns of Kansas

 Crazy Horse, the great Oglala Sioux war chief, Red Cloud, Oglala Sioux chief, and Standing Bear, Ponca chief, are familiar names in the history of the Great Plains Native Americans.

Barbecued Butter Beans

³/₄ cup brown sugar
¹/₃ cup dark corn syrup
2 or 3 drops hot pepper sauce
3 cans large lima beans, well
    drained

¹/₂ cup ketchup
2 teaspoons liquid smoke
1 medium diced onion
4 strips raw bacon

Combine; mix well. Turn into a 1¹/₂-quart casserole. Arrange bacon strips on top. Bake at 325° for one hour.

Our Daily Bread

Leather Britches Beans

Wash and drain a batch of firm green beans. Remove ends and strings. Use large darning needle with heavy white thread and pierce the pod near the middle of each, pushing them along with thread so that they are about ¹/₄-inch apart. Hang up the strings of beans in a warm, well-ventilated place to dry. They will shrivel and turn greenish-gray. To cook in the winter time, as the pioneers did, cover with water and soak overnight. Drain, renew water and parboil slowly for ¹/₂ hour. Drain again. Cook slowly with ham hock or salt pork until tender.

The Mormon Trail Cookbook

Mom's Baked Beans

2 cups (1 pound) navy beans
Water
1/4 pound bacon, sliced in
   pieces
1/2 cup chili sauce
1/2 teaspoon vinegar

1 medium onion, sliced
2 cups hot bean liquid
1 teaspoon salt
1/2 teaspoon dry mustard
1/2 cup dark molasses
Brown sugar to taste

Rinse and sort beans. Place beans in pan and cover with water. Add bacon; cover pan and simmer over low heat (do not boil) until just tender, about one hour. Drain bean and bacon mixture; reserve liquid. Transfer bean mixture to a 2-quart bean pot or casserole with cover. Add remaining ingredients. Mix gently. Cover and bake in a slow oven (300°) for 6 hours. Add bean liquid or hot water as needed. Brown sugar may be added to taste. Makes 8 servings.

Per serving: 125 calories; 3g fat; 3mg cholesterol.

Reader's Favorite Recipes

Baked Bean Casserole

1 1/2 pounds ground beef,
   browned
1/2 pound bacon, cut up and
   browned
1 large can pork and beans
1 can kidney beans, drained
1 can pinto beans, drained
1 can lima beans, drained

1 onion, diced
1/4 cup brown sugar
1 teaspoon dry mustard
1/4 teaspoon ginger
1/4 cup vinegar
1 cup catsup
3 tablespoons liquid smoke
Salt and pepper

Mix all together. Bake in a 300° oven for 2 hours.

Homemade Memories

MEATS

The buffalo roam on the range in South Dakota.

Prime Rib

Select a standing aged prime rib roast. Let stand at room temperature for one hour. Preheat oven to 375°. Season and place roast in shallow roasting pan. Do not cover or add water. Put in oven and bake just one hour. Turn off heat but do not open door any time until ready to serve. (I tie the oven door shut.) Regardless of the time the roast has been in the oven, 30-40 minutes before serving, turn oven on to 375°. Cook for remaining 30-40 minutes. The meat will be very brown and crisp on the outside and beautifully pink all the way through, medium-rare and very juicy. Use procedure for any size roast. (May be cooked in morning, let stand in an unopened oven all day, then cooked just before serving.)

Amana Lutheran Church 125th Anniversary Cookbook

Beef Brisket

MARINADE:

2 tablespoons liquid smoke
1 teaspoon garlic salt
1 teaspoon onion salt
1 teaspoon black pepper

1 teaspoon celery salt
2 tablespoons Worcestershire
  sauce

Combine marinade ingredients.

1 (3½ to 4-pound) beef brisket   1 bottle barbeque sauce

Place brisket fat-side-down in 9x13-inch container 2 inches deep. Rub marinade into top and sides of meat. Cover and marinate overnight. Next day, place meat fat-side-up, cover with foil and bake 5 hours at 250°. Uncover; remove fat. Pour ½ of barbeque sauce on top. Bake one hour, uncovered. Let stand till cold to slice ¼ to ⅜-inch thick.

Heavenly Delights

Mustard Roast Beef & Vegetables

1 (4-pound) boneless rump roast	3 large carrots
1½ teaspoons salt	4 small potatoes
Pepper to taste	4 small onions
1 tablespoon prepared mustard	2 large ribs celery

Season beef with ¾ teaspoon salt and pepper. Spread top and sides of roast with mustard. Place on small rack in lightly greased roasting pan. Peel and cut vegetables in chunks and place around rack in pan. Season with salt and pepper. Roast in preheated 325° oven 1½ hours or until meat thermometer registers desired doneness (rare 140°, medium 160°, well done 170°)—approximately 25 minutes per pound. Remove from oven; let stand about 10 minutes.

Taste the Good Life! Nebraska Cookbook

French Dip

½ cup soy sauce	3-4 peppercorns
1 beef bouillon	Water
1 bay leaf	1 (3-pound) rump roast
1 teaspoon thyme	French bread rolls
1 teaspoon garlic powder	

Put soy sauce, bouillon, bay leaf, thyme, garlic powder, and peppercorns in crockpot. Mix with 1 cup water. Put rump roast in and cover with water. Cook on low 8-10 hours; put sliced meat on rolls and use juice for dipping.

St. Joseph's Table

Working Man's Roast

1 (3-pound) rump roast
¼ teaspoon garlic powder
¼ teaspoon seasoned salt
⅛ teaspoon salt
⅛ teaspoon pepper

1 package onion soup mix
2 tablespoons Worcestershire
  sauce
1 can cream of mushroom soup

Put foil in a cake pan and place roast in pan. Mix together garlic powder, seasoned salt, salt, pepper, onion soup mix, Worcestershire sauce, and soup. Pour over roast. Seal foil and bake at 200° from 7:00 a.m. to 5:00 p.m. or for 10 hours.

Recipes from the Heart / Epsilon Omega Sorority

Peppery T-Bone Steaks & Chili Corn

4 ears fresh sweet corn, in
  husks
1-2 garlic cloves, minced
½ teaspoon coarse ground
  black pepper

2 well-trimmed beef T-bone
  steaks, cut 1-1½ inches thick
2 tablespoons butter
½ teaspoon chili powder
¼ teaspoon ground cumin

Pull back corn husks from each ear of corn leaving husks attached to base. Remove corn silk. Fold husks back around corn; tie at the end of each ear with string or a strip of one of the outside corn leaves. Soak corn in cold water 3-4 hours. Remove from water and place on grill over medium coals. Cook 20 minutes, turning often. Combine garlic and pepper; rub into both sides of beef T-bone steaks.

Place steaks on grill with corn; continue cooking, turning steaks once, and corn often. Grill 1-inch thick steaks 16-20 minutes for rare (140°) to medium (160°) or to desired doneness. Grill 1½-inch thick steaks 22-30 minutes (rare to medium) or to desired doneness. Remove corn when tender. Meanwhile, melt butter; add chili powder and cumin. Carve steaks into thick slices and serve with corn and seasoned butter.

282 calories per 3-ounce serving.

Taste the Good Life! Nebraska Cookbook

Garlic Marinated Sirloin Steak

2 (3-pound) sirloin steaks,
1¼-2 inches thick
⅓ cup Worcestershire sauce

2 teaspoons granulated
garlic
2 teaspoons lemon pepper

Coat steaks with Worcestershire sauce and rub on dry ingredients. Marinate meat in the refrigerator for 2 hours. Bring steaks to room temperature and sear for 2 minutes on each side over hot coals. Reduce heat to medium by spreading coals out and cook to taste (rare, 4 minutes each side; medium, 6 minutes each side; well done, 8 minutes each side). Serves 8-10.

All About Bar-B-Q Kansas City Style

Barbecued Steak

1 cup catsup
½ cup water
¼ cup vinegar
¼ cup chopped green pepper
¼ cup chopped onion
1½ tablespoons Worcestershire
sauce

1 tablespoon prepared mustard
2 tablespoons brown sugar
½ teaspoon salt
⅛ teaspoon pepper
4 pounds round steak, cut
½-inch thick

Combine all ingredients except steak in a saucepan. Bring to a boil, then simmer for about 5 minutes over low heat. Keep barbecue sauce hot. Cut steak into serving-size portions. Place pieces in a large roasting pan. Pour hot barbecue sauce over meat. Cover and bake at 325° for 1½-2 hours. Makes 8-10 servings.

Recipes & Remembrances / Courtland Covenant Church

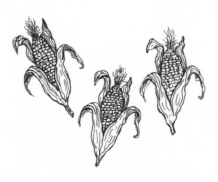

Marinated Flank Steak

1/4 cup soy sauce
2 tablespoons vinegar
1/2 cup oil
3 tablespoons honey

1 teaspoon ground ginger
1 teaspoon garlic salt
Green onions
1 flank steak

Mix all ingredients and marinate flank steak 4 hours or more. Broil or grill, and to serve, thinly slice across grain. Good to serve with Milanese Rice on page 167.

If It Tastes Good, Who Cares? I

Pepper Steak

1 pound round (or sirloin) steak, cut in 1/2-inch-thick strips
1 tablespoon paprika
2 tablespoons butter or oleo
2 cloves garlic, crushed
1 1/2 cups beef broth
1 cup sliced green onions, including tops

2 green peppers, cut in strips
2 tablespoons cornstarch
1/4 cup water
1/4 cup soy sauce
2 large fresh tomatoes, cut in eighths
3 cups hot cooked rice

Sprinkle strips of beef with paprika, and allow to stand while preparing other ingredients. Using a large skillet, brown meat in butter. Add garlic and broth. Cover and simmer for 30 minutes. Stir in onions and green peppers. Cover and cook for 5 minutes more. Blend cornstarch, water, and soy sauce. Stir into meat mixture. Cook, stirring until clear and thickened, about 2 minutes. Add tomatoes and stir gently. Serve over beds of fluffy rice. Makes 6 servings.

Our Daily Bread

Swiss Bliss Round Steak

2 pounds round steak, cut
  in serving-size portions
1 envelope onion soup mix
1 small can mushrooms,
  drained
1/2 green pepper, sliced

1 (1-pound) can tomatoes,
  drained, chopped (save juice)
1/2 cup juice from tomatoes
1 tablespoon A-1 Steak Sauce
1 tablespoon cornstarch

Use a 20-inch piece of aluminum foil. Butter middle. Arrange raw meat, overlapping, down the middle. Sprinkle onion soup, mushrooms, green pepper, and tomatoes. Mix juice, A-1 sauce, and cornstarch. Pour over meat and seal. Bake at 365° for 2 hours.

We Love Country Cookin'

Roast Beef Pastries

1 (4-ounce) can chopped
  mushrooms
1 onion, chopped
1 medium carrot, grated
1 celery stalk, chopped
2 tablespoons butter
1/2 teaspoon salt
4 tablespoons Dijon mustard

1 (10-ounce) package frozen
  patty shells (6), thawed
1 pound rare roast beef, sliced
  thin or shaved
1/2 cup grated Monterey Jack
  or Swiss cheese
1 egg, beaten with a teaspoon
  of water

Sauté mushrooms, onion, carrot, and celery in butter over medium heat, about 10 minutes, stirring occasionally. Remove from heat; stir in salt and one tablespoon mustard. On lightly floured surface, roll each patty shell into 7-inch circle; spread each circle with mustard to within one inch of edge. Cover mustard with sliced roast beef, dividing evenly. Spoon vegetable mixture over beef; sprinkle with cheese. Brush edge of each pastry circle with egg wash mixture. Bring 2 sides of pastry up and over filling to form package. Press edges firmly to seal. Brush with egg wash; place on ungreased pan. Bake at 425° for 15 minutes.

Recipes & Remembrances / Buffalo Lake

Waldorf Astoria Stew

3 pounds lean beef, cut into
   1-inch cubes
2 medium onions, chopped
2 cups carrots, cut in rounds
1 cup sliced celery
4 medium potatoes, peeled and
   cut into chunks

2 teaspoons salt
Dash pepper
2¹/₂ tablespoons tapioca
2 cups tomato juice

In a large kettle or Dutch oven, mix beef, chopped onions, carrot rounds, sliced celery, and potatoes. Season with salt and pepper; sprinkle mixture with tapioca. Pour the tomato juice over all. Cover and bake for 5 hours at 250°. Makes 8 servings.

Per serving: 435 calories; 19.2g fat; 112mg cholesterol.

Reader's Favorite Recipes

Ho Bo Delight

Each person assembles his own meal, starting with Fritos, and building up.

2 pounds ground beef
1 teaspoon chili powder
2 teaspoons oregano
4 tablespoons sugar
1 teaspoon salt
2 teaspoons cumin seed
1 tablespoon minced onion
2 cloves garlic
3 (8-ounce) cans tomato paste
2 (8-ounce) cans tomato sauce

5 cans water
1 cup Minute Rice
1 large package Fritos
1 pound shredded cheese
1 head lettuce, cut up
3 cups tomatoes, cut up
1 cup dark olives, sliced
1 cup green onion, chopped
1 pint sour cream
Picante sauce

Fry ground beef; drain off fat. Add chili powder, oregano, sugar, salt, cumin seed, minced onion, minced garlic, tomato paste and sauce, water, and rice. Bring to a boil. Simmer for 40 minutes.

To serve, put in separate dishes in this order: Fritos, meat mixture, cheese, lettuce, tomatoes, olives, green onions, sour cream, and picante sauce.

Cooking with Iola

Beef Potato Cakes

6 cups slightly seasoned dry
　mashed potatoes
1/4 cup sliced green onions
　with tops
2 cups finely cut cooked beef
　or 1 pound ground beef,
　cooked and drained

1 egg, slightly beaten
1/2 teaspoon garlic salt
1/8 teaspoon pepper
2-3 tablespoons flour
2-3 tablespoons margarine

Mix first 6 ingredients together. Shape into patties. Coat with flour. Heat margarine in 10-inch skillet. Cook patties until heated and brown, 4-5 minutes each side. Yields about 4 servings.

Red River Valley Potato Growers Auxiliary Cookbook

Picadillo

Probably Spanish explorers introduced this delicious blend of meat, spices and fruit in a pastry turnover.

1/2 pound ground beef
1/2 pound ground pork
1 onion, minced
1 clove garlic, minced
2 cups stewed tomatoes

1/2 teaspoon cinnamon
1/4 teaspoon ground cumin
1/8 teaspoon cloves
1 cup white raisins

Brown meats in skillet; drain off fat. Add onion and garlic. Add tomatoes, spices, and raisins with salt and pepper to taste. Simmer 5 minutes. Serve in a heated flour tortilla or empanada, or use as a taco filling.

Iola's Gourmet Recipes in Rhapsody

About 200 years ago, Lewis and Clark began their historic journey to explore the American frontier. They followed the Missouri River through present-day South Dakota, witnessing buffalo by the thousands, squirrels that barked, and bluffs that appeared to be on fire. The Lewis and Clark Visitor Center is at Gavins Point Dam, near Yankton, South Dakota.

Beulah's Beef Casserole

1½ pounds ground round
½ cup minced onion
2 teaspoons Worcestershire
  sauce
¼ teaspoon garlic salt

1 teaspoon curry powder
½ teaspoon parsley flakes
1½ cups cooked rice
1 (16 to 17-ounce) can
  tomatoes

Brown the ground meat lightly and spoon onto a plate covered with a paper towel to drain off fat. Mix all ingredients. Put into lightly sprayed casserole. Bake 30 minutes at 350°. (I usually cover the casserole for the first 20 minutes.)

Pioneer Daughters Cookbook

Crouton Hot Dish

1½ pounds hamburger
1 (7-ounce) box croutons
¼ pound butter
1 cup chopped celery

½ cup chopped onion
1½ cups water
1 can cream of celery soup
1-2 cans cream of chicken soup

Layer meat and croutons in pan. In saucepan mix together butter, celery, onion, and water. Heat until butter melts; pour over hamburger and stuffing mixture. Blend soups and pour over top. Bake for one hour at 350°. Turn off oven and let stand in oven for an additional 15 minutes.

Wyndmere Community Alumni Cookbook

Shipwreck Casserole

½-¾ pound hamburger
6 medium potatoes, peeled
1 large onion, sliced

1 can pork and beans
Salt and pepper to taste
1 can tomato soup

Brown hamburger, then place a layer of sliced potatoes in bottom of casserole. Layer on onions and pork and beans. Crumble hamburger on top. Salt and pepper, then pour tomato soup over top. Bake at 300° for 1½ hours.

Home at the Range II

Potato Pepperoni Hot Dish

This hot dish brings many compliments.

1¹/₂-2 pounds hamburger	¹/₄ teaspoon pepper
1 small onion, diced	1 teaspoon sugar
1 can Cheddar cheese soup	6-8 potatoes, sliced
1 can tomato soup	1 package pepperoni slices
1 cup milk	¹/₂ cup Parmesan cheese
¹/₂ teaspoon oregano	1 cup shredded mozzarella cheese

Brown hamburger and onion. Mix the soups, milk, and seasonings. Mix together the hamburger, potatoes, and soup mixture. Place in a 9x13-inch pan. Bake at 350° for one hour, or until potatoes are tender. Top with pepperoni slices. Bake for 5 minutes. Top with Parmesan and mozzarella cheese. Bake until cheese melts.

North Dakota...Where Food is Love

Cracked Wheat-Ground Beef Casserole

1 pound lean ground beef	1 (16-ounce) can tomatoes, cut up
2 stalks celery, chopped (1 cup)	1 cup cracked wheat
1 large green pepper, chopped	1 cup water
1 medium onion, chopped	¹/₂ cup raisins
1 clove garlic, minced	¹/₃ cup shelled sunflower seeds
1¹/₂ teaspoons salt	Cheddar cheese, sliced and
¹/₈ teaspoon pepper	halved diagonally (optional)

In skillet cook ground beef, celery, green pepper, onion, garlic, salt and pepper till meat is browned and vegetables are crisp-tender; drain off excess fat. Stir in undrained tomatoes, cracked wheat, water, raisins, and sunflower seeds. Turn mixture into a 2-quart au gratin dish or casserole. Bake, covered, in 375° oven for about 35 minutes or until wheat is tender and mixture is heated through. If desired, uncover and top with a few half slices of cheese during the last 5 minutes of baking. Serves 6.

Whole Wheat Cookery

Walking Taco

1½ pounds hamburger
1 small onion, chopped
1 teaspoon garlic salt
Salt and pepper to taste
10 (2¾-ounce) bags Fritos or
   nacho cheese Doritos chips

2 cups lettuce, shredded
1 cup tomatoes, chopped
1 cup shredded Cheddar cheese
1 cup sour cream
1 can black olives, drained
Taco sauce to taste

Brown hamburger, onion, garlic salt, salt and pepper. Cut ¼-inch top off chip bags. Crush chips slightly. Fill bags with cooked hamburger mixture. Top with lettuce, tomatoes, cheese, sour cream, and olives. Stick fork in bag and serve. Offer taco sauce.

Recipes from the Heart / Epsilon Omega Sorority

Mexican Crazy Crust

CRUST:
½ cup flour
½ teaspoon salt
½ teaspoon baking powder

¼ cup Crisco
½ cup sour cream or yogurt

FILLING:
1 pound ground beef, browned
½ cup chopped onion
1 teaspoon salt
2 teaspoons chili powder

¼ teaspoon hot pepper
1 (16-ounce) can pinto beans,
   undrained
1 (6-ounce) can tomato paste

TOPPING:
½ cup chopped tomato
½ cup shredded lettuce

½ cup shredded Cheddar cheese

Preheat oven to 425°. Combine crust ingredients. Spread batter in greased and floured 9 to 10-inch pie pan. Spread batter thinly on bottom, thicker on the sides. Brown ground beef with onion and drain. Add remaining filling ingredients. Pour over crust. Bake for 20-30 minutes or until crust is a deep brown. Remove from oven and top with tomato, lettuce, and cheese. Makes 4 servings. *Recipe from The Barn B&B Inn, Valley Falls, Kansas.*

Savor the Inns of Kansas

Pizza Cups

1 tube refrigerator biscuits
Pizza sauce
Hamburger (cooked),
  pepperoni, etc.

Mushrooms (optional)
Mozzarella cheese

Using a greased muffin pan, spread biscuits into muffin sections. Place a spoonful of pizza sauce into each biscuit. Place meat and sliced mushrooms on top of sauce. Top with mozzarella cheese. Bake at 350° for 15-20 minutes.

125 Years of Cookin' with the Lord

Köttbullar
(Swedish Meatballs)

This recipe has been adapted from an old recipe once used in a cooking course in the Royal Palace in Sweden.

1 pound lean beef or chuck,
  ground
1 medium potato, peeled
1 medium onion, peeled
1 teaspoon salt

$1/2$ teaspoon ground allspice
1 ($10^3/4$-ounce) can beef broth
  or consommé
1 soup can of water

Put the meat into a large mixing bowl. Grate the raw potato and the onion over the meat. Add salt and allspice. Mix well and form into balls the size of walnuts. Pour the beef broth and water into a 2-quart saucepan and bring to a boil. Carefully drop in all the meatballs, one at a time. Simmer 20 minutes. Remove the meatballs with a slotted spoon and put in a baking dish. Remove the fat from the broth by skimming or chilling until the solid cake can be lifted off. Add the broth to the meatballs; cover. Heat on top of stove or bake in oven for 30 minutes at 350°. These meatballs freeze well both before and after baking.

Measure for Pleasure

Norwegian Meatballs
(Kjoltboller)

1 pound lean pork
1 pound lean beef
2 large potatoes, boiled and
  mashed or 1 cup instant
  potatoes prepared with 1 cup
  boiling water

2 eggs
1 cup milk
1 small onion, finely chopped
Flour
Margarine

Grind meat finely. (May have butcher put it through grinder three times.) Mix all ingredients, except flour and margarine, well. Shape into balls the size of an egg. Dip balls in flour. Fry in butter or margarine. Put in a 9x13-inch pan. Rinse skillet with 1½ cups water. Pour over meat balls. Bake at 325° for 40 minutes. Turn temperature down to 300° for an additional 20 minutes. This will serve six generously. These meat balls freeze well, so can be made ahead.

Tried & True II

Sweet and Sour Meatballs

3 pounds hamburger
1½ cups quick oatmeal
2 (10-ounce) cans water
  chestnuts, chopped
1 teaspoon onion salt
1 teaspoon garlic salt
2 tablespoons soy sauce
2 eggs, beaten
1 cup milk

2 (15-ounce) cans crushed
  pineapple
2 cups light brown sugar
1 cup white vinegar
4 tablespoons soy sauce
2 cubes beef bouillon
6 tablespoons cornstarch
²/₃ cup chopped green pepper

Mix together hamburger, oatmeal, chopped chestnuts, onion and garlic salts, soy sauce, eggs, and milk. Form into meat balls. Fry or broil, turning occasionally until done. Drain pineapple into saucepan. Add brown sugar, vinegar, soy sauce, and bouillon. Bring to low boil. Thicken with cornstarch. Stir in green peppers and pineapple. Heat through but leave peppers crisp-tender. Serves 20.

St. Joseph's Table

Barbecued Meatballs

1 (13-ounce) can evaporated
   milk
3 pounds hamburger
2 cups 1-minute oatmeal,
   uncooked
2 eggs

1 cup chopped onion
1/4 teaspoon garlic powder
2 teaspoons chili powder
2 teaspoons salt
1/2 teaspoon pepper

Mix together and shape with ice cream scoop.

SAUCE:
2 cups catsup
1 1/2 cups brown sugar
2 teaspoons liquid smoke

1 1/2 teaspoons garlic
   powder
1/2 cup chopped onion

Mix and pour over meatballs and bake at 350° for one hour.

Note: Marinate meatballs in sauce overnight in refrigerator to enhance flavor.

A Century in His Footsteps

Upside-Down Meat Loaf

1/2 cup brown sugar
1/2 cup catsup
1 1/2 pounds ground beef
3/4 cup milk
2 eggs, beaten

1 1/2 teaspoons salt
1/4 teaspoon pepper
1/4 teaspoon ginger
1 small onion, grated
3/4 cup crushed cracker crumbs

Butter a 9x3x5-inch loaf pan well. Press brown sugar into bottom. Spread catsup over sugar. Mix remaining ingredients and shape into loaf. Put on top of catsup. Bake at 350° for one hour. Turn upside-down to serve. Let stand for 5-10 minutes before cutting. Serves 6-8.

North Dakota...Where Food is Love

Where's the beef? A good guess is Nebraska. There are approximately five million beef animals to the state's population of around 1.6 million people. Nebraska ranks second in the US in total red meat production.

Cheese-Filled Meat Loaf

1½ pounds ground beef
¾ cup quick rolled oats
¼ cup chopped onion
1 egg
½ teaspoon salt
½-1 teaspoon oregano
¼ teaspoon pepper
1 (8-ounce) package mozzarella
  cheese (large slices)
1 (8-ounce) can tomato sauce

Mix beef, oats, onion, egg, salt, oregano, and pepper. Divide meat mixture in 3 parts. In bread loaf pan (approximately 9x5x3 inches), layer ⅓ of meat mixture, ½ of cheese, ⅓ meat mixture, rest of cheese and top with last ⅓ of meat mixture. Seal edges as you put in layers. Top with tomato sauce. Bake at 350° for one hour.

Yesterday and Today Friendly Circle Cookbook

Border Burgers

2 pounds lean ground beef
1 (4-ounce) can diced green
  chiles
1½ cup finely shredded
  Cheddar cheese (divided)
½ teaspoon salt
½ teaspoon pepper
½ teaspoon cumin
4 hamburger buns, separated
2 (15-ounce) cans chili with
  beans, heated
1 cup chopped red onion

Combine ground beef, green chilies, ¾ cup Cheddar cheese, salt, pepper, and cumin in bowl; mix well. Shape into eight ¾-inch thick patties. Grill 4-6 inches above hot coals for 8 minutes for rare, 12 minutes for medium and 15 minutes for well-done, turning once or twice. Move patties to edge of grill. Place buns cut-side-down on grill. Grill for one minute or until light brown. Remove from grill. Arrange patties on buns on serving platter. Top with chili; sprinkle with cheese and onion. Yield: 8 servings.

The Kansas City Barbeque Society Cookbook

Sioux Sundries in Harrison, Nebraska, makes the world's largest hamburgers.

Blue Ribbon Barbecued Country Back Ribs

2 slabs country back pork ribs
Teriyaki sauce (enough to
  cover ribs)
Morton Nature's Seasons®
  Seasoning Blend, to taste

1 (12-ounce) can beer, room
  temperature
K.C. Masterpiece barbecue
  sauce (original)

Do not trim fat from ribs or parboil. Marinate overnight in the refrigerator in a mixture of teriyaki sauce and Morton's seasoning.

Prepare coals around sides of grill and let ash down, about 45 minutes. Stack ribs, one on top of the other, in the center of the grill. Leave in this position for 10 minutes, with the lid closed, at 300°. Rotate the stack, putting top slab on the bottom, and cook for 10 minutes more. Repeat the process on the other side of each slab of ribs. (This takes 40 minutes in all.) Allow heat to lower to 225° and continue rotating slabs, occasionally basting with beer to keep ribs moist on the outside. Turn every 20-30 minutes for about 2 hours. Baste with barbecue sauce for another hour, continuing to rotate ribs and letting fire die out naturally. Serves 4-6.

All About Bar-B-Q Kansas City Style

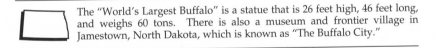

The "World's Largest Buffalo" is a statue that is 26 feet high, 46 feet long, and weighs 60 tons. There is also a museum and frontier village in Jamestown, North Dakota, which is known as "The Buffalo City."

Indoor/Outdoor Ribs

4 pounds pork ribs or beef
  short ribs
$1/2$ cup strong-flavored beer,
  room temperature
4 tablespoons light molasses
1 teaspoon liquid smoke

2 teaspoons Maggi gravy
  seasoning or Kitchen Bouquet
1 teaspoon sesame oil
8 slices white bread
Kansas City-style barbecue sauce

Place ribs in a large roasting pan. Pour beer around ribs and cover pan tightly with lid or heavy-duty foil. Bake at 400° for one hour. Combine molasses, liquid smoke, gravy seasoning, and sesame oil, and set aside. Remove ribs from oven, then remove from pan and pat dry with paper towels.

To finish ribs in the broiler, place on a rack, meaty-side up, and brush generously with browning sauce. Place rack 4-6 inches from heat and broil for 4-5 minutes, or until browned to taste. Turn ribs, brush with more sauce, and broil.

To finish on a barbecue grill, brush with browning sauce and grill over hot coals for 6 minutes, or until ribs are well charred. To serve, arrange each portion over 2 slices of bread and paint generously with barbecue sauce. Serves 4.

All About Bar-B-Q Kansas City Style

Chow Mein

$1/2$ cup butter
$1^1/2$ cups diced pork steak
1 cup chopped onion
1 cup diced celery

1 teaspoon salt
$1/8$ teaspoon pepper
1 cup hot water
1 can drained bean sprouts

THICKENING:
$1/3$ cup cold water
2 tablespoons cornstarch

2 teaspoons soy sauce
1 teaspoon sugar

Melt butter; add meat and sear. Add onions and fry 5 minutes. Add celery, salt, pepper, and hot water. Cook 5 minutes. Add bean sprouts and mix thoroughly. Heat to boiling point. Mix and add thickening ingredients. Serve over rice or chow mein noodles.

North Dakota...Where Food is Love

Orange-Glazed Pork Butt

½ cup frozen orange juice
  concentrate
½ cup honey
2 tablespoons fresh lime juice
2 tablespoons butter
1 teaspoon ground ginger

1 (5 to 7-pound) pork butt,
  trimmed
3 tablespoons garlic salt
1 tablespoon pepper
1 tablespoon ground ginger

Bring orange juice concentrate, honey, lime juice, butter, and one teaspoon ginger to a boil in saucepan. Boil for one minute. Remove from heat. Sprinkle pork with garlic salt, pepper, and remaining one tablespoon ginger. Place pork on grill rack in covered grill with water pan. Cook with lid down at 230° for 7-9 hours or to 165° on meat thermometer. Brush pork with orange glaze 30 minutes before end of cooking process. Yield: 25 servings.

The Kansas City Barbeque Society Cookbook

Dinner in a Skillet

6 lean pork chops
2 tablespoons chopped onion
1 green pepper, sliced in
  rings

1 can tomatoes (2½ cups)
⅓ cup rice
1 teaspoon salt
¼ teaspoon pepper

Brown the chops in hot fat, pour off any excess fat. Add onion and green pepper and pour tomatoes over the top. Sprinkle the rice around the chops, also the salt and pepper. Cover; cook over low heat until the chops are tender, about one hour.

St. Joseph's Table

William Frederick Cody, better known as Buffalo Bill Cody, helped arrange a world-famous buffalo hunt for Russian Grand Duke Alexis in 1872, and held America's first rodeo on July 4, 1882. He earned his nickname after the Civil War ended by supplying buffalo meat for the crew of the Kansas-Pacific Railroad. His 275-acre spread, including an 18-room Victorian mansion and vast barn, is near North Platte, Nebraska.

Ham Loaf

1¾ pounds ground cured ham
2½ pounds ground fresh pork
4 tablespoons ketchup
4 tablespoons horseradish
4 tablespoons chopped
   green pepper

1 cup mushrooms
1 cup cracker crumbs
2 eggs
1 cup milk
4 strips bacon

SAUCE:
½ cup prepared horseradish
½ cup mayonnaise
2 teaspoons prepared mustard

¼ cup chopped parsley
2 cups dairy sour cream

Combine ingredients for ham loaf and place in a 9x13-inch baking dish with 2 strips bacon on top and bottom of loaf. Bake at 350° for 1½ hours. Serve with sauce. Serves 12.

Our Daily Bread

Rosemary Pork Chops

1½ cups soy sauce
¾ cup water
¼ cup brown sugar

1 tablespoon dried rosemary, crushed
4 thick pork chops

Mix soy sauce with water, brown sugar, and rosemary. Marinate pork chops 3-4 hours. Bake uncovered at 350° up to one hour, depending upon thickness. May be grilled. Easy.

If It Tastes Good, Who Cares? II

Marinated Roast Pork

1 (3-pound) boneless single pork tenderloin
1 tablespoon Dijon mustard
½ teaspoon salt
¼ teaspoon pepper
¼ teaspoon crushed dry leaf thyme
¼ cup soy sauce

½ cup plus 1 tablespoon tawny port wine
2 teaspoons ground ginger
3 cloves garlic, minced
1 (10-ounce) jar red currant jelly
1 tablespoon soy sauce
2 tablespoons lemon juice

Remove any excess fat from the pork roast. Mix mustard, salt, pepper, and thyme and rub over pork roast outer surface. Place pork roast in self-sealing plastic bag.

Combine soy sauce, ½ cup wine, ground ginger, and garlic. Pour marinade over the roast and seal the bag, then refrigerate 8 hours or more; turning the bag occasionally. Transfer roast to 9x13-inch roasting pan. Reserve marinade. Insert meat thermometer. Cover loosely with aluminum foil; roast at 325° for one hour. Uncover and roast 1½-2 hours or until thermometer reads 155° for medium or 165° for well done. Baste frequently with reserved marinade.

Heat jelly, soy sauce, 1 tablespoon wine, and lemon juice in a small pan to boiling. Boil 5 minutes, stirring constantly. Pour jelly mixture over roasted meat and let stand at room temperature for 30 minutes. Baste pork with jelly mixture several times. Remove pork to serving platter and slice into serving pieces. Strain jelly from pan and pour over sliced meat. Serves 8.

Treasures of the Great Midwest

Herbed Pork Loin with Apricot Mustard Sauce

This dish freezes great! Plan on making extra sauce to go with leftovers, or other sandwich meats.

3-4 pounds pork tenderloin, trimmed
½ teaspoon dried rosemary
½ teaspoon dried dill weed

½ teaspoon dried thyme
½ teaspoon dried basil
1 tablespoon olive oil
1 large clove garlic, minced

Place pork flat in single layer in glass pan. Mix herbs, oil, and garlic; pour over meat and rub the oil mixture thoroughly onto all surfaces. Cover and refrigerate overnight or at least 6-8 hours.

Roast uncovered at 350° for about 20-25 minutes per pound of total weight to an internal temperature of 160°. (About 1½ hours; begin checking after one hour.) Let sit 10 minutes. Slice diagonally just before serving and spoon a strip of warm Apricot Mustard Sauce across slices. Pass extra sauce.

APRICOT MUSTARD SAUCE:
¾ cup apricot preserves, puréed
⅓ cup Dijon mustard
1½ teaspoons cornstarch

1½ teaspoons bottled brown bouquet sauce
⅓ cup soy sauce
¾ cup water

In processor or blender, purée preserves and transfer to small bowl. Stir in the mustard and cornstarch and gradually add remaining ingredients. Heat in pan on the stove over medium to high heat, stirring constantly, until sauce thickens and simmers one minute. Serves 8.

Presentations

Venison Marinade

½ cup dry red wine
¼ cup olive oil
1 tablespoon salt
1 tablespoon rosemary

½ teaspoon peppercorns
½ teaspoon cloves
1 clove garlic, cut up

Remove all fat and bluish tissue, and bones from venison. Combine all ingredients and shake. Marinate overnight, if possible.

Recipes from the Heart: 100 Years of Recipes and Folklore

Smoked Deer Ham

1 (5 to 8-pound) deer ham,
  trimmed neatly
½ cup Worcestershire sauce
1 cup Italian dressing
1 tablespoon cayenne red
  pepper

1 tablespoon salt
1 tablespoon pepper
1 cup chopped onions
½ cup soft butter

Put ham in large container; cover with mixture of all remaining ingredients. Can slice holes in meat so it can soak inside better. Cover good; soak overnight or about 10 hours. Can turn over about 2 or 3 hours to marinate. Put on smoker and let smoke for 6 hours; turn and smoke 4 more hours or until tender.

The Oregon Trail Cookbook

Pioneer Pickled Buffalo or Beef Tongue

1 (3-pound) beef tongue

Boil tongue approximately 4 hours or until tender. When cool, the rough may be removed with a sharp knife. Slice and soak in cold water for one hour. Skin when cooled.

PICKLING WATER:

2 cups water
2 cups plus 1 tablespoon
  vinegar

2 tablespoons pickling spice
1 teaspoon salt

Mix ingredients in saucepan; bring to a boil. Pour over drained beef tongue. One large onion may be sliced and added.

The Mormon Trail Cookbook

Bierocks

Use any yeast dough for hot rolls.

2 pounds hamburger
Garlic salt
Pepper

3-4 cups shredded cabbage
1 medium onion, chopped fine
1 tablespoon Worcestershire sauce

Brown hamburger and season. Drain well. Add cabbage, onion, and Worcestershire sauce. Simmer together 10 minutes.

Follow yeast dough recipe till ready to make rolls. Divide as for pan rolls; roll out thin (one at a time) and put some filling in each one. Pull all sides up and pinch together. Put on greased cookie sheet and let rise. Bake at 425° until golden brown, about 10 minutes. Brush with melted butter.

Note: These freeze well before or after baking. May use a chunk or slice of cheese in each Bierock.

Eastman Family Cookbook

PHOTO BY CHARLIE REIDEL, KANSAS DIVISION OF TRAVEL AND TOURISM

Built of native limestone, the magnificent Romanesque twin towers of the Cathedral of the Plains rise majestically above the surrounding plains. Victoria, Kansas.

Chicken Breast with Cranberry-Orange Sauce

2 large onions, sliced ½-inch
thick
6 boneless, skinless chicken
breast halves

¼ cup frozen orange juice
concentrate, thawed but not
diluted
¼ cup water

Place onion slices in bottom of ungreased 9x13x2-inch baking dish. Top with chicken. Mix orange juice concentrate and water in bowl. Baste breasts with orange juice mixture. Bake one hour at 350°, until cooked through and browned. Baste occasionally with orange juice mixture. When chicken is done, transfer to serving plates. Discard onions. Spoon Cranberry-Orange Sauce over chicken. Garnish with orange slices and serve. Makes 6 servings.

CRANBERRY-ORANGE SAUCE:

1 (16-ounce) can whole-berry
cranberry sauce
¾ cup unsweetened orange
juice

1 teaspoon grated orange rind
2 tablespoons brown sugar
2 teaspoons cornstarch
Orange slices, for garnish

Combine all sauce ingredients in small saucepan; stir well. Bring to a boil over high heat, stirring constantly. Reduce heat to medium, and cook one minute, stirring until thickened. Serve warm.

Recipes Worth Sharing

The World's Easiest Chicken

1 jar Russian dressing
1 small jar apricot jam

½ envelope onion soup mix
4 chicken breasts

In a large baking dish, combine Russian dressing, apricot jam, and onion soup mix. Place chicken breasts in dish; cover with the mixture. Bake at 350° for one hour. For best flavor, keep basting chicken with the mixture throughout the hour.

Favorite Recipes of Rainbow Valley Lutheran Church

Poulet Aux Quarante Gousses D'Ail
(Chicken with Forty Cloves of Garlic)

The aroma of France.

1 tablespoon butter
2 tablespoons olive oil
8 chicken thighs
Salt
Freshly ground pepper
1 head of garlic

1/2 cup dry white wine
1 can chicken broth
Basil
Thyme leaves
Cornstarch

In a large, deep skillet, warm butter and olive oil. Add the chicken, season on all sides, and brown on all sides.

Peel garlic cloves and distribute over chicken. Add wine and chicken broth. Sprinkle liberally with basil and thyme leaves. Cover and cook until chicken begins to fall off the bone (about 45 minutes). Remove chicken to a warm platter. Reduce stock slightly. Thicken with a little cornstarch mixed with cooled stock and serve over chicken. Don't discard the garlic. Spread the cloves over fresh slices of French bread.

If It Tastes Good, Who Cares? II

Honey Dijon Barbequed Chicken

2 (3-pound) chickens, cut into
  quarters
1/2 cup olive oil
1/2 cup white zinfandel
1/4 cup clover honey

2 tablespoons Dijon mustard
2 cloves of garlic, crushed
1 teaspoon pepper
1/2 teaspoon salt

Rinse chicken and pat dry. Place chicken quarters in 2 sealable plastic bags. Pour mixture of olive oil, wine, honey, Dijon mustard, garlic, pepper, and salt over chicken; seal. Marinate in refrigerator for 2-4 hours, turning occasionally. Drain, reserving marinade. Grill chicken with lid down over medium-hot coals for 20-30 minutes per side or until cooked through, basting frequently with reserved marinade. Yield: 8 servings.

The Kansas City Barbeque Society Cookbook

Hawaiian Chicken

1 whole chicken, cut up
  (or chicken breasts)
1/2 cup flour
1/3 cup salad oil
1 teaspoon salt
1/4 teaspoon pepper
1 (16-ounce) can sliced
  pineapple
1 cup sugar

2 tablespoons cornstarch
3/4 cup cider vinegar
1 tablespoon soy sauce
1/4 teaspoon ginger
1 chicken bouillon cube
1 large green pepper, cut in
  1/4-inch circles
Cooked rice

Coat chicken with flour. Heat oil; brown chicken on all sides. Put in greased 9x13-inch pan, skin-side-up. Salt and pepper. Drain pineapple, pouring syrup into 2-cup measure, adding water to make 1 1/4 cups. Add next 6 ingredients. Bring to a boil, stirring constantly. Boil 2 minutes. Pour over chicken. Bake at 350° for 30 minutes. Add pineapple and green pepper. Bake 30 minutes more. Serve with rice.

Wyndmere Community Alumni Cookbook

Oven Barbecued Chicken

Everyone wants this recipe.

5-6 pounds chicken thighs	**1 cup pineapple juice**
Garlic powder	**1½ cups catsup**
3 eggs, beaten	**1 cup white vinegar**
2 cups granulated sugar	**2 teaspoons soy sauce**

Wash chicken thighs and pat dry. Sprinkle with garlic powder and let set for about 5 minutes. Dip chicken in beaten eggs. Fry until nearly done. Spray large oven pan with non-stick spray. Mix together the granulated sugar, juice, catsup, vinegar, and soy sauce. Put chicken in pan and pour the sauce over chicken. Cover pan with aluminum foil and bake 30-45 minutes in 300° oven, or until sauce is thick. Put chicken on platter and spoon remaining sauce over top.

In the Kitchen with Kate

Mandarin Chicken with Broccoli

3 whole broiler-fryer chicken
  breasts, halved
1 teaspoon salt
1/4 teaspoon pepper
1/4 cup butter
1/2 cup minced onion
1 clove garlic, minced
2 teaspoons paprika

1 bunch fresh broccoli, cut up,
  steamed about 10 minutes
1 (11-ounce) can mandarin
  orange sections, drained
1 cup sour cream
1/3 cup mayonnaise (NOT salad
  dressing)
1/3 cup grated Parmesan cheese

Sprinkle chicken meat with salt and pepper. In large frying pan, melt butter over medium heat. Add onion and garlic; sauté 3 minutes. Stir in paprika. Remove pan from heat; add chicken to mixture, turning to coat. In large shallow baking pan, place chicken in single layer, skin-side-up. Cover with foil; bake in 375° oven about 40 minutes or until fork can be inserted in chicken with ease. Remove chicken from oven; place broccoli around chicken. Add mandarin orange sections. In medium bowl mix together sour cream and mayonnaise; spoon over chicken, broccoli, and orange segments. Sprinkle with Parmesan cheese. Return to oven; bake (uncovered) about 6 minutes longer, or until it turns golden. Serves 6.

Nutritional analysis: Cal 400; Carbo 10g; Prot 26g; Fat 20.3g; Chol 101mg; Dietary Fiber 1.7g; Vit A 3,781IU; Vit B1 .2mg; Vit B2 .5mg; Vit B6 .9mg; Vit B12 .6mcg; Folacin 80mcg; Niacin 8mg; Vit C 103mg; Vit E 3.5mg; Sod 618mg; Potas 421mg; Cal 219mg; Iron 2mg; Zinc 1.3mg.

REC Family Cookbook

Creamy Baked Chicken Breasts

8 chicken breast halves
8 slices Swiss cheese
1 can cream of chicken soup

1 cup herb seasoned croutons,
  crushed
1/4 cup melted butter

Arrange chicken in a lightly greased baking dish. Top with cheese slices. Spread soup evenly over all and top with crushed croutons. Drizzle with melted butter. Bake uncovered 45-50 minutes in a 350° oven. Use the extra sauce to top your baked potatoes.

Heavenly Delights

Apricot Chicken Stir-Fry

1/2 cup dried apricot halves, cut
   in half
1/4 cup hot water
1 tablespoon all-purpose flour
1 tablespoon chopped cilantro
   (optional)
1/2 teaspoon salt
1/8 teaspoon pepper
3/4 pound boneless skinless
   chicken breasts, cut into
   1/2-inch pieces

3 tablespoons cooking oil,
   divided
1 medium onion, halved and
   sliced
1 cup chopped celery
1/2 cup halved snow peas
1/2 teaspoon ground ginger
1 garlic clove, minced
1-2 tablespoons lemon juice
Hot cooked rice

In a small bowl, soak apricots in water and set aside (do not drain). Combine flour and cilantro, if desired, salt and pepper; sprinkle over the chicken and set aside. Heat one tablespoon oil in a large skillet or Wok over medium heat; stir-fry onion and celery for 2-3 minutes or until tender. Add peas, ginger, garlic, and apricots; stir-fry for 2 minutes. Remove and keep warm. Add remaining oil to skillet and stir-fry chicken for 6-7 minutes or until no longer pink. Sprinkle with lemon juice. Return apricot mixture to skillet and heat through. Serve over rice. Makes 4 servings.

Silver Celebration Cookbook

Lemon Teriyaki Glazed Chicken

1/2 cup lemon
1/2 cup soy sauce
1/4 cup sugar
3 tablespoons brown sugar
2 tablespoons water

4 cloves garlic, minced
3/4 teaspoon ground ginger
6-8 chicken breasts or chicken
   thighs

In skillet, combine all ingredients except chicken. Cook over medium heat 3-4 minutes. Add chicken. Simmer 30 minutes or until thoroughly cooked.

To Tayla with TLC

Juicy Baked Chicken and Mushrooms

A delicious low-calorie way to make chicken. The unflavored gelatin gives the chicken a saucy texture.

2 tablespoons dried parsley
2 tablespoons dried chives
8 ounces fresh mushrooms, sliced
2 (5 to 6-ounce) chicken breasts, skinned
1/3 cup lemon juice

1/2 teaspoon onion powder
1/2 teaspoon salt (optional)
1/2 teaspoon poultry seasoning
1 1/2 teaspoons unflavored gelatin granules (1/2 package)
1 teaspoon paprika

Mix parsley, chives, and mushrooms in a 1-quart casserole. Place chicken on mushrooms. Pour lemon juice over chicken. Sprinkle remaining ingredients over chicken in order given. Cover. Microwave at MEDIUM HIGH (70%) for 11-14 minutes or until tender. Let stand 3 minutes before serving. Yields 2 servings (approximately 160 calories per serving.)

Easy Livin' Microwave Cooking

Chicken Squares with Mushroom Sauce

3 cups diced, cooked chicken
1 cup cooked rice
2 cups soft bread crumbs
1/3 cup diced celery
1/4 cup pimiento, chopped

4 beaten eggs
2 teaspoons salt
1/4 teaspoon poultry seasoning
2 cups chicken broth

Combine chicken, rice, bread crumbs, celery, and pimiento. To the beaten eggs, add salt, poultry seasoning, and broth (or use 2 chicken bouillon cubes dissolved in 2 cups hot water, then cooled); mix thoroughly. Stir into chicken mixture. Bake in greased 9x9x2-inch baking dish at 350° for 55 minutes. Cut into squares and serve with Mushroom Sauce.

MUSHROOM SAUCE:
2/3 cup milk   1 can cream of mushroom soup

Add milk to soup. Heat thoroughly. Serves 9.

Sharing God's Bounty

Chicken and Stuffing Casserole

4 cups stuffing mix
1 cup melted butter
4 cups chopped cooked chicken
2 cans cream of chicken soup
1 (13-ounce) can evaporated milk
1 (10-ounce) package frozen peas, thawed
1/4 cup minced onion
1 (2-ounce) jar chopped pimento, drained

Combine stuffing mix with melted butter in bowl; mix well. Press half the mixture into 9x13-inch baking dish. Combine chicken, soup, evaporated milk, peas, onion, and pimento in bowl; mix well. Spread in prepared dish; top with remaining stuffing mix. Bake at 350° for one hour. Yields 8 servings.

Y Cook?

Broccoli and Chicken Casserole

20 ounces chopped broccoli, cooked, drained
1 large chicken, cooked and cubed

Put cooked broccoli in 9x13-inch pan. Put cubed chicken over broccoli.

SAUCE:

1 cup sharp Cheddar cheese, shredded
2 cans cream of chicken soup
1 cup mayonnaise
1 tablespoon lemon juice
1/2 teaspoon curry powder, if desired
Buttered crumbs, to cover casserole

Combine and mix cheese, creamed chicken soup, mayonnaise, lemon juice, and curry powder and spread over chicken and broccoli. Sprinkle buttered crumbs over top. Bake at 350° for 30-45 minutes or until top is browned.

90th Anniversary Trinity Lutheran Church Cookbook

Speedy Overnight Casserole

3 cups chopped cooked chicken or turkey
2 cups large elbow macaroni, uncooked
1 can cream of mushroom soup
1 can cream of chicken soup
1 soup can milk
1 soup can chicken broth
1 small onion, chopped
1 small can water chestnuts, sliced
1/2 teaspoon salt
1/2 pound grated cheese (save some for topping)
1 cup crushed potato chips

Mix all ingredients except chips. Put in 9x13-inch pan. Sprinkle reserved cheese and potato chips on top. Cover with foil. Refrigerate overnight. Bake, covered, for 1½ hours at 350°. This freezes well.

Home at the Range III

Sour Cream 'n' Dill Chicken

8-10 chicken pieces, skinned
Black pepper to taste
1 can cream of mushroom soup, undiluted
1 envelope dry onion soup mix
1 (8-ounce) carton sour cream
1 tablespoon lemon juice
1 tablespoon fresh dill, chopped or 1 teaspoon dill weed
1 (4-ounce) can sliced mushrooms, drained
Paprika
Cooked egg noodles (optional)

Place chicken in a single layer in 9x13-inch baking dish. Sprinkle with pepper. Combine soup, soup mix, sour cream, lemon juice, dill, and mushrooms; pour over chicken. Sprinkle with paprika. Bake in 350° oven one hour, uncovered, until chicken is tender. Serve over egg noodles, if desired. Yields 4-6 servings.

Norman Lutheran Church 125th Anniversary Cookbook

A few Kansas facts: Kansas' name is from the Kansa or Kaw Indians. The cottonwood tree is often called the "pioneer of Kansas" because of its abundance on the plains. The official state song of Kansas is "Home on the Range."

Swiss Chicken Cutlet

3 tablespoons margarine or
  butter
$1/4$ cup all-purpose flour
$1/2$ teaspoon salt
$1/8$ teaspoon pepper
$2^{1}/_{2}$ cups milk
$1/2$ cup dry white wine

5 whole boneless chicken
  breasts, skinned and halved
2 eggs, well beaten
1 cup dry bread crumbs
$1/4$ cup vegetable oil
1 cup shredded Swiss cheese

Heat oven to 350°. In 2-quart saucepan, melt butter; stir in flour and seasonings until bubbly (1 minute). Stir in milk and continue cooking over medium heat, stirring constantly until thickened. Remove from heat and stir in wine. Pour half into greased 13x9-inch baking dish. Dip chicken in eggs and coat with bread crumbs.

In 10-inch skillet, heat 2 tablespoons oil and place 5 breast halves in oil. Cook over medium heat until browned (2-3 minutes on each side). Place browned chicken in sauce and repeat with remaining chicken. Cover with remaining sauce. Bake for 30-40 minutes or until chicken is fork tender. Sprinkle with cheese and bake for 2-4 minutes or until cheese is melted. Serves 10.

Note: Chicken can be prepared ahead. Cook chicken until no longer pink and place in sauce. Cover and refrigerate for several hours or overnight. Increase baking time to 50-60 minutes. This is a rich entrée and the wine will give it a special taste.

Silver Celebration Cookbook

Chicken Rice Supreme

1 package onion soup (dry)	1 cup rice, uncooked
1 can cream of mushroom soup	1 fryer, cut in pieces
1½ soup cans of water	Salt and pepper to taste

Mix onion soup, mushroom soup, and water. Put rice in a 13x9x2-inch pan. Pour half of liquid over rice. Place chicken, skin-side-up, on rice. Salt and pepper and add rest of liquid. Cover and bake 1½ hours in 350° oven. Remove cover last 20 minutes to brown chicken.

Home at the Range I

Fantastic Chicken Fajitas

1 pound boneless chicken breast or thigh meat	½ teaspoon hot pepper sauce
1 teaspoon each garlic powder, oregano, ground cumin, and seasoned salt	1 tablespoon cooking oil
	1 medium onion, peeled and sliced
2 tablespoons orange juice	1 green pepper, seeded and sliced
2 tablespoons vinegar	4 flour tortillas

Slice chicken into ¼-inch strips. Mix together garlic, oregano, cumin, salt, orange juice, vinegar, and hot pepper sauce. Marinate chicken strips in mixture for 10 minutes. Heat oil in heavy skillet until hot. Stir-fry chicken strips, onion, and green pepper until chicken is no longer pink, about 3-5 minutes. Serve with flour tortillas and accompany with sliced green onion, shredded lettuce, and salsa, if desired. Serves 4.

Heavenly Recipes

Kansas ranks first in the US in quail and prairie chicken harvest.

Chicken Loaf with Mushroom Sauce

CHICKEN LOAF:

1 (4-pound) chicken cooked
  and diced
2 cups soft bread crumbs
1 cup cooked rice
1 teaspoon salt (less if chicken
  is salted)
1/2 teaspoon paprika

1/4 cup chopped pimiento
4 beaten eggs
1/2 stick margarine
1 1/2 cups milk
3 cups chicken broth, divided
  (reserve 2 cups for sauce)

Combine in order given. Cook in loaf pan at 325° for 45-60 minutes (use custard test). Let stand 15-20 minutes before cutting in suitable servings. Serve with Mushroom Sauce.

MUSHROOM SAUCE:

1/4 cup butter
1/2 pound fresh mushrooms,
  diced
1/4 cup flour
2 cups chicken broth, heated

2 egg yolks
1/4 cup cream
1/8 teaspoon paprika
1/2 tablespoon lemon juice

Melt 2 tablespoons butter; add mushrooms and cook 5 minutes, but do not brown. Melt remaining butter in double boiler, add flour and mix. Stir in hot stock. Cook until thick. Beat egg yolks and cream together. Add to mixture and cook. Add paprika and lemon juice. Serves 18.

Note: If using canned mushrooms, make the sauce in double boiler as above, and add mushrooms with paprika and lemon juice. Substitute the juice from canned mushrooms for part of the chicken stock.

Measure for Pleasure

Hot Chicken Sandwich

1 loaf Pepperidge Farm Bread
3 cups chopped, cooked chicken
3 hard-boiled eggs, chopped
2 tablespoons chopped onions
1 cup sliced ripe olives
1 small can mushrooms
²/₃ cup mayonnaise
1 can mushroom soup
1 cup sour cream
Slivered almonds
Paprika

Remove crust from bread and butter on both sides. Put 8 slices of bread in 9x13-inch pan. Mix together chicken, eggs, onions, olives, mushrooms, and mayonnaise. Put on bread. Put 8 slices of bread on top. Mix soup and sour cream together. Put on top of bread. Sprinkle with slivered almonds and paprika. Bake at 325° for 30 minutes.

St. Joseph's Table

Carrot, Cheese 'n Chicken Pie

Pastry for 1-crust 9-inch pie
1 (10³/₄-ounce) can mushroom
  soup
¹/₃ cup milk
2 whole skinless, boneless
  chicken breasts, cooked and
  cubed (1-inch)
1 (16-ounce) bag frozen carrot,
  broccoli and cauliflower,
  thawed and drained
1¹/₂ cups shredded mozzarella
  cheese

Place rolled-out pie crust in pan; set aside. In bowl stir together soup and milk. Fold in chicken cubes, vegetables, and cheese. Spoon into pie crust. Bake in 400° oven 40 minutes or until pie is bubbly. Serves 6.

Pumpkin, Winter Squash and Carrot Cookbook

Sour Cream Chicken Enchiladas

1 pint fat-free sour cream
2 cans cream of chicken soup
1 (7-ounce) can diced chiles
1 bunch green onions, chopped
1 dozen flour tortillas
2 tablespoons butter or margarine
3-4 chicken breasts, boned and cooked
1-2 cups Cheddar cheese, divided

Mix sour cream, soup, chiles, and onions. Spread tortillas with a tablespoon of this mixture and add diced chicken and cheese. Roll up and put in shallow, greased 9x13-inch pan. Spread remaining mixture over the rolled tortillas. Bake at 350° for 40 minutes. Remove and sprinkle grated cheese over top. Return to oven until cheese melts. Serves 8-12.

Feed My Lambs

Chicken Pot Pie

How wonderful! Chicken pot pie you can make without deboning a chicken and peeling vegetables.

2 (9-inch) deep dish frozen pie shells
1 (10-ounce) can chunk chicken, drained
1 (15-ounce) can mixed vegetables, drained
1 (2.8-ounce) can French fried onion rings
2 (11-ounce) cans condensed cream of chicken soup
¼ teaspoon salt

Prick bottom pie shell all over with fork. Bake, uncovered, at 375° for 10 minutes. Combine chicken, vegetables, onion rings, soup, and salt. Fill bottom pie shell with mixture. Place second pie shell on top. Prick with fork 6 places. Set on a foil-covered oven rack to catch spills. Bake, uncovered, at 375° for 40 minutes. Yields 6 servings.

The Give Mom a Rest (She's on Vacation) Cookbook

Fort Leavenworth is the oldest continuously garrisoned military installation west of the Mississippi. Leavenworth is the oldest city in Kansas, founded in 1854.

Cheese-Stuffed Chicken in Phyllo

8 skinless, boneless chicken breast halves, about 1¹/₂-2 pounds
Salt and pepper
4 cups chopped fresh spinach
1 cup chopped onion
2 tablespoons olive oil
4 ounces cream cheese, cubed and softened
1 cup shredded mozzarella cheese, about 4 ounces

¹/₂ cup crumbled feta cheese, about 2 ounces
¹/₂ cup shredded Cheddar cheese
1 beaten egg yolk
1 tablespoon all-purpose flour
¹/₂ teaspoon nutmeg
¹/₂ teaspoon ground cumin
16 (18x14-inch) sheets phyllo dough (usually available in frozen food department)
²/₃ cup margarine or butter, melted

Place each chicken breast between two sheets of heavy plastic; pound with the flat side of a metal mallet until ¹/₄ inch thick. Season with salt and pepper; set aside. In a large skillet cook spinach and onion in hot oil until onion is tender. Remove from heat. Stir in cream cheese until blended. Stir in remaining cheeses, egg yolk, flour, nutmeg, and cumin. Place about ¹/₄ cup of the spinach mixture on each chicken breast half; roll up jellyroll style. It's not necessary to seal ends.

Place one sheet of phyllo on work surface. Keep remaining sheets covered with a damp towel to prevent drying out. Brush with some of the melted margarine or butter. Place another phyllo sheet on top of first; brush with margarine. Place one chicken roll near short side of phyllo; roll chicken and phyllo over once. Fold in long sides and continue rolling from short side. Repeat with remaining chicken, phyllo and margarine. Brush with margarine or butter. Bake, uncovered, in 350° for 30-35 minutes or until chicken is no longer pink. Serves 8.

Iola's Gourmet Recipes in Rhapsody

Guilt-Free Gourmet Turkey Burgers

1 pound lean ground turkey	1 egg white
1 small shredded zucchini	1 tablespoon parsley
1/2 cup dry bread crumbs or crushed cornflakes	1/2 teaspoon salt
	1/2 teaspoon pepper
Onion, chopped	1/2 green or red bell pepper,
2 tablespoons Worcestershire sauce	shredded
	1 carrot, peeled and shredded

Combine all ingredients in large bowl; mix well. Form into patties (will be soft). Use spatula to transfer to broiler pan or fine wire vegetable rack for grilling. Cook well. Excellent with BBQ sauce, lettuce and tomato garnish.

Kearney 125th Anniversary Community Cookbook

Turkey Casserole

1 pound ground turkey	1 (15-ounce) can black beans, drained
1/3 cup chopped onion	
1 clove garlic, minced	1/4 cup water
1 tablespoon vinegar	1 (16-ounce) jar salsa, (mild or medium)
2 teaspoons chili powder	
1 1/2 teaspoons crushed dried oregano	6 (6-inch) corn tortillas, cut into 1-inch wide strips
1/2 teaspoon ground cumin	3/4 cup shredded Cheddar
Dash of ground red pepper (optional)	cheese (reduced fat)

Cook turkey, onion, and garlic in skillet. Drain fat. Add vinegar, chili powder, oregano, cumin, and red pepper, if desired. Cook and stir for one minute. Stir in beans and water. Remove from heat.

In a 2-quart baking dish, place 2 tablespoons of salsa, half of tortilla strips and top with turkey mixture and half of the remaining salsa. Repeat layers. Cover and bake in a 325° oven for 30 minutes. Uncover and sprinkle with cheese. Bake 5-10 minutes more or till cheese is melted. Makes 6 servings.

Recipes 1978-1998

Apple-Smoked Turkey

1 (10 to 13-pound) turkey
1 cup balsamic vinegar
1/4 cup water
3 tablespoons paprika

2 tablespoons sea salt
2 tablespoons lemon pepper
1/4 teaspoon marjoram

Rinse turkey thoroughly and place in a large roasting pan. Combine the vinegar, water, paprika, sea salt, lemon pepper, and marjoram in a glass jar; shake to blend and pour over turkey. Marinate for one hour or until turkey comes to room temperature, spooning marinade over the turkey several times. Build an indirect fire in a kettle grill or water smoker and add a handful of water-soaked apple wood chunks to the charcoal. Remove turkey from the marinade and place in the smoker. Smoke for 4-5 hours at 225° until a meat thermometer inserted in the thickest part of the turkey thigh registers 170°. When the turkey is smoked, the meat will have a pink color. Serves 6-8.

Que Queens Easy Grilling & Simple Smoking

Turkey à la King

5 tablespoons butter
3 tablespoons flour
1/2 cup chicken broth
1 cup cream (or half-and-half)
1/4 pound mushrooms, sliced
1 green pepper, cut in strips
3 cups diced, cooked turkey
  or chicken

1 (4-ounce) jar pimento
Salt and pepper
Paprika
1 (10-ounce) package frozen
  pastry shells (puff pastry),
  baked

In large saucepan over low heat, melt 2 tablespoons of the butter; stir in flour. Remove from heat and stir in broth and cream, stirring constantly until smooth. Put back on heat and cook on medium, stirring until thick. Set aside. In 10-inch skillet, sauté mushrooms and green pepper in remaining butter. Cook until pepper is wilted and mushroom liquid evaporated. Stir into above sauce with turkey and pimento, and season with salt, pepper, and paprika. Heat through. Serve on baked pastry shells.

To Tayla with TLC

Crock-Pot Dressing

1 cup butter
2 cups onion, chopped
1 cup celery, chopped
13 cups dried bread cubes
1 teaspoon poultry seasoning

1½ teaspoons salt
1½ teaspoons sage
½ teaspoon pepper
4 cups chicken broth
2 well-beaten eggs

Melt butter; add onion and celery; simmer. Mix all and cook in crockpot on low for 6-8 hours.

Years and Years of Goodwill Cooking

Duck and Wild Rice Trail Casserole

2 pounds wild ducks
4 stalks celery
1 large onion, halved
Salt and pepper
1 (6-ounce) package long grain
   and wild rice
1 (4-ounce) can sliced
   mushrooms

½ cup chopped onion
½ cup melted oleo
¼ cup all-purpose flour
¾ cup half-and-half
¾ cup white wine
2 tablespoons chopped fresh
   parsley
½ cup slivered almonds

Cook ducks with seasonings (celery, onion, salt and pepper), covered with water in Dutch oven for one hour or until tender. Remove ducks from stock. Let cool; strain stock and reserve. Cut meat into bite-sized pieces and set aside.

Cook rice according to directions on package. Drain mushrooms, reserving liquid. Add enough duck broth (stock) to make 1½ cups. Sauté chopped onion in oleo until tender; add flour, stirring until thick and smooth. Gradually stir in mushroom broth liquid. Cook over medium heat, stirring constantly, until thick and bubbly. Stir in duck, rice, half-and-half, wine and parsley. Spoon into a greased 2-quart shallow casserole. Sprinkle almonds on top. Cover and bake at 350° for 15-20 minutes until liquid is absorbed. Let rest 5 minutes before serving. Serves 6-8.

Note: You may substitute 3 cups cooked chicken for duck.

The Oregon Trail Cookbook

Quail Cook-in-a-Bag

1 tablespoon flour
1 large oven cooking bag
6 quail
Salt and pepper to taste
1 cup onion, chopped
1/2 cup green pepper, chopped

1 pound fresh mushrooms,
 sliced
1 bay leaf
1 cup dry sherry
Juice of 1/2 lemon
1 cup water

Grease a large roasting pan. Put flour in oven cooking bag and shake, making sure that the inside of bag is evenly coated. Split birds lengthwise in half and sprinkle flesh with salt and pepper. Place birds in the bag and add the onion, green pepper, mushrooms, bay leaf, sherry, lemon juice, and water. Tie the bag, lay in pan, and punch 12 holes in the top of the bag. Roast at 350° for 45 minutes. This method of roasting creates its own gravy and bastes the birds at the same time.

The Oregon Trail Cookbook

Creamed Pheasant

1 pheasant
2 tablespoons oil
2 tablespoons flour
2 teaspoons chicken bouillon
1/2 cup water
1 can cream soup (celery,
 chicken or mushroom)

1 cup sour cream
2 cups half-and-half
1 cup water
Salt and pepper to taste

Fry pheasant in oil until brown. Take out of pan. To pan add flour, and bouillon dissolved in 1/2 cup water. Add soup, sour cream, half-and-half, 1 cup water, and salt and pepper. Add pheasant and bake at 350° until pheasant is soft.

Cookin' with Farmers Union Friends

Flint Ridge Pheasant

Those of us who cook for hunters always welcome a new recipe for fish or fowl. Here's one that we cheered for! This casserole is also wonderful for chicken; use 3 skinless, boneless chicken breast halves.

2 cups cooked wild rice
  (²/₃ cups dry)
1 cup julienned (matchstick)
  1-inch carrot strips, cooked
5 slices bacon
1-2 tablespoons oil, butter or
  margarine
2 skinless, boneless pheasant
  breast halves, cut in 2x2-inch
  pieces
Salt and pepper to taste
5 medium mushrooms, sliced

5 green onions, sliced
1 can cream of chicken soup
¼ cup cream or milk
¼ cup sherry or dry, white
  wine
1 cup (4 ounces) shredded
  mozzarella cheese
1 (14-ounce) can artichoke
  hearts, drained, quartered
¼ cup grated Parmesan
  cheese

Put the wild rice in 9x9x2-inch baking dish that has been sprayed with nonstick vegetable spray. Layer the carrots over the wild rice.

In large skillet, cook bacon until crisp; drain and crumble over the carrots. Pour off grease from skillet and add a tablespoon or two of oil. Sauté the pheasant until well browned on both sides (about 10 minutes). Transfer to baking dish.

In same skillet, sauté the mushrooms and green onions until tender, adding additional oil if needed. Add soup, cream and sherry, and mix well. Add mozzarella and gently stir in artichokes. Spread over the pheasant layer. Sprinkle with Parmesan. Cover dish with foil sprayed with nonstick vegetable spray. Bake at 350° for 30 minutes; remove foil and bake 15 more minutes until bubbly throughout. Serves 4-5.

Presentations

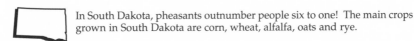

In South Dakota, pheasants outnumber people six to one! The main crops grown in South Dakota are corn, wheat, alfalfa, oats and rye.

River Roast Wild Goose

1 young wild goose (about 10
  pounds) with giblets
Salt and pepper
8 medium onions, peeled
2-3 branches fresh sage or
  1 tablespoon dried sage,
  crushed

8 thick slices fatty bacon
2 tablespoons flour
1 cup strong stock made from
  giblets

Preheat oven to 325°. Rinse goose, drain and pat dry with paper towels, inside and out. Sprinkle cavity and all surfaces with salt and pepper. With a sharp knife, cut a quarter inch deep X in the root end of each onion. Fill goose body with onions and the fresh or dried sage. Close the cavity and tie legs together with butchers cord. Place in roasting pan on rack, breast-side-up. Cover with bacon slices and roast for about 2 hours. Remove bacon strips and dust goose with half of the flour. Continue roasting until crisp and done, about 30 minutes more. Transfer to heated platter and keep warm.

Skim fat from pan juices and add remaining flour to juices, stirring over medium heat until smooth and thickened. Add stock slowly, stirring. Bring to boil and adjust seasoning with salt and pepper to taste. Serve on side as sauce. Serves 6. Serve with hot applesauce and baby Brussels sprouts.

The Oregon Trail Cookbook

Football is king in Lincoln, where the five-time National champions University of Nebraska Cornhuskers always draw capacity crowds.

Orange Roughy Almondine

4 (4-ounce) orange roughy
  fillets
1 teaspoon plain gelatin, dry
1/2 teaspoon seasoned salt or
  substitute

2 tablespoons snipped fresh
  parsley
1 1/2 tablespoons lime juice

Place fish fillets in a flat 1 1/2-quart microwave-safe casserole. Sprinkle with gelatin, salt substitute, parsley, and lime juice. Cover with a lid or vented plastic wrap. Microwave for 4-6 minutes at HIGH (100%), or until fish flakes easily with a fork. Let stand 5 minutes. Serve fish topped with Toasted Almonds.

TOASTED ALMONDS:
1 tablespoon regular
  polyunsaturated margarine

1/4 cup sliced almonds

Mix margarine and almonds in a 9-inch glass dish. Microwave uncovered for 1 1/2-3 minutes at HIGH (100%), until almonds are toasted, stirring often.

Nutritional analysis per serving (3-ounce cooked fillet): Cal 162; Carbo 2g; Fat 10g; Prot 14g; Chol 17mg; Sod 54mg. Diabetic exchanges: Lean meat 2.25; Fat 1.0.

Easy Livin' Low-Calorie Microwave Cooking

Platte River Catfish Fillets

2 tablespoons lemon juice
2 tablespoons white wine
1/2 cup dry bread crumbs
1/4 teaspoon salt

1/8 teaspoon garlic powder
1/8 teaspoon pepper
1 pound catfish fillets
2 teaspoons oil

Heat oven to 450°. Spray 15x10x1-inch baking pan with non-stick cooking spray. In shallow dish, combine lemon juice and wine. In another shallow dish, combine bread crumbs, salt, garlic powder, and pepper. Dip fillets in liquid, then dip in crumbs to coat. Arrange coated fillets on sprayed pan; drizzle with oil. Bake at 450° for 8-10 minutes or until fish flakes easily with fork. Makes 4 servings.

The Oregon Trail Cookbook

Salmon Supreme

Season this casserole as pleases your family.

1 cup uncooked rice
1 can salmon and some juice
1 medium onion, chopped
¹/₂ cup butter or margarine
2-3 slices American cheese,
   cut up

Paprika
Onion salt
Pepper
Buttered bread crumbs

Cook rice. Add salmon and juice, chopped onion, butter, cheese and seasonings. Mix well and turn into greased casserole. Top with buttered bread crumbs. Bake at 350° for 30-35 minutes.

Heart of the Home Recipes

Orange and Herb Salmon

Halibut steaks, sea bass or snapper may be substituted for salmon.

¹/₂ tablespoon olive oil
Zest of 1 orange, finely grated
¹/₄ cup orange juice, freshly
   squeezed
2 teaspoons garlic, minced
2 teaspoons dried tarragon

Salt to taste
Coarsely ground black pepper
   to taste
4 salmon steaks
2 teaspoons freshly snipped
   chives

Combine olive oil, orange zest, orange juice, garlic, tarragon, salt and pepper in medium mixing bowl to make marinade. Place salmon steaks in oven-proof dish. Pour marinade over steaks. Marinate for at least one hour at room temperature (or let marinate in refrigerator overnight). Preheat grill or oven to 450°. Place steaks directly on the grill; spoon some of the marinade over steaks. If preparing in the oven, fish may be baked in marinade. Bake for 7-8 minutes, turning after 4 minutes or until salmon is just cooked through. Fish should flake easily when tested with a fork. Place on serving platter and sprinkle with chives. Serves 4.

Treasures of the Great Midwest

Lemon Salmon with Cucumber Sauce

4 (4-ounce) salmon steaks, fresh   2 green onions, thinly sliced
  or frozen, thawed   1 lemon, sliced

Arrange salmon in a 10-inch flat microwave-safe casserole with thickest portions toward outside. Top with onion and lemon slices. Cover loosely with plastic wrap or waxed paper. Microwave for 7-9 minutes at MEDIUM HIGH (70%), or until fish flakes easily with a fork. Let stand 3 minutes.

CUCUMBER SAUCE:

½ cup low-fat cottage cheese   ½ medium cucumber, peeled
3 tablespoons nonfat plain   and sliced
  yogurt   Lemon and cucumber slices to
½ teaspoon lemon juice   garnish (optional)
¼ teaspoon seasoned salt
  substitute

Purée all sauce ingredients using a blender or food processor. Refrigerate or heat. (Sauce can be served chilled or heated.) To heat, microwave for 2-3 minutes at MEDIUM (50%). Serve chilled or heated sauce over salmon. Garnish with additional lemon slices and cucumber slices, if desired. Yields 4 servings.

VARIATION:

Omit cottage cheese and use ⅔ cup yogurt total. Proceed as directed. For white fish fillets with cucumber sauce, substitute one pound of any white fish fillets for the salmon steaks.

Nutritional analysis per serving (¼ recipe): Cal 175; Carbo 4g; Fat 5g; Prot 24g; Chol 62mg; Sod 198mg. Diabetic exchanges: Lean meat 3; Vegetable 0.5.

Easy Livin' Low-Calorie Microwave Cooking

BBQ Salmon

8 large cloves of garlic, finely chopped
1 teaspoon salt
¼ cup finely chopped fresh parsley
2 tablespoons minced sun-dried tomatoes
¼ cup olive oil
1 (1½-pound) salmon fillet

Sprinkle garlic with salt in shallow dish; mash together with blade of knife. Combine with parsley, sun-dried tomatoes, and olive oil in bowl; mix well. Let stand, covered, in refrigerator for 8 hours or longer. Cut 2 lengthwise slits to but not through skin with sharp knife. Spread half the garlic mixture over fillet and into slits. Place salmon skin-side-down on greased grill rack in covered grill. Grill with lid down over low heat for 10-15 minutes; spread with remaining garlic mixture. Cook with lid down over medium heat for 15 minutes or until fish flakes easily. Yield: 4 servings.

The Kansas City Barbeque Society Cookbook

Walleye Whopper

BATTER:
1 cup cold water
¼ cup dry white wine
1 cup all-purpose flour
1½ teaspoons baking powder
¼ teaspoon salt

Combine water and wine. Whisk in flour, baking powder, and salt until smooth.

4 (4 to 6-ounce) skinless boneless walleye fillets
¼ cup all-purpose flour
Cooking oil for deep-fat frying
4 warm buns
4 lettuce leaves
Tartar sauce

Rinse fillets and pat dry with paper towels. Halve crosswise. Coat fillets with flour, dip in batter. Fry fillets in large skillet of hot oil for 3-5 minutes. Remove; drain on paper towels. Keep warm. Serve on buns with lettuce and tartar sauce. Makes 4 sandwiches.

Kearney 125th Anniversary Community Cookbook

Balsamic Mustard Grilled Swordfish

4 large swordfish steaks	4 tablespoons olive oil
3 tablespoons balsamic vinegar	½ cup Dijon mustard

Rinse fish thoroughly and place in a glass dish. Combine the vinegar, oil, and mustard, and pour over fish. Marinate, refrigerated, for 15-30 minutes. Drain the fish and reserve the marinade. Grill the swordfish over a hot fire for 5-6 per side (10 minutes per inch of thickness), basting with the marinade several times while cooking. The fish is done when it just begins to flake apart. Serves 4.

Note: Marinate fish for about 30 minutes only, as it tends to get mushy if over-marinated.

Que Queens: Easy Grilling & Simple Smoking

Baked Shrimp

2 pounds large shrimp (about 32)	3 large garlic cloves, minced
1 cup butter, melted	2 teaspoons basil
¼ cup dry white wine	1 teaspoon Worcestershire sauce
¼ cup minced parsley	¾-1 teaspoon hot pepper sauce
2 tablespoons fresh lemon juice	½ teaspoon salt
	½ cup dry unseasoned bread crumbs

Preheat oven to 450°. Shell and devein shrimp, leaving tails intact. In a shallow 2-quart baking dish, combine butter, wine, parsley, lemon juice, garlic, basil, Worcestershire sauce, hot pepper sauce and salt. Mix well. Remove ¼ cup of this mixture and set aside. Add shrimp to baking dish and mix thoroughly. Combine bread crumbs with reserved butter sauce and sprinkle over shrimp. Bake 10-15 minutes. Serve immediately.

Incredible Edibles

Wichita businesswoman, Louise Caldwell Murdock, who died in 1915, bequeathed her wealth to a trust established to create a public collection of contemporary artworks by American painters, potters, sculptors and weavers. The Wichita Art Museum displays this incredible collection of contemporary American art.

Ham 'n Broccoli Quiche

1 (15-ounce) package
  refrigerated pie crust
1 cup milk
4 eggs, slightly beaten
$1/4$-$1/2$ teaspoon dry mustard
$1/8$ teaspoon pepper

1 cup cubed, cooked ham or
  turkey ham
$1^1/_2$ cups shredded Cheddar cheese
1 cup frozen broccoli cuts, thawed
1 tablespoon chopped onion

Prepare pie crust according to package directions for filled one-crust pie using a 9-inch pan. (Refrigerate remaining crust for later use.) Heat oven to 350°. Combine milk, eggs, dry mustard, and pepper; set aside. Layer ham, cheese, broccoli, and onion in crust-lined pan. Pour egg mixture over ham, cheese, and broccoli. Bake at 350° for 40-50 minutes or until knife inserted in center comes out clean. Cool 5 minutes; cut into wedges. Refrigerate any remaining quiche. Makes 6-8 servings.

Feed My Lambs

Hash Brown Quiche

3 cups frozen hash browns,
  thawed and pressed between
  paper towels
$1/3$ cup melted margarine
4 ounces hot pepper cheesse

4 ounces Swiss cheese
6 ounces ham
Salt to taste
2 eggs
$1/2$ cup cream

Put well-dried hash browns in 9-inch pie plate, pressing some up sides. Drizzle with melted margarine. Bake 10 minutes at 400°.

Process balance of ingredients in food processor. Pour over hash brown crust. Bake 35-45 minutes at 350° or until knife comes out clean. Let stand 10 minutes before serving. Can be served hot, cold, or at room temperature for lunch, brunch or an appetizer.

If It Tastes Good, Who Cares? II

Tex-Mex Quiche

1 teaspoon chili powder
1 unbaked 9-inch pie shell
1 cup shredded Cheddar cheese
1 cup shredded Monterey Jack
1 tablespoon all-purpose flour
3 eggs, well beaten

1½ cups half-and-half cream
1 can green chiles, drained
  and chopped
1 (2½-ounce) can sliced ripe olives
1 teaspoon salt
¼ teaspoon pepper

Sprinkle chili powder over inside of the pie shell. Combine cheeses with flour and place in pie shell. Combine eggs, cream, chiles, olives, salt and pepper. Pour over cheese. Bake at 325° for 45-55 minutes or until knife inserted in center comes out clean. Yields 6 servings.

Incredible Edibles

Rice and Sour Cream Casserole

3 cups sour cream
2 cans green chilies, drained
  and chopped
3 cups cooked rice (measure
  exactly)

Salt
Pepper
¾ pound Monterey Jack
  cheese, sliced
½ cup Cheddar cheese

Mix sour cream and chopped chilies. Layer rice, salt, pepper, sour cream mixture, and Jack cheese (two layers of each) in buttered casserole. Top with Cheddar cheese. Bake in 350° oven until hot and bubbly, 30 minutes to one hour.

Our Daily Bread

Milanese Rice

2 tablespoons butter or oleo
2 tablespoons olive oil
1 cup raw rice
1 medium onion, chopped
1 clove garlic, minced
1 cup crumbled crisp bacon

2 tablespoons dry white wine
1 small can mushrooms
2 cans chicken broth
Salt and pepper
1/2 cup Parmesan cheese

Heat butter and oil in heavy skillet. Add rice, onion, and garlic, and brown until rice is golden. Add balance of ingredients; cover and bake at 350° about 45 minutes or until rice is dry. Freezes well. (Be sure to use the olive oil, as it gives the rice a wonderful flavor.) Double or triple the recipe and freeze in zip-lock bags.

If It Tastes Good, Who Cares? I

Wild Rice Casserole

1 cup wild rice, uncooked
1 chopped onion
1 1/2 cups chopped celery
1 teaspoon seasoned salt
3/4 cup white wine

2 tablespoons butter
1 quart chicken broth
1 pound sliced fresh mushrooms
Salt and pepper to taste

Combine wild rice, onion, celery, seasoned salt, wine, butter, and broth. Add salt and pepper to taste. Gently mix in the sliced mushrooms. Place in a casserole and bake at 325° for 1 1/2-2 hours.

Incredible Edibles

Easy Pasta Bake

1 pound ground beef
1 (8-ounce) package
   mostacciolli, cooked
1 (30-ounce) jar spaghetti sauce

1/2 cup Parmesan cheese
1 (8-ounce) package shredded
   mozzarella cheese

Brown ground beef in large skillet; drain. Stir in cooked pasta, spaghetti sauce, and Parmesan cheese. Spoon into 9x13-inch baking dish. Top with mozzarella cheese. Bake at 375° for 20 minutes. Serves 8-10.

Taste of Coffeyville

Pasta with the Works

4 cups cooked corkscrew macaroni (about 3 cups dry)

½ cup thinly sliced pepperoni (2 ounces)

1 medium green pepper, cut into strips

2 cups spaghetti sauce with mushrooms

⅓ cup pitted ripe olives, cut in half

1 cup shredded mozzarella cheese (4 ounces)

Grated Parmesan cheese

Boil macaroni and drain. In skillet over medium heat, cook pepperoni and pepper until pepper is tender-crisp, stirring often. Stir in spaghetti sauce and olives over medium to high heat; heat to boiling. Reduce heat to low. Cover; cook 10 minutes, stirring occasionally. Remove from heat. Add macaroni and mozzarella cheese. Toss to coat. Serve with Parmesan cheese. Makes 4 main-dish servings.

Norman Lutheran Church 125th Anniversary Cookbook

Vermicelli

So easy and always a big hit.

1 small package vermicelli

1 stick butter (not margarine)

2 cans beef broth

1 can mushrooms

1 tablespoon soy sauce

1 or 2 chopped green onions

Lightly brown broken pieces of vermicelli in butter. Add beef broth, mushrooms, and soy sauce. Simmer until liquid is absorbed. Add green onions just before noodles are done.

If It Tastes Good, Who Cares? I

Mock Lasagna Rolls with Cheese Filling

Low-calorie eggplant substitutes for the pasta.

1 large eggplant, peeled and sliced lengthwise into 6-inch by ¼-inch-long thin slices
1 small onion (⅔ cup), finely chopped
2 cloves garlic, minced
1 teaspoon olive oil
2 teaspoons water
¼ cup grated Parmesan cheese
½ cup grated mozzarella cheese (optional)

1¼ cups low-fat cottage cheese, drained
1 teaspoon Italian seasoning
1 teaspoon dried chives
1 large egg white
1 (16-ounce) jar sugar-free spaghetti sauce with mushrooms*
Parmesan cheese and chives to garnish (optional)

Place eggplant slices in a 10-inch or 12x8-inch flat microwave-safe casserole. Cover with lid or vented plastic wrap. Microwave for 10-11 minutes at HIGH (100%), or until tender, rearranging once. Drain and set aside. Combine onion, garlic, olive oil, and water in a small microwave-safe dish. Microwave uncovered for 2-3 minutes at HIGH (100%), or until tender-crisp. Stir in cheeses, Italian seasoning, chives, and egg white until mixed. Place 2 spoonfuls of cheese mixture on each slice, distributing more toward one end. Start at that end and roll up. Place rolls seam-side-down in the flat casserole. Pour spaghetti sauce over rolls. Cover with vented plastic wrap or lid. Microwave for 12-13 minutes at HIGH (100%), rearranging rolls halfway through cooking. Sprinkle each roll with a dash of Parmesan cheese and chives to garnish, if desired. Let stand 2 minutes. Yields 6 servings.

*Use no-salt-added variety for lowest sodium values, if desired.

Variation: For Mock Lasagna Rolls with Meat Filling, add ½ pound cooked ground turkey, veal, or lean ground beef with cheese filling.

Nutritional analysis per serving (⅙ recipe): Cal 128; Carbo 14g; Fat 3g; Prot 11g; Chol 7mg; Sod 286mg. Diabetic exchanges: Lean meat 1; Vegetable 3.

Easy Livin' Low-Calorie Microwave Cooking

Manicotti

SHELL:

1 egg
½ cup milk
½ teaspoon sugar
1 tablespoon salt

¼ cup vegetable oil
¼ cup melted butter
2 cups flour
½ teaspoon baking powder

Mix all ingredients, adding enough water to make the batter watery. Pour on a griddle like a pancake or use a crepe maker. The thinner the shells, the better. Makes approximately 25 shells which can be frozen to use later. Layer with waxed paper.

FILLING:

4 pounds ricotta cheese
2 teaspoons parsley
½ teaspoon black pepper
2 eggs

½ cup grated Parmesan or
    Romano cheesee
Tomato sauce

Blend ricotta cheese, parsley, pepper, and eggs until smooth. Fill each crepe with about 3 ounces of the filling and roll. Set in baking dish. Cover with your favorite tomato sauce and sprinkle cheese on top. Bake for 20 minutes at 350°. Makes 25 crepes.

Note: Can also use prepared manicotti shells; boil per package directions. Then assemble as above and bake.

To Tayla with TLC

Cavatini

1 pound hamburger
1 green pepper, diced
1 small onion, diced
Pepperoni slices
1 can sliced mushrooms
1 (6-ounce) can tomato paste

1 (29-ounce) can pizza sauce
1 package spaghetti sauce mix
1 cup water (or less)
1 package mixed pasta
8 ounces mozzarella cheese,
    shredded

Brown hamburger. Add green pepper and onion, and brown. Drain and add pepperoni slices, mushrooms, tomato paste, pizza sauce, spaghetti sauce mix and water. Simmer. Cook pasta and drain. Mix pasta with remainder and put in 9x13-inch baking dish and top with mozzarella. Bake 30 minutes at 350°.

Recipes from the Heart / Epsilon Omega Sorority

Meatless Lasagna Rolls

You'll never miss the meat!

1 (10-ounce) package frozen
　chopped spinach
1 clove garlic, minced, or ¼
　teaspoon garlic powder
½ medium onion (½ cup),
　chopped
½ cup (2 ounces) chopped
　mushrooms (optional)
1 tablespoon water
2 large egg whites, slightly
　beaten
¼ teaspoon ground nutmeg
1 teaspoon Italian seasoning

1 (8-ounce) carton low-fat
　cottage cheese, lightly drained
¼ cup (1 ounce) shredded
　part-skim mozzarella cheese
¼ cup grated Parmesan
　cheese, divided
6 curly-edged (3x12-inch) lasagna
　noodles, cooked according to
　package directions and drained
1 (16-ounce) jar sugar-free
　spaghetti sauce*
Parsley sprigs or chopped fresh
　parsley to garnish (optional)

Place spinach package on a paper plate or paper towel-lined glass pie plate. (If box is wrapped in foil, remove wrapping.) Microwave for 6-7 minutes at HIGH (100%), or until spinach is cooked. Discard packaging and drain spinach well, using strainer. Pat with paper towels to absorb any liquid. Set aside.

Combine garlic, onion, mushrooms, and water in a 1-quart microwave-safe bowl or casserole. Cover with lid or vented plastic wrap. Microwave for 3-3½ minutes at HIGH (100%), or until tender. Stir in egg whites, nutmeg, Italian seasoning, cottage cheese, mozzarella cheese, 2 tablespoons Parmesan cheese, and spinach into cooked onion mixture; blend well. Spread ⅙ spinach mixture on each lasagna noodle. Starting with narrow end, carefully roll up each noodle, enclosing filling (like a jellyroll). Place seam-side-down in a 10-inch microwave-safe casserole that has been sprayed with vegetable coating.

Pour spaghetti sauce over rolls. Cover lightly with waxed paper. Microwave for 12-14 minutes at MEDIUM HIGH (70%), or until rolls are hot, gently rearranging rolls halfway through cooking time. Serve garnished with remaining 2 tablespoons Parmesan cheese and parsley sprigs, if desired. Yields 6 servings.

*Use no-salt-added variety for lowest sodium values, if desired.

Nutritional analysis per serving (1 roll): Cal 218; Carbo 31g; Fat 3g; Prot 16g; Chol 9mg; Sod 339mg. Diabetic exchanges: Bread 1; Lean meat 1; Vegetable 3.

Easy Livin' Low-Calorie Microwave Cooking

Chicken Lasagna

2 cups chicken breasts, cut into 1-inch cubes
3 cups sliced mushrooms
2 cloves garlic, minced
1 large onion, chopped
1 teaspoon dried oregano
1 teaspoon dried basil
1 teaspoon dried thyme
2 tablespoons olive oil
1 (28-ounce) can Italian tomatoes
1 (15-ounce) can tomato sauce

3 tablespoons freshly ground Romano cheese
2 cups grated carrots
1/2 teaspoon salt
1 teaspoon freshly ground black pepper
1 (8-ounce) package lasagna noodles, cooked and drained
1/2 cup freshly ground Romano cheese
6-8 slices mozzarella cheese

Sauté chicken, mushrooms, garlic, onion, oregano, basil, and thyme in olive oil until chicken loses its pink color. Stir in tomatoes and tomato sauce, 3 tablespoons Romano cheese, carrots, salt, and pepper. Simmer 10-15 minutes. In oiled 9x13-inch baking dish, place half lasagna noodles, top with half the sauce mixture, Romano, and mozzarella cheeses. Repeat layers. Cover and bake at 350° for 20 minutes. Uncover and bake 10 minutes or until bubbly. Let rest 5 minutes in pan before serving.

To Tayla with TLC

Vegetable or Garden Lasagna

8 ounces bulk sweet or hot Italian sausage
2 cups sliced zucchini
2 cups cubed, peeled eggplant
2 cups chopped red and/or green bell pepper
1/2 cup chopped onion
2 cloves garlic, chopped
1 cup chicken broth, divided
1 (26 to 28-ounce) jar spaghetti sauce
2 cups small curd cottage cheese (can use low-fat or regular)
1/4 cup Italian-style bread crumbs
8 ounces uncooked lasagna noodles
1 cup shredded mozzarella cheese
1/3 cup grated Parmesan cheese

In a 3-quart saucepan, cook sausage until no longer pink. Drain. Return sausage to pan. Stir in zucchini, eggplant, peppers, onion, garlic and 1/4 cup chicken broth. Cover and simmer 5 to 10 minutes or until vegetables are slightly tender. Stir in spagetti sauce and remaining chicken broth. Cover and simmer another 5 to 10 minutes. In another bowl, combine cottage cheese and bread crumbs.

To assemble: Spray bottom of 9x13-inch pan with non-stick coating. Spread with about 1/2 cup vegetable-meat sauce. Layer with 1/3 of the noodles, 1/3 of vegetable-meat sauce, 1/2 of cottage cheese and 1/3 of mozzarella and Parmesan cheeses. Repeat, ending with mozzarella and Parmesan cheeses. Cover tightly with aluminum foil. Bake at 350° for about 1 hour until mixture is bubbly. Uncover and bake another 5 to 10 minutes to brown top. Let stand for 10 minutes at room temperature before cutting. Makes 12 servings.

Two Sisters II

In North Dakota, there is a stretch of the Great Plains known as the Missouri Plateau. Its topography is starkly varied. Many flat-topped buttes stand as high as 600 feet above the plains, and in the southwest, there is a strip of Badlands, which are spectacular formations produced by the erosion of soft sedimentary rocks.

Mindi's Special Spaghetti Sauce

½ pound hamburger
½ pound Italian sausage
1 small onion, chopped
1 green pepper, chopped
1 red pepper, chopped
1 large carton fresh
  mushrooms, chopped

1 fresh garlic clove, minced or
  chopped
1 large can whole tomatoes
1 (15-ounce) can tomato sauce
2 teaspoons Worcestershire sauce
1 package spaghetti seasoning
1 can water

Fry hamburger and sausage. Mix other ingredients with water. Add to hamburger mixture and simmer for one hour.

Cookin' with Farmers Union Friends

Fargo North High School Girls Swim Team Spaghetti Sauce

⅛ cup olive oil
1 onion, chopped
1 clove garlic, minced
1 green pepper, chopped
4 sprigs parsley, cut finely
½ teaspoon basil

2 teaspoons salt
1½ pounds lean ground beef
1 large can Italian plum tomatoes
4 cans tomato paste
1 large can water
1 teaspoon sugar

Pour olive oil into 5 or 6-quart pan. Place onion, garlic, green pepper, parsley and basil in the pot and let brown lightly. Add salt and ground beef and let brown. Add tomatoes and let simmer ½ hour. Stir occasionally. Add tomato paste and the plum tomato can of water. Stir very well. Bring to boil and let simmer for 2 hours. Stir often. Add more water if desired and sugar. Simmer 2 more hours.

Y Winners . . . Cookbook of Champions

Lentil Spaghetti Sauce

1 medium onion, chopped
1 clove garlic, minced
2 tablespoons oil
1½ cups dried lentils, washed
1 dried hot pepper, crumbled
1 teaspoon salt (optional)
½ teaspoon pepper
4 cups water

2 beef bouillon cubes
¼ teaspoon dried basil, crumbled
¼ teaspoon dried oregano, crumbled
1 (16-ounce) can tomatoes
1 (6-ounce) can tomato paste
1 tablespoon vinegar
Pasta of choice

Sauté onion and garlic in oil for 5 minutes. Add lentils, red pepper, salt, pepper, and water. Cover and simmer for 30 minutes. Add remaining ingredients and simmer uncovered about 1 hour, stirring occasionally. Serve over spaghetti, macaroni, noodles or rice. Yields 10 servings; 6½ cups.

Note: May substitute 4 cups fat-skimmed beef broth for 2 beef bouillon cubes, and omit 4 cups water.

North Dakota American Mothers Cookbook

Freezer Tomato Sauce

2 large onions, chopped
2 cloves garlic, minced
⅓ cup oil
12 large tomatoes
2 cups water
1 (12-ounce) can tomato paste
2 envelopes instant beef broth

2 teaspoons salt
½ teaspoon pepper
¼ cup sugar
2 teaspoons basil
2 tablespoons oregano
3 bay leaves

Sauté onions and garlic in oil until translucent. Wash tomatoes, cut out center core. Blend in blender. Add to onions and garlic. Cook for 5 more minutes. Add water, paste, beef broth, and all spices. Simmer for one hour. Cool completely and pour into freezer containers. Freeze.

Cooking with Iola

Spaghetti Pizza

12 ounces spaghetti
2 eggs
1/2 cup milk
4 cups shredded mozzarella
  cheese (divided)

1 (32-ounce) jar spaghetti sauce
1 pound ground beef, cooked,
  drained

Break spaghetti into 2-inch pieces. Cook using package directions; rinse and drain. Combine with eggs, milk, and one cup mozzarella cheese in bowl; mix well. Spread in greased 10x15-inch baking pan. Bake at 400° for 15 minutes. Spread with spaghetti sauce. Crumble ground beef over top; sprinkle with 3 cups mozzarella cheese. Bake at 350° for 30 minutes. May add olives, mushrooms, onions, and green peppers or other favorite pizza toppings. Yields 16 servings.

Y Cook?

German Pizza

1 pound ground beef
1/2 medium onion, chopped
1/2 green pepper, diced
1 1/2 teaspoons salt, divided
1/2 teaspoon pepper
2 tablespoons butter or
  margarine

6 medium potatoes (about 2 1/4
  pounds), peeled and shredded
3 eggs, beaten
1/3 cup milk
2 cups (8 ounces) shredded
  Cheddar or mozzarella cheese

In a 12-inch stove-top or electric skillet over medium heat, brown beef with onion, green pepper, 1/2 teaspoon salt and pepper. Remove meat mixture from skillet and drain fat. Reduce heat to low. Melt butter; spread potatoes over butter and sprinkle with remaining salt. Top with beef mixture. Combine eggs and milk; pour over all. Cook, covered, until potatoes are tender, about 30 minutes. Top with cheese. Cover and heat until cheese is melted, about 5 minutes. Cut into wedges or squares to serve.

Sisters Two II

Taco Pizza

1¼ cups cornmeal
1½ cups all-purpose flour
2 teaspoons baking powder
1½ teaspoons salt
²/₃ cup milk
⅓ cup margarine, melted
1 pound ground beef
1 (6-ounce) can tomato paste
1 (14½-ounce) can diced
  tomatoes, undrained

1 envelope taco seasoning mix
¾ cup water
1½ cups shredded Cheddar cheese
1 cup shredded Monterey Jack
  cheese
2 cups chopped lettuce
1 cup diced fresh tomato
½ cup sliced ripe olives
½ cup sliced green onions

In a medium bowl combine the cornmeal, flour, baking powder, and salt. Add milk and butter; mix well. Press onto the bottom and sides of a 14-inch pizza pan. Bake at 400° for 10 minutes or until edges are lightly browned. Cool.

In a large skillet brown beef; drain. Stir in the tomato paste, canned tomatoes, taco seasoning, and water. Bring to a boil. Simmer, uncovered, for 5 minutes. Spread over crust. Combine cheeses; sprinkle 2 cups over the meat mixture. Bake at 400° for 15 minutes or until cheese melts. Top with remaining ingredients in order listed. Makes 4-6 servings.

Kearney 125th Anniversary Community Cookbook

Better-Than-the-Box Macaroni and Cheese

1 (8-ounce) package (4 cups)
  elbow macaroni
Cooking spray
1 tablespoon all-purpose
  flour
1 small onion, minced

½ teaspoon salt
½ teaspoon dry mustard
Dash pepper
1¾ cups skim milk
4 ounces extra sharp Cheddar
  cheese, shredded (1 cup)

Preheat oven to 350°. Cook elbow macaroni as label directs; drain. Meanwhile, spray a 2-quart casserole with cooking spray. In 2-quart saucepan, combine flour and next 4 ingredients. Gradually stir in skim milk. Over medium-high heat, cook until mixture is slightly thickened, stirring constantly. Reduce heat to low; add cheese; cook until cheese is melted, stirring occasionally. In casserole, combine macaroni and cheese mixture. Bake 30 minutes or until heated through and bubbly. Serves 4.

Y Winners . . . Cookbook of Champions

CAKES

The Badlands' lunar-like landscape was once a wooded forest where dinosaurs roamed.
North and South Dakota.

Rave Reviews Coconut Cake

"Rave Reviews" says it all.

1 package Duncan Hines
  Yellow Cake Mix
1 package instant vanilla
  pudding
1¹/₃ cups water
4 eggs

¹/₄ cup oil
2 cups coconut
1 cup pecans, finely chopped
1 can cream cheese frosting
Extra coconut [³/₄ cup]
Margarine [2 teaspoons]

With an electric mixer, blend 2 minutes the cake mix, pudding, water, eggs, oil, coconut, and pecans. Pour into a greased and floured 9x13-inch pan. Bake about 45 minutes at 325°. Top with frosting. Sprinkle with extra coconut that has been sautéed in a little melted margarine until golden.

If It Tastes Good, Who Cares? II

Chocolate Sheet Cake

2 cups sugar
2 cups flour
1 stick oleo
¹/₂ cup shortening
4 tablespoons cocoa
1 cup water

¹/₂ cup buttermilk
2 eggs
1 teaspoon soda
1 teaspoon cinnamon
1 teaspoon vanilla
Dash of salt

Mix together sugar and flour. Bring to boil oleo, shortening, cocoa, and water. Pour over dry ingredients and beat until smooth. Add remaining ingredients. Pour into large oiled sheet cake pan. Bake for 20 minutes at 400°.

ICING:

1 stick oleo
4 tablespoons cocoa
6 tablespoons milk

1 pound powdered sugar
1 teaspoon vanilla
¹/₂ cup pecans

Bring oleo, cocoa, and milk to boil and add powdered sugar; beat smooth. Add vanilla and nuts. Spread onto warm cake.

Blew Centennial Bon-Appetit

Rum Flavored Bundt Cake

1 cup chopped nuts
1 box yellow cake mix
1 (3-ounce) box instant vanilla
  pudding
4 eggs

½ cup cold water
½ cup cooking oil
3-4 tablespoons rum flavoring
  (or according to taste)*

Preheat oven to 325°. Grease and flour tube or bundt pan. Sprinkle nuts over bottom of prepared pan. Mix remaining ingredients together according to box directions. Pour batter over nuts. Bake one hour. Cool. Invert on serving plate and prick top. Drizzle glaze on cake and brush on sides. Allow cake to absorb glaze. Repeat until the glaze is used up.

GLAZE:

½ cup butter or margarine
¼ cup water

1 cup white granulated sugar
3-4 tablespoons rum flavoring*

Melt butter in saucepan; stir in water and sugar. Boil 5 minutes, stirring constantly. Add flavoring.

*Instead of flavoring, ½ cup dark amber rum (divided) may be used in both cake and glaze.

Yesterday & Today Friendly Circle Cookbook

Almost Better Than Harrison Ford Cake

1 package German chocolate
  cake mix
1 can sweetened condensed milk

1 jar caramel topping
1 (8-ounce) carton Cool Whip
Heath bar crumbles

Make and bake cake according to package directions and pour into a greased and floured 9x13-inch pan. Remove from oven and poke holes in cake with the handle of a wooden spoon. Pour condensed milk over all the holes. Pour caramel topping over all. Frost with Cool Whip and sprinkle with crumbles. Refrigerate.

Recipes from the Heart / Epsilon Omega Sorority

Prairie Beer Cake

1 cup butter
2 cups brown sugar, firmly
  packed
2 eggs, well beaten
3 cups sifted flour
1/2 teaspoon salt
2 teaspoons baking soda

1 teaspoon cinnamon
1/2 teaspoon allspice
1/2 teaspoon cloves
2 cups beer
2 cups plumped raisins
1 cup coarsely chopped nuts

Preheat oven to 350°. In a large bowl, cream butter until soft. Gradually add sugar, creaming until light and fluffy. Add beaten eggs and blend well. Sift together flour, salt, soda, and spices. Reserve about 2 tablespoons of the flour mixture and beat the rest into the batter. Slowly add beer and blend thoroughly (it may foam while beating).

Using reserved flour, toss with fruit and nuts until lightly coated. Fold into batter, blending thoroughly. Pour into greased and floured 10-inch tube pan. Bake in preheated oven at 350° for 1 hour 15 minutes. Cool in pan for 10 minutes, then carefully turn out of pan onto a rack. Cover and refrigerate overnight. Dust lightly with powdered sugar.

Homemade Memories

Black Russian Cake

Such a special, delicious cake.

1 package Duncan Hines
  Yellow Cake Mix
1 (3.9-ounce) package Jell-O
  Instant Chocolate Pudding
1 cup oil

4 eggs
1/4 cup vodka
1/4 cup Kahlua
3/4 cup water

Beat all ingredients with mixer very well. Pour into a greased bundt pan and bake at 350° for 50-60 minutes. Cool 1/2 hour in pan. Sift powdered sugar over top, or glaze with mixture of 1/2 cup sifted powdered sugar and enough Kahlua to make a glaze consistency. Serves 14.

A Cooking Affaire I

Ugly Duckling Pudding Cake

1 (2-layer) package yellow
  cake mix
1 (3½-ounce) package lemon
  flavor instant pudding
1 (16-ounce) can fruit cocktail,
  including syrup
1 cup coconut, flaked
4 eggs
¼ cup oil
½ cup firmly packed brown
  sugar
½ cup chopped nuts (optional)

Blend all ingredients except brown sugar and nuts in large mixer bowl. Beat 4 minutes at medium speed of electric mixer. Pour into greased and floured 9x13-inch pan. Sprinkle with brown sugar and nuts. Bake at 325° for 45 minutes or until cake springs back when lightly pressed and pulls away from sides of pan. Do not under bake. Cool in pan 15 minutes. Spoon hot Butter Glaze over warm cake. Serve warm or cool, with prepared whipped topping, if desired.

BUTTER GLAZE:
½ cup butter or margarine
½ cup granulated sugar
½ cup evaporated milk
1½ cups flaked coconut

Combine butter, sugar, and milk in saucepan; boil 2 minutes. Stir in coconut.

90th Anniversary Trinity Lutheran Church Cookbook

Tourists enjoy the beautiful scenery of the Black Hills with such attractions as Wind Cave National Park, Badlands National Park, Jewel Cave National Monument, Custer State Park, the Mammoth Site, and the historic mining town of Deadwood, South Dakota. Leading these attractions is Mount Rushmore National Memorial and Crazy Horse Memorial.

Punch Bowl Cake

1 chocolate cake, baked and
   cut into small pieces
1 large package chocolate
   pudding, prepared

1 jar caramel sauce
1 (12-ounce) container Cool Whip
3 Skor or Heath bars, broken
   into pieces

Put cake pieces in bowl (glass looks best). Mix in chocolate pudding, then caramel sauce. Spread Cool Whip on top. Sprinkle candy on top. Refrigerate. Dip out with ice cream scoop. Rich and very yummy!

Rainbow's Roundup of Recipes

Poppy Seed Cake

$^3/_4$ cup whole poppy seed
$^3/_4$ cup cold water
$2^1/_4$ cups cake flour
$1^1/_3$ cups sugar
$2^1/_2$ teaspoons baking powder
$^1/_2$ teaspoon salt

$^1/_2$ cup soft shortening
$1^1/_2$ teaspoons vanilla
$^1/_4$ cup milk
3 egg whites, stiffly beaten
   (save yolks)

Soak poppy seed in cold water for 30 minutes. Heat oven to 350°. Grease well and flour 2 round layer cake pans. Sift dry ingredients into a mixing bowl. Add shortening, vanilla, and poppy seed-water combination, and beat 2 minutes at medium speed. Scrape sides and bottom often. Add milk, then fold in egg whites. Pour into prepared pans. Bake 30-35 minutes. Cool.

NUT FILLING:

1 cup sweet cream
$1^1/_4$ cups sugar
4 egg yolks

1 cup ground nuts
$^1/_2$ cup coconut
1 teaspoon vanilla

Stir together the cream and sugar in saucepan till sugar is dissolved. Beat egg yolks slightly and add to cream mixture. Cook till thickened, about 7 minutes. Stir constantly. Cool, then add nuts and coconut, then vanilla. Cool and spread between layers and on top of the last layer. Let filling flow onto the sides.

Homemade Memories

Garden Eggplant Pudding Cake

1 package yellow cake mix
   with pudding
1/2 cup sour cream
1/4 cup oil
2 cups peeled and grated
   eggplant

4 eggs
1/2 teaspoon each nutmeg and
   cinnamon
1/8 teaspoon each ground
   cloves and salt

Combine all ingredients and beat 4 minutes. Pour into greased and floured 10-inch bundt pan. Bake 50-55 minutes in 350° oven. Sprinkle powdered sugar on top.

Iola's Gourmet Recipes in Rhapsody

Scrumptious Pumpkin Cake

1/3 cup oil
3 eggs
2 cups pumpkin
1/3 cup sugar
1/2 cup milk

1 box chocolate cake mix with
   butter
1 cup chocolate chips
1 cup chopped pecans

In large mixer bowl, mix on high one minute: oil, eggs, pumpkin, sugar, and milk. Blend in cake mix, then beat on high 2 minutes. Stir in chips and nuts. Pour mixture into greased and floured jellyroll pan. Bake in 350° oven for 25-30 minutes or until toothpick comes out clean. Frost with fudge frosting when cake is cool, or sprinkle with confectioners' sugar. Refrigerate leftovers. It tastes even better the next day!

Pumpkin, Winter Squash and Carrot Cookbook

Nebraska Braggins: Nebraska has the third highest high school graduation rate in the US. The 911 emergency system was developed and first used in Nebraska. The world's largest porch swing (in Hebron) holds 25 adults. Kool-Aid was invented in Hastings. Halsey is home to the world's largest hand-planted forest, covering 22,000 acres. Marlon Brando's mother gave Henry Fonda acting lessons at the Omaha Community Playhouse.

Spice Cake

1 egg	1 teaspoon baking powder
2 cups sugar	1 teaspoon soda
2 tablespoons butter	1 teaspoon salt
1 cup raisins	1 teaspoon allspice
1 teaspoon ginger	1 teaspoon cloves
1 teaspoon cinnamon	3 cups flour
2 cups buttermilk	

Mix all ingredients together; bake in greased, floured pan(s) at 350° for 30-45 minutes.

EASY PENUCHE ICING:

½ cup butter	1¾-2 cups sifted
1 cup brown sugar, packed	confectioners' sugar
¼ cup milk	

Melt butter. Add brown sugar. Boil over low heat for 2 minutes, stirring constantly. Stir in milk. Stir until it comes to a boil. Cool to lukewarm. Gradually add sifted confectioners' sugar. Beat until of spreading consistency. Hot water can be added if needed.

Eastman Family Cookbook

Rhubarb Cake Quicky

1 box yellow or vanilla cake mix	1 cup sugar
3 cups rhubarb, thinly sliced	1 pint whipping cream, NOT
½ cup nuts, chopped	whipped

Mix cake as directed and pour into greased and floured 13x9-inch pan. Sprinkle rhubarb and nuts over cake batter. Sprinkle sugar over rhubarb and nuts. Pour *unwhipped* cream over top. Bake in 350° oven for 40 minutes.

Ritzy Rhubarb Secrets Cookbook

Rosh Hashanah Apple and Honey Cake

Eating honey at Rosh Hashanah signifies the hope for a sweet new year.

¹/₃ cup pareve margarine	1 teaspoon cinnamon
²/₃ cup sugar	Dash nutmeg
1 large egg	¹/₂ cup chopped nuts
¹/₃ cup honey	(optional)
¹/₂ cup whole wheat flour	2 cups peeled shredded
¹/₂ cup white flour	Delicious apples
³/₄ teaspoon baking soda	

Microwave pareve margarine in a glass custard cup for 15-20 seconds at HIGH (100%) to soften. Using a food processor or electric mixer and mixing bowl, process/beat margarine and sugar until light and creamy. Beat in honey and egg. Add flours, soda, and spices; process/beat until blended. Fold in nuts and apples. Pour batter into an 8- or 9-inch round microwave-safe baking dish that has been sprayed with vegetable coating and dusted with sugar. Place on an inverted glass pie plate in the microwave oven. Microwave uncovered for 10-12 minutes at HIGH (100%) or until no longer doughy. Let stand 10 minutes covered loosely with waxed paper or plastic wrap. Cut into wedges and serve drizzled with Hot Honey Sauce. Yields 1 (8 or 9-inch) round cake.

HOT HONEY SAUCE:

¹/₄ cup honey	1¹/₂ tablespoons hot tap
¹/₄ cup sugar	water

Combine honey, sugar, and water in a 2-cup measure. Microwave uncovered for 1-1¹/₂ minutes at HIGH (100%) until boiling and thickened. Serve warm over cake wedges.

Easy Livin' Microwave Cooking for the Holidays

Badlands National Park in South Dakota is literally nature in the raw. The harsh landscape was created by millions of years of erosion. The Badlands' haunting lunar-like landscape was once a wooded forest where dinosaurs roamed. The Lakota Indians called it "mako sica," meaning "land bad." French Canadian trappers in search of beaver called the region "les mauvaises terres a traverser"—bad land to travel across.

Carrot Cake

This is such a moist cake. Everyone asks for the recipe.

2 cups flour	1½ cups oil
2 teaspoons baking powder	4 eggs
1½ teaspoons soda	2 cups grated carrots
2 teaspoons cinnamon	1 small can crushed pineapple
1 teaspoon salt	½ cup chopped nuts
2 cups sugar	

Sift flour, baking powder, soda, cinnamon, and salt. Cream sugar and oil. Add eggs, beating after each addition. Stir in sifted ingredients, carrots, pineapple and nuts. Bake in 3 (8 or 9-inch) greased and floured pans in 350° oven for 35-40 minutes. Cool before icing.

CREAM CHEESE ICING:

1 (1-pound) box powdered sugar	1 teaspoon vanilla
1 stick margarine	1 (8-ounce) package Philadelphia cream cheese

Combine ingredients and beat. Icing may be tinted with a few drops of green food coloring.

Heart of the Home Recipes

Fruit Cocktail Cake

This recipe is fast and simple to make, takes no eggs or shortening.

1 (16 to 17-ounce) can fruit
  cocktail
1 cup flour, sifted
1 cup and 2 tablespoons sugar
$1/4$ teaspoon salt

1 teaspoon soda
1 teaspoon vanilla
$1/2$ cup brown sugar
$1/2$ cup pecans

Put first 6 ingredients together in pan or mixing bowl and stir with a spoon; do not beat. Pour into greased 8x8-inch pan. Top with brown sugar and pecans. Bake at 350° for 55-60 minutes.

More Heart of the Home Recipes

Swedish Pineapple Cake

2 cups sugar
$2-2^{1}/4$ cups flour
2 eggs
2 teaspoons soda

1 (20-ounce) can crushed
  pineapple, undrained
1 teaspoon vanilla
$3/4$ cup chopped nutmeats

Combine sugar, flour, eggs, soda, pineapple, vanilla, and nutmeats in bowl. Do not use a mixer, but mix until all dry ingredients are moistened. Pour batter into 2 or 3 round 8-inch cake pans or a 9x13-inch pan, greased and floured. Bake for 25-40 minutes (depending on pan size) in 350° oven. Frost with either a cream cheese frosting or Fluffy Pudding Frosting.

FLUFFY PUDDING FROSTING:
4 ounces instant vanilla
  pudding
1 cup cold milk

$1/4$ cup powdered sugar
$4^{1}/2$ cups Cool Whip or
  whipped cream, thawed

Mix pudding mix, milk, and sugar with wire whisk 1-2 minutes or until well blended. Stir in whipped topping gently. Spread on cake layers and around sides. Store frosted cake in refrigerator.

Iola's Gourmet Recipes in Rhapsody

Simply Great Pineapple Cake

1 box yellow or lemon cake mix
   with pudding in the mix
¾ cup vegetable oil

4 eggs, unbeaten
1 (11-ounce) can mandarin
   oranges with juice

Mix ingredients in order given. Blend; beat with electric mixer, medium speed, for 2 minutes. Bake at 325° in 3 (8-inch) greased and floured pans for 20-24 minutes, or at 350° in 9x13-inch pan for 28-34 minutes. When cool, spread with the following icing.

ICING:

1 (13½-ounce) can crushed
   pineapple
1 (3½-ounce) package dry
   instant vanilla pudding mix

1 (12-ounce) container whipped
   topping
Dash of salt

Mix crushed pineapple and instant pudding. Fold in the topping; spread on cake. Serves 15. Store cake in refrigerator.

Nutritional Analysis: Cal 370; Carbo 44g; Prot 4g; Fat 19.5g; Chol 73mg; Vit A 330IU; Vit C 11mg; Sod 234mg; Potas 119mg; Cal 66mg.

REC Family Cookbook

Raspberry Walnut Torte

1¼ cups flour
⅓ cup powdered sugar
½ cup soft margarine
1 (10-ounce) package frozen red
   raspberries, thawed, drained
   (reserving juice)
¾ cup chopped walnuts

2 eggs
1 cup sugar
½ teaspoon salt
½ teaspoon baking powder
1 teaspoon vanilla
Whipped topping

Combine one cup flour, powdered sugar, and margarine; blend well. Press mixture into bottom of 13x9-inch pan. Bake at 350° for 15 minutes. Cool. Spoon drained raspberries over crust; sprinkle with walnuts. Beat eggs with sugar in small mixing bowl until light and fluffy. Add salt and ¼ cup flour, baking powder, and vanilla; blend well. Pour over walnuts/raspberries. Bake at 350° for about 30-35 minutes until golden brown. Cool. Cut into squares. Serve with whipped topping and sauce.

SAUCE:
½ cup water
½ cup sugar
Reserved raspberry juice

2 tablespoons cornstarch
1 tablespoon lemon juice

Combine water, sugar, reserved raspberry juice, and cornstarch in saucepan, or glass bowl if using microwave. Cook, stirring constantly, until thickened and clear. Stir in lemon juice. Cool.

Our Daily Bread

Chocolate Raspberry Cheesecake

1½ cups (18) finely crushed creme-filled chocolate cookies
2 tablespoons butter
4 (8-ounce) packages cream cheese, softened
1¼ cups sugar
3 eggs
1 cup sour cream
1 teaspoon vanilla
1 cup (6 ounces) semisweet chocolate chips, melted
⅓ cup seedless raspberry preserves
1-2 packages frozen raspberries

Mix cookies and softened butter and press into bottom of buttered 9-inch springform pan. Combine 3 packages cream cheese and sugar until well blended. Add eggs, one at a time, mixing well after each. Blend in sour cream and vanilla; pour over crust. Combine remaining package cream cheese and melted chocolate until smooth and well blended. Add preserves and mix well. Drop spoonfuls of chocolate onto plain batter. Do not swirl. Bake at 325° for 1 hour 20 minutes. Cool before removing rim from pan. Serve with sieved raspberry sauce (1-2 packages frozen raspberries pushed through food mill or strainer to remove seeds.) Serve 2 tablespoons sauce per slice of cheesecake.

Y Winners...Cookbook of Champions

Chocolate Chipper Frosting

Use this frosting any time you need a delicious chocolate frosting. It works well drizzled on bundt cakes, too.

FOR 9x13-INCH CAKE OR BARS:
1½ cups sugar
⅓ cup butter or margarine
⅓ cup milk
1 cup chocolate chips

In a 1-quart microwave bowl, combine sugar, butter, and milk. Microwave for 2-3 minutes at HIGH (100%) until mixture boils. Stir in chocolate chips until smooth. (Halve recipe for 8x8-inch cake.) Frost cake or brownies immediately.

Easy Livin' Microwave Cooking

God's Country White Chocolate Cheesecake

We endure plenty of ribbing when it comes to the prairie—people unfamiliar with its beauty think this must be "God's country, because no one else would want to live there." Maybe He knows something they don't and plans to visit when a sliver of this cake will be waiting at His place—it's truly a little slice of heaven.

1-3 tablespoons butter or
  margarine, softened
1 cup finely chopped, lightly
  toasted macadamia nuts
24 ounces white chocolate,
  chopped or broken
3/4 cup heavy cream, scalded
3 (8-ounce) packages cream
  cheese
1 cup sugar

1/4 cup flour
4 eggs, room temperature (let
  sit out 30 minutes)
1 tablespoon vanilla or 1/4 cup
  white crème de cacao
Sweetened whipped cream
12-14 macadamia nuts and/or
  12-14 fresh raspberries dipped
  in 1 ounce melted white
  chocolate

Coat sides and bottom of 8 or 9-inch springform pan with butter. Sprinkle macadamia nuts over buttered surface, turning pan and shaking to distribute evenly. Chill in freezer 15 minutes.

Partially melt chocolate in double boiler or microwave. Add scalded cream, whisking until chocolate is melted and mixture is smooth. Set aside.

Beat the cream cheese, sugar, and flour. Add the chocolate mixture, then eggs, one at a time. Stir in vanilla and pour into prepared pan. Bake 20 minutes at 425°; reduce heat to 300° and bake 45-55 minutes more until cheesecake is nearly set. Turn off oven. Cool in oven 30 minutes. Cool one hour on rack, then refrigerate 6-24 hours.

At least 2 hours before serving, prepare raspberry sauce. Chill. Line baking sheet with waxed paper. Partially melt one ounce white chocolate, then stir until smooth. Dip macadamia nuts and raspberries halfway into melted chocolate. Invert onto waxed paper. Chill. Serve thin wedges of cheesecake with a small spoonful of Raspberry Sauce; garnish with whipped cream and top with a dipped macadamia nut and/or raspberry. Serves 12-14.

Presentations

Raspberry Sauce

(Serve with God's Country White Chocolate Cheesecake)

2 cups fresh or frozen
  raspberries
½ cup sugar

2 tablespoons framboise or
  raspberry schnapps (optional)

Combine berries and sugar in processor (reserve some berries for garnish.) Purée sauce, strain, add liqueur, chill. Makes 1½ cups.

Presentations

Chocolate Chip Cheesecake

2 cups crushed Oreos
2 tablespoons margarine,
  melted
3 eggs
2 (8-ounce) packages cream
  cheese, softened

¾ cup sugar
1 teaspoon vanilla
½ cup whipping cream
1¼ cups miniature semisweet
  chocolate chips
1 teaspoon shortening

Combine crushed Oreos and margarine and press in bottom and up sides of 10-inch springform pan. In large bowl beat eggs. Add cream cheese, sugar, and vanilla. Beat until smooth. Add whipping cream; blend well. Stir 1 cup chips in by hand. Pour into crust. Bake at 325° for about 60-75 minutes or until center is set. Edges will just begin to brown. (To minimize cracking, place shallow pan half full of hot water in oven while baking.) Cool. Melt remaining chips and shortening in microwave. Drizzle over cooled cheesecake. Refrigerate several hours.

Kearney 125th Anniversary Community Cookbook

North Dakota is called the Peace Garden State, in reference to the International Peace Garden, the only building built directly on the US-Canadian border. The Peace Garden is home to the International Music Camp, which hosts hundreds of young musicians from around the world each summer.

Miracle Cheese Cake

1 (12-ounce) can evaporated
  milk
1 (3-ounce) package lemon
  Jell-O
3 tablespoons lemon juice

1 cup boiling water
1 (8-ounce) package cream cheese
1 cup sugar
1 teaspoon vanilla

Night before making: Put egg beaters and bowl into freezer. Put can of milk in fridge.

Dissolve Jell-O in boiling water. Add lemon juice and cool well but not yet syrupy. Cream together cream cheese, sugar, and vanilla. Add to well-cooled Jell-O. Mix well. Whip cold evaporated milk and fold into above mixture. Be sure it is well mixed.

CRUST:
35 graham crackers, crushed
¹⁄₄ cup sugar

1 stick margarine, melted

Mix crumbs, sugar, and margarine. Put all but ¹⁄₂ cup into 9x13-inch pan. Add cheese cake mixture and sprinkle crumbs on top. Make night before planning to serve or at least 4 hours before serving. Can top with spoon of cherry pie filling when serving, if desired.

Pioneer Daughters Cookbook

Quick and Easy Frosting

1 package instant pudding
¹⁄₄ cup powdered sugar

1 cup cold water
1 (8-ounce) container Cool Whip

Combine pudding mix, sugar and water in a small bowl. Beat slowly with beater at low speed for one minute. Fold in Cool Whip. Keep in the refrigerator.

Cookin' with Farmers Union Friends

The big boys are buried at the Mammoth Site of Hot Springs, South Dakota. There lies in-situ (bones left as found) the largest concentration of Columbian and woolly mammoth bones discovered in their primary context in the world.

Blender Red-Raspberry Cheesecake

RASPBERRY-CHEESE FILLING:

1 (8-ounce) package Neufchâtel cheese

2 cups (16 ounces) low-fat cottage cheese, drained

½ cup Egg Substitute or Egg Beaters or 2 large eggs

½ cup sugar or 12-14 packets sugar substitute

3 teaspoons cornstarch dissolved in 2 tablespoons skim milk

1 cup fresh or frozen red raspberries, cleaned and stems removed

2 drops red food coloring (optional)

Unwrap Neufchâtel cheese and place in a 2-quart microwave-safe bowl. Microwave for 40-60 seconds at MEDIUM-HIGH (70%), or until softened. Using a food processor, blender, or electric mixer and bowl, combine cheese and remaining filling ingredients until blended. Pour filling back into 2-quart bowl. Microwave for 7-8 minutes on HIGH (100%), or until very hot, stirring twice.

Microwave for 5-7 minutes at MEDIUM HIGH (70%), or until almost set (center will jiggle slightly). Let cool. Refrigerate at least 4 hours. Yields 1 (9-inch) cheesecake.

VARIATION:

Substitute one cup fresh or frozen blueberries or sliced strawberries for the raspberries.

Nutritional analysis per serving (¹/₁₀ cheesecake): Cal 167; Carbo 13g; Fat 8g; Prot 10g; Chol 22mg; Sod 304mg. Diabetic exchanges: Bread 5; Fat .75; Fruit .25; Lean meat 1.25.

Easy Livin' Low-Calorie Microwave Cooking

Cheesecake Cups

Great for holiday entertaining—serve in red baking cups.

CUPS:

6 vanilla wafers
12 baking cups
1 (8-ounce) package cream
  cheese
1/3 cup brown sugar

1 egg
1 teaspoon vanilla
1/2 can cherry pie filling or 1/4
  cup sour cream and 6 large
  strawberries

Place 2 medium-size paper baking cups in each cup of a micro-wave muffin pan or in 6 custard cups. Place a vanilla wafer in each cup. Set aside. Microwave cream cheese in a 2-quart mi-crowave bowl for 1-2 minutes at DEFROST (30%) until soft. Stir in brown sugar, egg, and vanilla and beat until smooth. Pour into baking cups. Microwave 6 cups for 7-8 minutes at DEFROST (30%). Remove paper baking cups from dish(es). Cool at least one hour. Garnish with cherry pie filling and/or sour cream and sugar-sprinkled strawberries before serving. Keep refrigerated. Yields 6 servings.

Easy Livin' Microwave Cooking

Hedemora Bundt Cake

1¹/₃ cups flour
1¹/₃ cups sugar
3 eggs

³/₄ cup hot melted butter
1 teaspoon almond flavoring
Powdered sugar

Mix flour and sugar in a medium mixing bowl. Beat eggs until frothy. With mixer on medium speed, alternate hot melted but-ter and beaten eggs. Then blend in the flour and sugar mixture. Add the almond flavoring. Pour into a greased and floured bundt pan. Bake 45 minutes at 350°. It does not rise high! Cool 10 minutes and turn onto a plate and sprinkle generously with pow-dered sugar.

Measure for Pleasure

COOKIES
and
CANDIES

Castle Rock, a beautiful 70-foot-high chalk spire, is visible for miles. Several important fossil discoveries have been made at this 70-million-year-old natural landmark in northwest Kansas.

Marshmallow Krispie Bars

1 (14-ounce) package caramels
3/4 cup margarine, divided
1 (14-ounce) can sweetened
  condensed milk

2 (10-ounce) packages
  miniature marshmallows
8 cups crisp rice cereal

Melt caramels with 1/4 cup margarine and condensed milk in saucepan over low heat, stirring to mix well; set aside. Melt 1/2 cup margarine and 1 1/2 packages marshmallows in saucepan over low heat, stirring to mix well. Pour over cereal in large bowl; mix well. Press half the mixture in buttered 10x15-inch dish. Sprinkle with remaining 1/2 package marshmallows. Spread caramel mixture over marshmallows. Top with remaining cereal mixture. Let stand until firm. Cut into bars. Yields 70 servings.

Y Cook?

Interstate Bar Cookies

1/2 cup oleo, softened
1 (2-layer) package cake mix
  (any flavor)
3 eggs
1 (8-ounce) package cream
  cheese, softened

1 cup brown sugar
1 cup powdered sugar
1 teaspoon vanilla

Combine oleo, cake mix, and one egg, beaten. Press into 9x13-inch pan. Beat together cream cheese, brown sugar, powdered sugar, 2 eggs, and vanilla. Pour over crust. Bake at 325° for 45 minutes. Cool. When cool, dust top of cookies with additional sifted powdered sugar.

125 Years of Cookin' with the Lord

Deadwood, South Dakota, is known as the final resting place of many legendary characters from the Old West; Wild Bill Hickok, who had 21 notches on his gun; Calamity Jane, a hard-living woman who looked, dressed, drank, cussed and shot like a man; Poker Alice Tubbs, who liked her whiskey neat and her cigars big; and Potato Creek Johnny, who found a chunk of gold the size of a candy bar—the biggest ever found in the Hills.

Easy Lemon Bars

1 package 1-step angel food
    cake mix
1 (21-ounce) can lemon pie
    filling

Powdered sugar icing
Lemon extract flavoring

With a spoon, stir together cake mix and pie filling (do not use electric mixer). Pour into ungreased jellyroll pan (10½x15½) and bake in 350° oven for 20-25 minutes. When baked, frost with a powdered sugar frosting (2 cups powdered sugar thinned with a little milk) flavored with lemon extract.

Note: For diabetics, replace lemon pie filling with sugar-free yogurt—I use lemon, but you can use your choice of flavors— and then I do not frost the bars.

125 Years of Cookin' with the Lord

Butterscotch Bars

No bake.

2 eggs, beaten
¾ cup margarine
1 cup sugar
2½ cups crushed graham
    crackers

½ cup coconut
½ cup chopped walnuts
    2 cups miniature marshmallows
1 (6-ounce) bag butterscotch chips
3 tablespoons peanut butter

Add sugar to beaten eggs and margarine. Boil slowly for 2 minutes and let cool. Add graham cracker crumbs, coconut, walnuts, and marshmallows. Press this into a 9x13-inch pan and top with butterscotch chips melted with peanut butter.

Kelvin Homemakers 50th Anniversary Cookbook

Blarney Stones

4 eggs
2 cups sugar
1 cup boiling water
2 cups flour

3 teaspoons baking powder
1/2 teaspoon salt
1 teaspoon vanilla

Beat eggs slightly and add sugar. Beat thoroughly for 5 minutes. Slowly stir in boiling water. Add dry ingredients and mix. Add vanilla. Pour into a greased and floured 9x13-inch pan. Bake at 350° for 25-30 minutes. After it has cooled, turn it out and cut into bars. Frost with frosting:

FROSTING:

1 (3-ounce) package cream
  cheese, softened
3/4 cup softened oleo
1 teaspoon vanilla

1 (1-pound) box powdered
  sugar
1 (22-ounce) can salted peanuts,
  coarsely ground

Combine the cream cheese, oleo, vanilla, and powdered sugar. Beat until smooth. Frost bars on all sides. Roll in peanuts.

Heavenly Delights

Cashew Bars

1 1/2 cups flour
3/4 cup brown sugar
1/2 cup butter
1 teaspoon salt
1 cup butterscotch chips

2 tablespoons butter
1/2 cup white syrup
1 tablespoon water
1/2 cup cashews or peanuts

Mix flour, brown sugar, butter, and salt as for pie crust. Press into 9x13-inch pan. Bake 10 minutes at 350°. Cool completely. Cook over low heat, just enough to melt chips, butter, syrup, and water. Put nuts evenly on cooled crust. Pour butterscotch mixture over nuts and crust. Bake 10 minutes at 350°. Cool somewhat before cutting.

Feed My Lambs

Almond Bark Oatmeal Bars

1 cup butter
2 cups brown sugar
2 eggs
1 teaspoon vanilla

2 1/2 cups flour
1 teaspoon soda
1 teaspoon salt
3 cups oatmeal

FILLING:
1 (14-ounce) package light
  almond bark
1 can sweetened condensed
  milk

3 tablespoons butter
3/4 cup chopped nuts
2 teaspoons vanilla

Cream butter and sugar; add rest of ingredients and mix well. Press two-thirds of the mixture into bottom of 10x15-inch pan. Mix and spread filling over crust and sprinkle with rest of crust mixture. Bake in 350° oven 25 minutes.

Norman Lutheran Church 125th Anniversary Cookbook

Almond Bars

FIRST LAYER:
1/2 cup powdered sugar
1 cup margarine, softened

2 cups flour

SECOND LAYER:
1 (8-ounce) package cream
  cheese
2 eggs

1/2 cup white sugar
1 teaspoon almond flavoring

TOPPING:
1/4 cup margarine
1 1/2 cups powdered sugar

1 1/2 tablespoons milk
1 teaspoon almond flavoring

Combine ingredients in First Layer and press into 9x13-inch pan. Bake at 350° for 15 minutes. Beat Second Layer ingredients until creamy, and pour over First Layer immediately after removing from oven. Bake for 15 minutes. Let cool. Mix Topping ingredients and spread over bars. May put slivered almonds on top.

Heavenly Recipes

Apple Brownies

½ cup margarine
1 cup sugar
1 egg
½ teaspoon baking soda
½ teaspoon baking powder
1 teaspoon cinnamon

1 cup all-purpose flour
2 cups coarsely chopped apples
½ cup nuts, chopped
2 tablespoons sugar
½ teaspoon cinnamon

Preheat oven to 350°. Cream margarine and one cup sugar; add egg, beat well. Sift in baking soda, baking powder, cinnamon, and flour. Mix well. Fold in apples and nuts. Pour into lightly greased 9x9-inch pan. Mix 2 tablespoons sugar and ½ teaspoon cinnamon. Sprinkle over batter. Bake for 35-40 minutes. Cool in pan before cutting. Serves 12.

Treasures of the Great Midwest

Apple Bars

2½ cups flour
1 teaspoon salt
1 cup shortening
2 egg yolks
Milk [about ½ cup]

1 cup cornflakes
12 apples, peeled and sliced
1-1½ cups sugar
1 teaspoon cinnamon
2 egg whites

Cut flour and salt into shortening. Beat egg yolks and add milk to make ⅔ cup. Mix well and add to flour mixture. Roll ½ of the dough between 2 sheets of waxed paper to fit a jellyroll pan. Crush cornflakes and spread on dough. Add apples, sugar, and cinnamon. Roll the rest of the dough for top. Beat egg whites and brush on top. Bake at 350° for 50-60 minutes. Frost with powdered sugar icing.

Incredible Edibles

Carrot Bars

4 eggs, beaten until thick	2 cups flour
1½ cups oil	1 teaspoon salt
2 teaspoons soda	3 jars baby food carrots
2 teaspoons cinnamon	

Beat eggs, oil, soda, cinnamon, flour, and salt well. Add baby food carrots and mix well. Bake in greased and floured [11x17-inch] cookie sheet with sides at 350° for 30 minutes.

FROSTING:

4 tablespoons oleo, melted	1 teaspoon vanilla
1 (8-ounce) package cream cheese, softened	3-4 cups powdered sugar

Add melted oleo to cream cheese and vanilla; mix well and add powdered sugar; mix well and spread on carrot bars.

Recipes & Remembrances / Courtland Covenant Church

Wild Bill Hickok, Bat Masterson, and Wyatt Earp all tried to keep the peace in notorious "cowtowns" like Dodge City, Abilene, and Wichita, Kansas. You can still saddle up and hit the trails to relive the rugged past.

Rhubarb Dream Bars

CRUST:

2 cups flour   1 cup butter or margarine
³/₄ cup powdered sugar

Combine flour and sugar. Cut in butter until crumbs form. Press into 15x10-inch pan. Bake in 350° oven for 15 minutes (or a little less). While crust is baking, prepare filling.

FILLING:

4 eggs   ¹/₂ teaspoon salt
2 cups sugar   4 cups rhubarb, diced
¹/₂ cup flour

Blend eggs, sugar, flour, and salt until smooth. Fold in rhubarb. Spread over hot crust and bake in 350° oven 35-40 minutes until filling is lightly browned. Cut bars when cool.

Ritzy Rhubarb Secrets Cookbook

Loaun's Raisin Bars

If you have raisin fans in the family, this will be a favorite.

2 cups raisins   1¹/₄ cups brown sugar
3 tablespoons flour   2 cups quick oatmeal
³/₄ cup sugar   1¹/₂ teaspoons soda
1 cup water   1¹/₄ cups margarine, melted
2 cups flour

Boil raisins, 3 tablespoons flour, sugar, and water until thick. Mix 2 cups flour with brown sugar, oatmeal, and soda. Add melted margarine and mix until crumbly. Put ¹/₂ crumb mixture in pan. Cover with filling, and put remaining crumb mixture on top. Bake 20-30 minutes at 325°.

A Taste of Prairie Life

Sour Cream Raisin Bars

BAR:

1³/₄ cups oatmeal	1 teaspoon baking soda
1³/₄ cups flour	1 cup margarine, melted
1 cup brown sugar	

Preheat oven to 350°. Combine oatmeal, flour, brown sugar, and soda. Add margarine and mix thoroughly. Pat ²/₃ of mixture into bottom of a 9x13-inch pan. Bake for 15-20 minutes. Cool.

FILLING:

4 eggs yolks	2 cups sour cream
1¹/₂ cups sugar	2 cups raisins
3 tablespoons cornstarch	

Mix and bring to a boil. Reduce heat. Boil 5-10 minutes, stirring constantly to avoid scorching. Pour over crumb layer and cover with remaining crumbs. Bake for 20 minutes. Cool and cut into bars.

Regent Alumni Association Cookbook

Date Bars

1 cup white sugar
4 level tablespoons butter
2 eggs, well beaten
1 pound dates, finely-chopped

4 tablespoons hot water
1 teaspoon baking powder
1½ cups flour (approximately)

Combine all ingredients together. Bake in 9x13-inch pan at 350°
until golden brown; cool. Cut into squares and roll in powdered
sugar.

Our Heritage

Seven Layers of Sin Bars

1 stick butter, melted
1½ cups graham cracker
   crumbs
1 cup chocolate chips
1 cup butterscotch chips

1 cup chopped pecans
1 cup flaked coconut
1 (14-ounce) can sweetened
   condensed milk

First pour melted butter in bottom of 9x13-inch pan. Secondly
sprinkle graham cracker crumbs over butter. The third layer will
be chocolate chips, followed by butterscotch chips. The fifth layer
will be chopped pecans, the sixth will be flaked coconut. For the
seventh layer, pour the milk over the top. Bake at 350° for 25
minutes.

Recipes & Remembrances / Buffalo Lake

Rocky Road Fudge Bars

BARS:

1/2 cup butter
1 (1-ounce) square unsweetened
  chocolate
1 cup sugar
1 cup flour

3/4 cup nuts
1 teaspoon baking powder
1 teaspoon vanilla
2 eggs

Preheat oven to 350°. Grease and flour 9x13-inch pan. In large saucepan over low heat, melt butter and chocolate. Add remaining bar ingredients. Mix well and spread in prepared pan.

FILLING:

6 ounces cream cheese,
  softened
1/2 cup sugar
2 tablespoons flour
1/4 cup butter
1 egg

1/2 teaspoon vanilla
1/4 cup chopped nuts
1 (6-ounce) package chocolate
  chips
2 cups miniature marshmallows
  (or 2 cups regular size, cut-up)

In small bowl, combine cream cheese with next 5 ingredients. Blend until smooth and fluffy. Stir in nuts. Spread over chocolate mixture. Sprinkle with chocolate chips. Bake 25-30 minutes or until toothpick inserted in center comes out clean. Sprinkle with marshmallows and bake 2 minutes longer.

FROSTING:

1/4 cup butter
1 (1-ounce) square unsweetened
  chocolate
2 ounces cream cheese

1/4 cup milk
1 pound powdered sugar
  (about 3 1/2 cups)
1 teaspoon vanilla

In large saucepan over low heat, melt butter, chocolate, cream cheese, and milk. Stir in powdered sugar and vanilla until smooth. Immediately pour over marshmallows.

Yesterday and Today Friendly Circle Cookbook

Wesson Oil Brownies

¾ cup flour, sifted
½ teaspoon baking powder
¾ teaspoon salt
2 eggs
1 cup granulated sugar
⅓ cup pure vegetable oil

2 (1-ounce) squares unsweetened
  chocolate, melted and cooled
1 teaspoon vanilla
½ cup coarsely chopped nuts
Confectioners' sugar

Preheat oven to 350°. Sift dry ingredients together; set aside. In a large bowl, beat eggs; add granulated sugar in 3 additions. Add oil, chocolate and vanilla; blend. Add flour mixture all at once and mix well. Stir in chopped nuts. Spread batter into a well-oiled 8x8x2-inch pan. Bake for 25-30 minutes or until top springs back to the touch. Cool in pan; dust with confectioners' sugar before cutting into squares. Makes 16 brownies.

Per brownie: 183 calories; 11g fat; 26.6mg cholesterol.

Reader's Favorite Recipes

German Chocolate Caramel Brownies

1 (14-ounce) package caramels
1 (5-ounce) can evaporated
  milk, divided
1 package German chocolate
  cake mix

¾ cup margarine, melted
1 cup chocolate chips (6 ounces)

Melt caramels and ⅓ cup evaporated milk together. Mix together cake mix, margarine, ⅓ cup evaporated milk, and chocolate chips. Grease 9x13-inch pan. Press ½ dough in pan; spread with caramel mixture. Top loosely with rest of dough. Bake 30 minutes at 350°.

Home at the Range II

Some of North Dakota's historical sites are military forts including Forts Abercrombie, Buford, Clark, Dilts, Mandan, Pembina, Ransom, Rice, Seward, Totten, and Union. Other notable landmarks are Sitting Bull's Grave Historic Site, Writing Rock Historic Park, and Theodore Roosevelt National Park.

Triple Fudge Brownies

1 (3.9-ounce) package instant
   chocolate pudding mix
1 (18¼-ounce) package
   chocolate cake mix

2 cups (12 ounces) semisweet
   chocolate chips
Confectioners' sugar

Prepare pudding according to package directions. Whisk in cake mix. Stir in chocolate chips. Pour into greased 15x10x1-inch baking pan. Bake at 350° for 30-35 minutes or until the top springs back when lightly touched. Dust with confectioners' sugar. Yields 4 dozen.

Recipes from the Heart / Epsilon Omega Sorority

Cornflake Macaroons

2 egg whites, beaten stiffly
1 cup granulated sugar
1 teaspoon vanilla

1 cup Angel Flake Coconut
1½ cups crushed cornflakes

Beat egg whites stiff. Gradually add sugar and vanilla. Fold in coconut and cornflakes. Drop by teaspoonful onto greased baking sheet. Bake 20 minutes in 325° oven.

Iola's Gourmet Recipes in Rhapsody

Chocolate Chip Pudding Cookies

1¹/₂ cups butter or margarine,
  softened
3 eggs
1 cup brown sugar
¹/₂ cup white sugar
1¹/₂ teaspoons vanilla

3¹/₃ cups flour
1¹/₂ teaspoons baking soda
2 (4-ounce) packages instant
  vanilla pudding powder
2 cups chocolate chips

Cream butter, eggs, sugars, and vanilla together and mix well. Sift flour, soda, and pudding powder together and add to creamed mixture. Add chocolate chips. Mix well. Drop by teaspoon onto ungreased baking sheets. Bake at 350° for 10-12 minutes just until golden; do not overbake.

Note: Cook-and-serve pudding can be used, but increase flour about ¹/₂ cup. Also, can use chocolate or tapioca.

Kelvin Homemakers 50th Anniversary Cookbook

Chocolate-Peppermint Cream Cookies

1¹/₂ cups brown sugar
³/₄ cup butter
2 tablespoons water
2 cups chocolate chips

2 eggs
3 cups flour
1¹/₄ teaspoons baking soda
1 teaspoon salt

In a saucepan, stir over low heat the brown sugar, butter, and water. Add chocolate chips; stir to melt chips. Beat in eggs and add flour, baking soda, and salt. Shape into balls and bake on cookie sheet at 350° for 8-10 minutes. Cool. Sandwich each pair together with 1 teaspoon Peppermint Cream.

PEPPERMINT CREAM:
3 cups powdered sugar,
  divided
¹/₃ cup soft butter

¹/₈ teaspoon peppermint extract
Dash of salt
¹/₄ cup milk

Mix one cup powdered sugar, butter, extract, and salt. Beat in 2 cups powdered sugar alternately with milk.

Lakota Lutheran Church Centennial Cookbook

Peanut Butter Middles

A grandchildren favorite.

1¹/₂ cups flour
¹/₂ cup cocoa
¹/₂ teaspoon soda
¹/₂ cup brown sugar
¹/₂ cup granulated sugar

¹/₂ cup margarine, softened
¹/₄ cup peanut butter
1 egg
1 teaspoon vanilla

Combine flour, cocoa, and soda and set aside. Beat together brown and granulated sugars, margarine, peanut butter, egg, and vanilla. Add flour mixture. Form mixture into 40 balls.

FILLING:
1 cup peanut butter   1 cup powdered sugar

Blend peanut butter and powdered sugar and form into 40 balls. Wrap the chocolate mixture balls around the filling mixture balls and place on ungreased baking sheet. Flatten with a glass dipped in granulated sugar. Bake at 375° for 7-9 minutes or until slightly cracked.

In the Kitchen with Kate

Chocolate Waffle Cookies

1¹/₂ cups sugar
1 cup shortening (or ¹/₂
   margarine and ¹/₂ shortening)
4 eggs

2 tablespoons vanilla
2 cups flour
¹/₂ cup cocoa
¹/₄ teaspoon salt

Blend sugar, shortening, and eggs well. Add vanilla and stir in flour, cocoa, and salt. Drop by spoonfuls onto hot waffle iron, close and bake one minute. While still warm, frost with chocolate frosting.

Heavenly Delights

The name Nebraska is derived from a Siouan expression meaning "flat or broad water," referring to the Platte River.

Chocolate Malt Ball Cookies

³/₄ cup brown sugar
1 teaspoon vanilla
1¹/₃ sticks margarine or
  vegetable shortening
1 egg
1³/₄ cups all-purpose flour
¹/₃ cup cocoa

¹/₂ teaspoon salt (if desired, or
  if shortening is used)
¹/₂ cup malted milk powder (not
  chocolate)
³/₄ teaspoon baking soda
2 cups malted milk balls,
  crushed

Beat together brown sugar, vanilla, and margarine in large bowl until mixed; beat in egg and mix well. Mix together flour, cocoa, salt, malted milk powder and baking soda. Add to creamed mixture and mix until blended. Stir in malted milk ball pieces. (To crush, put candy in sealable plastic bag and pound with rolling pin or a heavy spoon). Drop on ungreased cookie sheet by rounded tablespoonfuls 2 inches apart. Bake one sheet at a time at 375° for 7-9 minutes or until cookies are set. Do not overbake. Cool 2 minutes before removing to sheets of foil to cool completely. Makes about 3 dozen cookies.

In the Kitchen with Kate

Ginger Snaps

Bet you can't eat just one!

³/₄ cup shortening
1 cup sugar
¹/₄ cup molasses
1 egg
2 cups flour

¹/₄ teaspoon salt
2 teaspoons soda
1 teaspoon ginger
1 teaspoon cinnamon
1 teaspoon cloves

Mix shortening and sugar, add molasses and egg. Mix well. Add dry ingredients and mix. Roll into 1¹/₂-inch balls, flatten with bottom of glass dipped in sugar. Bake at 350° for 11-12 minutes. Very crispy and crunchy.

Wyndmere Community Alumni Cookbook

Soft Oatmeal Cookies

1½ cups raisins
1 cup shortening
1 cup brown sugar
1 teaspoon cinnamon
¼ teaspoon nutmeg
2 eggs, well beaten

1 teaspoon soda
2 cups flour
½ cup strong coffee
2 cups oatmeal
1 cup chopped nuts

Boil raisins in a small amount of water. Cream shortening, sugar, and spices; add well beaten eggs. Sift soda with flour; add alternately with coffee. Add oatmeal, drained raisins, and nuts; drop from spoon. Bake in a moderate oven (350°) for 10-12 minutes.

Favorite Recipes of Rainbow Valley Lutheran Church

Swedish Spritz Cookies

1 cup shortening, butter or
  margarine
¾ cup sugar
1 egg or 3 egg yolks

2¼ cups sifted all-purpose flour
½ teaspoon baking powder
Dash of salt
1 teaspoon almond extract

Cream shortening, adding sugar gradually. Add egg; beat well. Add flour, baking powder, and salt, mix well. Add almond extract. Fill cookie press. Form cookies on aluminum cookie sheet in an S-shape or desired shape. Bake in 400° oven for 10-12 minutes until golden. Yields about 5 dozen cookies.

125 Years of Cookin' with the Lord

No Bake Cookies

2 cups sugar
1 cup milk
½ cup butter or Crisco
½ cup cocoa

3 cups oatmeal
1 teaspoon vanilla
Pinch of salt

Boil sugar, milk, butter, and cocoa to a full boil. Remove from stove and add oatmeal, vanilla, and salt. Drop onto waxed paper by teaspoonful and chill.

The Hagen Family Cookbook

Swedish Gingies

1 cup butter, softened
1½ cups white sugar
1 egg, beaten
1½ tablespoons grated
 orange rind
2 tablespoons dark corn syrup

1 tablespoon water
3¼ cups sifted flour
2 teaspoons soda
2 teaspoons cinnamon
1 teaspoon ginger
½ teaspoon cloves

Cream butter and sugar. Add egg and beat. Add rind, corn syrup, and water. Sift dry ingredients together and add to mixture. Mold with hands into 2 rolls about 10 inches long and 2 inches thick. Chill overnight or longer. Slice thinly with a sharp knife. Bake at 350° about 10 minutes. May sprinkle with sugar or top with almond half.

Measure for Pleasure

Snickerdoodles

We find these to be extra good anytime.

1 cup shortening (part
 margarine)
1½ cups sugar
2 eggs
2¾ cups sifted flour

2 teaspoons cream of tartar
1 teaspoon soda
½ teaspoon salt
2 tablespoons sugar
2 teaspoons cinnamon

Cream shortening, sugar, and eggs. Sift flour, cream of tartar, soda and salt together. Add to creamed mixture. Roll dough into balls the size of small walnuts. Roll in a mixture of sugar and cinnamon. Place about 2 inches apart on ungreased cookie sheet. Bake in 400° oven 8-10 minutes, until light brown, but still soft. Cookies puff at first, then flatten out and have crinkled tops.

More Heart of the Home Recipes

Brown Sugar Cutouts

These caramelly cookies are wonderful!

1 cup margarine or butter,
  softened
1 cup firmly packed brown
  sugar
1 teaspoon vanilla

1 egg
2½ cups flour
½ teaspoon soda
½ cup chopped nuts
  (optional)

In large bowl, beat margarine and brown sugar until light and fluffy. Add vanilla and egg; blend well. Lightly spoon flour into measuring cup; level off. Stir in flour and baking soda; mix well. Cover with plastic wrap; refrigerate 1-2 hours for easier handling.

On floured surface, roll out dough, ⅓ at a time, to ⅛-inch thickness. (Refrigerate dough not being rolled). Cut out cookies with 2-inch cutter. Place 1 inch apart on ungreased cookie sheets. Bake at 375° for 5-8 minutes. Remove from cookie sheets immediately. Cool completely. Makes 4 dozen cookies.

I Love Recipes

Best in the West Sugar Cookies

These are the "melt-in-your-mouth" kind of cookies.

1 cup powdered sugar
1 cup white sugar
1 cup butter
1 cup oil
2 eggs
1 teaspoon vanilla

4 cups plus 4 heaping
  tablespoons flour
1 teaspoon salt
2 teaspoons baking soda
1 teaspoon cream of tartar

Cream powdered sugar, white sugar, butter, and oil. Beat in eggs and vanilla. Sift and add remaining ingredients. Place walnut-size balls of dough on non-stick cookie sheet and flatten with fork. Bake 8-10 minutes at 375°.

The Best Little Cookbook in the West

Lollipop Cookies

Will need wooden sticks and cookie decorations.

1 cup (2 sticks) butter,
  softened
1½ cups firmly packed
  brown sugar
2 eggs
2½ cups all-purpose flour
2 teaspoons baking powder

1 teaspoon each: cinnamon and
  nutmeg
½ teaspoon salt
¼ teaspoon baking soda
¼ cup milk
2½ cups quick cooking oats
  (not instant), uncooked

Cream butter and sugar in large mixing bowl until light and fluffy. Beat in eggs. Combine flour, baking powder, spices, salt, and baking soda. Add to butter mixture alternately with milk; mix well. Stir in oats. Cover and refrigerate 1 to 2 hours.

Preheat oven to 375°. Shape dough into 1½-inch balls. Place about 3 inches apart on unbuttered cookie sheets. Insert wooden stick (parallel with cookie sheet) halfway into each ball of dough. Flatten, using a flat bottom glass dipped in granulated sugar. Bake 13-15 minutes or until lightly browned. Cool on cookie sheet, 2-3 minutes. Transfer cookies to wire racks. Cool completely. Decorate as desired.

Sharing Our "Beary" Best II

Date Pinwheel Cookies

½ cup butter, softened	2 cups flour
½ cup sugar	½ teaspoon soda
½ cup brown sugar	½ teaspoon salt
1 egg	½ teaspoon cinnamon

Cream butter and sugars together until light and fluffy. Add egg and beat well. Sift together flour, soda, salt, and cinnamon. Stir into creamed mixture and blend well. Chill dough about 4 hours.

Roll on floured board into a rectangle ¼-inch thick. Spread with date filling. Roll up jellyroll fashion; wrap in waxed paper. Chill 6-8 hours or overnight.

Slice about ⅓-inch thick. Place on a lightly greased cookie sheet. Bake at 375° for 10-12 minutes.

FILLING:

1 (6½-ounce) package pitted dates, cut up	½ cup water
⅓ cup sugar	½ cup walnuts, chopped

Combine chopped dates, sugar, and water. Cook over medium heat, stirring occasionally until jam-like. Cool; stir in chopped nuts.

Home at the Range II

Almond Cookie Brittle

1 cup (2 sticks) butter or margarine, softened	1½ teaspoons almond extract
1 cup sugar	2 cups all-purpose flour
1 teaspoon salt	1 cup sliced almonds

Preheat oven to 350°. Combine butter, sugar, salt, and almond extract, and beat until creamy. Stir in flour gradually, beating until blended. Fold in nuts, then press dough into a jellyroll pan. Bake for 20-25 minutes (the shorter time it bakes, the chewier it stays; longer baking produces a crispier cookie). Leave in pan to cool, then break apart like peanut brittle. Store in an airtight container. Makes about 2 dozen pieces.

Variation: Chocolate Chip Version: Replace the almond extract with vanilla extract, use walnuts or pecans in place of almonds and add one cup chocolate chips!

Que Queens: Easy Grilling & Simple Smoking

Old-Fashioned Toffee

This is a delicious family favorite!

1½ cups (6 ounces) chopped
   walnuts or pecans
2 sticks (1 cup) butter

1½ cups brown sugar, packed
4 cubes (8 ounces) chocolate
   almond bark (or chocolate chips)

Spread nuts in a buttered 9x13-inch pan. Set aside. Combine butter and brown sugar in a 2-quart microwave-safe bowl. Microwave for 2 minutes at HIGH (100%). Stir until butter and brown sugar are completely dissolved. Microwave again for 7-9 minutes at MEDIUM-HIGH (70%), until mixture reaches 290° (soft crack stage), stirring two times (with a clean spoon each time). Pour syrup mixture over nuts. Microwave almond bark or chips in a 1-quart microwave-safe bowl for 2-3 minutes at MEDIUM-HIGH (70%). Stir. Spread over toffee. Cool and enjoy! Yields 2 pounds candy.

Easy Livin' Microwave Cooking for the Holidays

No Cook Candy

1 cup dry milk
1 cup peanut butter

1 cup honey
½ teaspoon vanilla

Combine all ingredients and shape into bite-size rolls. Roll in wheat germ or coconut.

The Eastman Cookbook

Snow White Chocolate Fudge

The dried apricots are an added surprise and neutralize the sweetness.

2 cups sugar
³/₄ cup sour cream
¹/₂ cup oleo
1 (12-ounce) package white
    chocolate bits

1 (7-ounce) jar marshmallow
    creme
³/₄ cup walnuts, chopped
³/₄ cup dried apricots, chopped

Mix together sugar, sour cream, and oleo in heavy saucepan. Bring to boil and boil 7 minutes, stirring constantly or until candy thermometer reaches 234°. Remove from heat; stir in white chocolate bits until they are melted. Add other ingredients and beat until well blended. Pour into 9-inch pan and cut into squares when cool. Makes 2¹/₂ pounds.

Home at the Range IV

3-Minute Microwave Fudge

1 pound powdered sugar
    (3³/₄ cups)
¹/₂ cup cocoa
1 stick margarine (¹/₂ cup)

¹/₄ cup milk
1 teaspoon vanilla
¹/₂ cup chopped peanuts (dry
    roasted)

Combine powdered sugar and cocoa in a 2-quart microwave-safe bowl. Place the stick of margarine on top of the mixture. Pour the milk over all. Do not stir! Microwave on HIGH (100%) for 3 minutes. Stir well and add the vanilla and peanuts. Pour into a greased 8x8-inch pan. Cool 20 minutes. Cut into squares. Yields 64 pieces.

Easy Livin' Microwave Cooking

If you're fascinated with fossils, you'll really "dig" Ashfall Fossil Beds where paleontologists unearth the bones of prehistoric rhinosauruses, three-toed horses, and mastodons. Volcanic ash buried them there at a watering hole 10 million years ago.

Bob's Peanut Butter Fudge

2 cups sugar
³/₄ cup cream
¹/₄ cup peanut butter
2 tablespoons corn syrup

¹/₈ teaspoon salt
1 cup peanuts (optional)
1 teaspoon vanilla

Combine sugar, cream, peanut butter, corn syrup, and salt. Cook to 234° (soft ball stage). Remove from heat and cool to 110°. Beat vigorously until fudge holds its shape. Add peanuts and vanilla, beat one minute and turn into buttered 8-inch square pan.

Recipes & Remembrances / Courtland Covenant Church

Peanut-Buttered Popcorn

3 quarts popped corn (¹/₂ cup unpopped)
1¹/₂ cups unblanched whole almonds, mixed nuts or peanuts

1 cup sugar
¹/₂ cup honey
¹/₂ cup light corn syrup
1 cup peanut butter
1 teaspoon vanilla

In a large roasting pan, combine popcorn and nuts; keep warm in a 250° oven. Butter sides of a heavy 1¹/₂-quart saucepan; combine sugar, honey, and corn syrup in pan. Bring mixture to boiling, stirring constantly. Boil hard for 2 minutes; remove from heat. Stir in peanut butter and vanilla. Immediately pour over popcorn mixture, stirring to coat well. Cool; break into bite-size pieces. Makes 3 quarts.

Home at the Range IV

Apricot Nuggets

These easy-to-make candies add a tasty note to a plate of Christmas confections.

1 pound powdered sugar	**¹/₂ teaspoon vanilla**
6 tablespoons melted butter	**1 (11-ounce) package dried**
or margarine	**apricots, ground (about 1¹/₂ cups)**
2 tablespoons orange juice	**1 cup chopped pecans**

Combine sugar, butter, orange juice, and vanilla. Add apricots. Mix, then knead in bowl until ingredients are well mixed. Form into 1-inch balls. Roll in chopped nuts. Store in refrigerator or freezer in covered container. Makes 6 dozen candies.

In the Kitchen with Kate

Peanut Clusters

The chocolate bark/butterscotch chips combination is my family's favorite, but they are all delicious. This is a recipe that children can easily make on their own. It is foolproof. If the mixture is too thin to drop into nice mounds, let it cool a little to thicken.

1 (24-ounce) package almond	**4²/₃ cups (24 ounces) salted**
bark, vanilla or chocolate	**peanuts**
2 cups (12 ounces) baking	
chips (chocolate, vanilla,	
or butterscotch)	

Melt almond bark and chips together in the microwave or place in a low oven. Keep away from all water. Stir until smooth. Stir in peanuts. Drop teaspoonsful onto waxed paper. Let cool to harden. Yields 5 dozen.

The Give Mom a Rest (She's on Vacation) Cookbook

Pastor Jeff's Rocky Road Candy

1 (12-ounce) package
   semisweet chocolate chips
1 cup peanut butter

1 package miniature
   marshmallows
1/4 cup chopped nuts

Microwave chips and peanut butter on HIGH for 2-3 minutes. Stir well. Fold in marshmallows and nuts. Spoon into slightly buttered 9x13-inch pan. Chill until firm; cut into squares.

Yesterday and Today Friendly Circle Cookbook

Holiday Chocolate Almond Wedges
(Candy Pizza)

2 cups (12 ounces) semisweet
   chocolate chips
8 cubes (16 ounces) white
   almond bark, divided
1 cup salted dry-roasted
   peanuts
1 cup miniature or 11 large
   marshmallows

1 cup crisp rice cereal
1/2 cup red candied cherries,
   chopped
1/2 cup green candied cherries,
   chopped
1/2 cup (2 ounces) slivered
   almonds or shredded coconut

Combine chocolate chips and 6 cubes (12 ounces) of the almond bark in a 2-quart microwave-safe bowl. Microwave for 3½-4½ minutes at MEDIUM-HIGH (70%), stirring twice. (Remember, the chips and bark will look soft and shiny but not melted; they will look melted only after stirring.) Stir until smooth.

Stir in peanuts, marshmallows, and cereal. Spread into a buttered 12-inch pizza pan. Sprinkle red and green cherries and almonds over the chocolate-cereal mixture. Microwave remaining 2 cubes (4 ounces) of white almond bark in a microwave-safe bowl for 1-1½ minutes at MEDIUM-HIGH (70%). Stir until smooth. Drizzle over the mixture in the pan. Chill slightly until firm. Cut into wedges. Enjoy! Yields 10-14 wedges.

Easy Livin' Microwave Cooking for the Holidays

Salted Nut Rolls

1 (7-ounce) jar marshmallow
creme
1 (12-ounce) package peanut
butter chips
1 can Eagle Brand condensed
milk

1 (24-ounce) jar dry roasted
peanuts
½ bag caramels
2 tablespoons milk

Melt marshmallow cream, chips, and condensed milk in microwave (2-3 minutes on HIGH). Put half the peanuts on bottom of a greased 9x13-inch pan. Pour marshmallow mixture over peanuts. Microwave marshmallows and milk on HIGH until melted (about 2½-3 minutes). Pour melted caramels over marshmallow mixture. Top with remaining peanuts.

Regent Alumni Association Cookbook

Meringue Mushrooms

So pretty served in a napkin-lined basket or your favorite crystal dish.

1/2 cup (3-31/2) egg whites, room temperature
Scant 1/4 teaspoon salt
1/4 teaspoon cream of tartar
1 cup sugar

1 teaspoon vanilla extract
Cocoa
Summer coating chocolate (or chocolate chips)

Cover 2 cookie sheets with aluminum foil. Beat egg whites until foamy. Add salt and cream of tartar, beating until very stiff. Add sugar, a rounded teaspoon at a time. Add vanilla. Beat an additional 7-8 minutes after all sugar has been added. Total beating time is 15-18 minutes.

Using a 15-inch pastry bag and a #9 decorating tip, shape stems 1 to 13/4-inches high. Place 1/2 to 1-inch apart. For caps, make even rounds about 11/2 to 13/4-inches wide and 3/4-inches high with tops smooth on the other cookie sheet. Put cocoa in a tea strainer and lightly dust across both cookie sheets. Bake stems on top shelf and caps on bottom shelf of oven for one hour in 225° oven. Turn heat off and open oven door slightly until meringues are cool. Melt chocolate in top of double boiler. With cap upside down, spread layer of chocolate just to edge. Attach stem. Let set at room temperature until firm. Store in non-airtight container. Will keep for weeks.

Cooking with Iola

PIES
and
OTHER DESSERTS

Entrance to Fort Mandon, winter home of Lewis and Clark 1804-1805.
Washburn, North Dakota.

Old-Fashioned Lemon Meringue Pie

1½ cups sugar
½ teaspoon salt
1½ cups water, divided
4 tablespoons butter
⅓ cup cornstarch

4 eggs, separated
¼ cup lemon juice
2 tablespoons lemon rind
1 (9-inch) baked pie shell

Combine sugar, salt, one cup of water and butter. Heat until sugar is dissolved. Blend cornstarch with ½ cup of cold water and add slowly to the hot mixture. Cook on low heat until clear, about 8 minutes. Beat egg yolks and add slowly; cook 3 minutes, stirring continually. Remove from heat and add lemon juice and rind. Cool. Pour in a baked pie shell. Set aside.

MERINGUE:

⅔ cup egg whites
¼ teaspoon salt

¼ teaspoon cream of tartar
⅔ cup sugar

Beat egg whites until foamy; add salt and cream of tartar. Continue beating and add sugar gradually until stiff peaks form. Pile on the lemon filling, sealing edges. Brown in a 375° oven for 10-15 minutes.

Taste the Good Life! Nebraska Cookbook

Wonderful Walnut Pie

This pie is wonderful!

1 unbaked 9-inch pie shell
1/2 cup brown sugar, packed
1/2 cup soft butter
3/4 cup granulated sugar
3 eggs
1/2 teaspoon salt

1/4 cup white corn syrup
1/2 cup light cream
1 cup broken walnut meats
1/2 teaspoon vanilla
7 walnut halves

In top of double boiler, cream together brown sugar and butter. Stir in granulated sugar, eggs, salt, corn syrup and cream. Cook over hot, but not boiling water for 5 minutes, stirring constantly. Remove from heat. Stir in broken nuts and vanilla. Pour into crust. Bake in 350° oven for 50 minutes. Arrange walnut halves around top of pie and bake 15 minutes longer. Cool on wire rack. Serve with ice cream or whipped cream or plain.

Note: For toasty nuts on top, bake pie for 15 minutes, then arrange nuts on top and bake 50 minutes longer.

In the Kitchen with Kate

Edith's Buttermilk Raisin Pie

One of my favorite pies.

1 1/2 cups raisins
1 cup water
2 eggs
2/3 cup sugar

1 teaspoon vinegar
1 tablespoon cornstarch
1 cup buttermilk
1 baked pie crust shell

Boil raisins in water until tender. Combine all other filling ingredients. Add this to the raisins and cook, stirring constantly until thickened. Pour into the baked shell. Serve with whipped topping.

A Taste of Prairie Life

Pie Crust

¼ cup milk
½ cup oil

2 cups sifted flour
1 teaspoon salt

Mix milk and oil together and add to flour and salt. Roll out between wax paper. Bake at 400° about 10 minutes. Makes enough for 2 crusts.

Recipes 1978-1998

Christmas Fruit Pie

This is a pretty red and white dessert, perfect to serve at Christmas time.

2 cups crushed pineapple, drained
1½ cups sugar
2 tablespoons flour
1 can sour pie cherries with juice
2 teaspoons red food coloring

1 (3-ounce) package orange Jell-O
1 teaspoon vanilla
5-8 bananas, chopped
1 cup chopped pecans
2 pie shells, baked
2 pints whipping cream
4 tablespoons sugar

Drain pineapple. Mix together sugar and flour; add drained pineapple, cherries with juice, and red food coloring. Cook until thick. Add box of Jell-O and vanilla; stir until Jell-O is melted. Cool 3 hours or overnight. Slice bananas lengthwise into quarters, then slice into small chunks. Add bananas and nuts to chilled mixture. Fill pastry shells. Mix 4 tablespoons sugar with whipping cream and whip; top pies. Refrigerate.

Taste of Coffeyville

America's First Lady of Flying, Amelia Earhart, was born on July 24, 1897, in Atchison, Kansas. Memorabilia of the famed aviator is on display there at the home owned by The Ninety-Nines, an international women's aviation group Earhart helped found in 1929.

Cottage Cheese Pie

A family favorite as a child.

2 cups cottage cheese
3 eggs
1/2 cup cream
2/3 cup sugar

1/4 teaspoon salt
1 unbaked pie crust
Cinnamon

Mix first 5 ingredients together. Put into pastry-lined pie pan.
Sprinkle with cinnamon. Bake at 375° until filling is set. Serve
warm or cooled.

Yesterday and Today Friendly Circle Cookbook

Miracle Custard Pie

2 cups milk
4 eggs
1/2 cup sugar
1/2 cup flour

1/4 cup margarine or butter
1 teaspoon vanilla
1/2 teaspoon salt
1 cup flaked coconut

In a blender container, combine milk, eggs, sugar, flour, and butter or margarine, vanilla, and salt. Cover; blend about 10 seconds or until well mixed. Stir in coconut. Pour into greased 9-
inch pie plate. Bake at 350° for 40 minutes or until a knife inserted comes out clean. Cool and chill.

A Century in His Footsteps

Baked Earth Dried Apple Pie

Soak 2 cups of dried apples in water overnight. Drain off water
and mix apples with 1/2 cup sugar and 1 teaspoon each of allspice and cinnamon. Line an 8-inch pan with a crust. Add the
apple mixture. Dot with 3 tablespoons of butter and cover with
a second crust. Make a few slashes in the top for ventilation and
bake at 350° for about one hour or until the crust is golden brown.

The Mormon Trail Cookbook

Pineapple-Rhubarb Pie

3 cups rhubarb, cut up
1 cup crushed, drained
   pineapple
1 cup sugar

3 tablespoons tapioca
2 tablespoons lemon juice
$1/2$ teaspoon grated lemon rind
Pastry for 2-crust, 9-inch pie

Blend rhubarb, pineapple, sugar, tapioca, lemon juice, and rind. Put in unbaked pie shell. Top with crust. Bake in 375° oven for 40-50 minutes. Cover with foil last 10 minutes to prevent over-browning.

Ritzy Rhubarb Secrets Cookbook

Sweet Potato Pie

Pastry for single-crust pie
$1^1/2$ cups mashed sweet
   potatoes
$2/3$ cup brown sugar
1 tablespoon butter or
   margarine, melted

1 egg, slightly beaten
1 cup milk
1 teaspoon ground cinnamon
$1/2$ teaspoon ground ginger
$1/3$ teaspoon allspice
$1/8$ teaspoon salt

Line a pie plate with pastry, forming a high collar. Combine sweet potatoes, brown sugar, melted butter or margarine, egg, milk, spices and salt. Ladle into pie shell, and bake at 450° for 15 minutes; reduce heat and continue baking at 350° for 30 minutes or until a knife inserted in the center comes out clean. Makes 6 servings.

Per serving: 218 calories; 5.28g fat; 43mg cholesterol.

Reader's Favorite Recipes

Springtime Simply Strawberry Pie

1 (3-ounce) box strawberry
  Jell-O
1 (3-ounce) box vanilla
  pudding (not instant)

2 cups water
2 cups sliced strawberries
Pie crust

Combine Jell-O, pudding, and water. Cook until thickened. Add strawberries and gently blend. Turn into prepared graham cracker crust or regular pie crust. Chill 3-4 hours. Garnish with whipped cream for serving.

Recipes & Remembrances / Courtland Covenant Church

Magic Peach Cobbler

This is very good!

1½ cups butter
3 cups sugar
3 cups flour
4½ teaspoons baking powder

3 cups milk
1 large can sliced peaches
1½ cups sugar for topping

Melt butter in [9x13-inch] cake pan. Mix 3 cups sugar, flour, baking powder, and milk. Pour over butter in pan. Do not stir. Add peaches on top of this. Place 1½ cups sugar on top of peaches. Bake at 350° for one hour. You may substitute other fruit of your choice. Makes 10-12 servings. *Recipe by Trix's Riley Roomer, Riley, Kansas.*

Savor the Inns of Kansas

"I Like Ike" was the campaign slogan for Eisenhower, and an awful lot of people surely liked him. The home, library, and final resting place of the former president and five-star general can be seen at the Eisenhower Center in Abilene, Kansas.

Wild Gooseberry Cobbler

2 cups sugar, divided	2 teaspoons baking powder
1 cup flour	1/8 teaspoon salt
2 tablespoons butter	2 cups gooseberries
3/4 cup milk	1 cup hot water

Cream one cup sugar, flour, and butter; add milk, baking powder, and salt. Mix. Pour batter into an 8x8-inch baking dish. On top of batter, spread gooseberries (or any other fruit) over which sprinkle remaining one cup sugar. Add one cup (or less) hot water over all. Bake in moderate oven (350°) for 30 minutes.

The Oregon Trail Cookbook

Grilled Stuffed Apples

4 large baking apples	2 tablespoons chopped
1/2 cup raisins	maraschino cherries
1/2 cup dry sherry	1/8 teaspoon cinnamon
2 tablespoons chopped	1/8 teaspoon ground cloves
walnuts	1/8 teaspoon nutmeg
2 tablespoons brown sugar	1 tablespoon butter

Core apples, enlarging hole slightly. Place each apple on 12x8-inch sheet of heavy-duty foil. Spoon mixture of raisins, sherry, walnuts, brown sugar, cherries, cinnamon, cloves, and nutmeg into apples; dot with butter. Fold and seal foil loosely. Grill over low heat for one hour or until apples are done to taste. Serve with vanilla ice cream. Yield: 4 servings.

The Kansas City Barbeque Society Cookbook

Bonanza farms were immense lands broken for agriculture, measured not by acres but by square miles. Worked by legions of horses and hired hands, some were a hundred times larger than the typical eastern farm. The Bagg Bonanza Farm near Mooreton, North Dakota, is America's only intact bonanza farm.

Apple Dumplings

4-6 tablespoons butter or solid
  shortening
1³/₄ cup all-purpose flour
3 tablespoons sugar
¹/₂ teaspoon salt

3 teaspoons baking powder
³/₄ cup milk
4 medium apples, peeled and
  sliced

Preheat oven to 375°. Cut shortening into dry ingredients with pastry blender or knives until mixture is consistency of coarse cornmeal. Make well in the center of these ingredients. Pour in milk. Stir lightly until all ingredients are moistened and dough cleans the sides of the bowl; not more than ¹/₂ minute. Turn dough onto lightly floured surface. Knead 10 times. With floured rolling pin, roll dough into 9x12-inch rectangle about ¹/₂-inch thick. Cover with apples. Starting on the long end, roll-up jellyroll-style. Pinch side edge together. Cut tube into 10-12 slices and place in greased 9x13-inch cake pan. Pour sauce over slices and bake for 45 minutes or until apples are tender.

SAUCE:
1 cup white sugar
1 cup brown sugar, packed
1 cup margarine

2 cups water
1 teaspoon cinnamon

Combine all ingredients in saucepan; bring to a full boil. Boil one minute. Pour over sliced apple roll.

St. Joseph's Table

Sulphured Apples

Peel and fill a market basket ⅓ full of apples quartered and the quarters cut into about 3 pieces. The apples must be free from all bruises and other blemishes.

In the bottom of a large barrel, place a pot of red coals. Sprinkle 3 tablespoons of sulphur on the coals. Hang the basket of apples by its handle on a rod laying across the top of the barrel, being sure the basket does not touch the coals. Cover the barrel top with an old piece of carpet and let smoke 45 minutes. When smoked, store apples in crocks or jars.

When ready to use, wash the apples good or put on the stove with some water and bring to a boil and pour the water off. They taste like fresh apples. Can be used for pies or sauce.

Egg Gravy

Danish Pudding

This is an old family recipe.

6 eggs	1 teaspoon vanilla
1 quart milk	1½-2 cups brown sugar
2 tablespoons flour dissolved in	
2 tablespoons cold water	

Beat eggs well. Add milk and flour/water mixture. Add vanilla. Lightly spray 8-10 custard cups or heart molds with Pam. Sprinkle brown sugar to cover bottom of each dish. Fill with egg/milk mix. Set in baking pan of hot water. Bake at 350° until knife inserted in center is clean. Chill well. To serve, invert on serving plate. Garnish with a strawberry or other fruit. Makes 8-10 servings. *Recipe from Bedknobs & Biscuits, Basehor, Kansas.*

Savor the Inns of Kansas

Nebraska ranks #1 in popcorn production and first in great northern bean production.

Edith's Auction Day Pudding

If you've ever sat at a bull sale on a bad day, you'll know why Mom and I would rather be home baking!

1 cup pitted dates, chopped	1 teaspoon baking soda
1 cup boiling water	1/2 teaspoon baking powder
1/2 cup white sugar	1/2 teaspoon salt
1/2 cup brown sugar	1 cup chopped nuts
1 egg	11/2 cups brown sugar
2 tablespoons butter, melted	11/2 cups boiling water
11/2 cups flour	1 tablespoon butter

Combine dates and boiling water. Set aside. Stir together white sugar, brown sugar, egg, and butter. Add dry ingredients. Stir in nuts and the date mixture. Pour into 11x7-inch baking dish. Pour on sauce made with brown sugar, water, and butter. Bake at 375° for 40 minutes. Cut in squares, invert and serve with whipped cream.

The Best Little Cookbook in the West

Bread Pudding

4 cups milk	3 eggs, beaten
3 tablespoons butter, melted	1 cup coconut
2 teaspoons vanilla	4 cups white French bread, cut
11/2 cups sugar	into 1/2 to 3/4-inch chunks
1 cup raisins	

In a large bowl, mix all ingredients, adding bread chunks last. Pour into 9x13-inch glass baking dish. Bake at 350° for one hour. Top with Sour Cream Sauce.

SOUR CREAM SAUCE:

1/2 cup packed brown sugar	1/2 cup dairy sour cream

Combine in a small bowl. Microwave at MEDIUM for 1-2 minutes or until warm and sugar melts. Stir well after one minute. Serve warm over dessert. Makes one cup.

Tried & True II

Indian Pudding

2 quarts milk, divided	1¹/₂ teaspoons cinnamon
2 cups sugar	1 teaspoon nutmeg
1¹/₃ cups coarse cornmeal	¹/₂ cup butter
or grits	4 or 5 eggs, beaten
1 teaspoon salt	1 cup (or more) raisins

Put one quart of milk in saucepan to heat. Mix sugar, cornmeal, salt, cinnamon, and nutmeg well; add to milk. Stir until it boils. Add butter and rest of milk and the eggs, which have been beaten separately. Divide into 2 large or 3 small pudding pans. Bake at 325° for 2 hours. When pudding begins to set, stir in raisins. If pudding seems too stiff, add more milk as it bakes or when re-heating. Can be kept in refrigerator a long time.

INDIAN PUDDING SAUCE:

2 tablespoons butter	2 cups sugar
2 teaspoons cinnamon	2 tablespoons cornstarch
¹/₄ teaspoon nutmeg	2 cups water
¹/₄ teaspoon ginger	

Melt margarine. Add cinnamon, nutmeg, and ginger; boil a minute. Mix sugar and cornstarch, then add to margarine mix. Add water and boil until thick.

The Mormon Trail Cookbook

Grandmother's Swedish Rice Pudding

1¹/₂ cups rice	6 cups milk
3 cups water	1¹/₂ cups sugar
1 stick cinnamon	

Combine rice, water, cinnamon. Boil slowly in large pot until rice absorbs the water. Add milk and sugar. Boil gently (about 1 hour) and stir often until milk is absorbed. Remove cinnamon. Pudding will be smooth and creamy. Serve as main dish or dessert; hot or cold. Add sugar to taste. Serves 8.

Measure for Pleasure

Old-Fashioned Shortcake

2 cups all-purpose flour
1 tablespoon baking powder
1 teaspoon salt
1 tablespoon granulated
  sugar
6 tablespoons fat (butter,
  margarine or shortening)

¾ cup milk
1 beaten egg (optional)
Melted butter, margarine or
  shortening
1 quart fresh or cooked fruit or
  berries
Whipped cream, as desired

Sift dry ingredients together twice; cut in fat until mixture resembles coarse corn meal. Add milk all at once, mixing until the dough leaves the side or cleans the bowl. An egg also may be added (with the milk) for a richer dough, if desired. Dough should be soft.

Turn onto lightly floured board and knead about 20 times or until dough is just smooth. Divide dough into 2 equal parts. Pat and roll out one portion to fit a pie or cake pan, making a layer about ¼-inch thick. Brush top with melted butter, margarine or shortening. Shape second portion of dough the same way and lightly place over the dough already in the pan. Bake at 425° for 12-15 minutes or until light golden brown. Cool slightly. Gently separate layers. Add fruit as filling; top with whipped cream as desired. Makes 8 servings.

Per serving: 222 calories; 9g fat; 23mg cholesterol.

Reader's Favorite Recipes

Kid's Favorite Dessert

2 (3-ounce) boxes strawberry
  Jell-O
2 packages regular vanilla
  pudding

5 cups boiling water
1 large container Cool Whip
Graham cracker crumbs
  (about 2 cups)

Put Jell-O, pudding and boiling water in large bowl and mix well. Refrigerate. When slightly thickened, add Cool Whip. Cover bottom of 9x13-inch pan with graham cracker crumbs. Pour in dessert. Sprinkle additional crumbs on top. Chill several hours. Cuts into nice firm servings.

Home at the Range II

Pistachio Ambrosia

1 (16-ounce) can chunky
  pineapple
1 (8-ounce) can crushed
  pineapple
1 (3-ounce) package instant
  pistachio pudding mix
1 cup chopped pecans

1 cup shredded coconut
  (optional)
12-16 ounces whipped
  topping
1 cup miniature
  marshmallows

Mix both pineapples with all their liquid. Sprinkle powdered pudding mix on top. Mix and let stand 3-5 minutes. Mix nuts and coconut together in separate bowl, then add to the pineapple-pudding mixture. Blend in the topping and marshmallows. Refrigerate for at least 2 hours. Serve well chilled.

Recipes 1978-1998

Cherry Blossom Dessert

1½ cups oatmeal
1½ cups flour
1 cup packed brown sugar
1 cup melted butter
¼ teaspoon salt

⅛ teaspoon ground
  cinnamon
2 cans cherry pie filling
1 teaspoon almond extract for
  each can

Preheat oven to 350°. Mix first 6 ingredients until crumbly. Pat ⅔ of mixture into a 9x13-inch pan. Mix cherry pie filling and almond extract and spread on oatmeal crust. Top with remaining crumbs and bake for 40 minutes, or until lightly browned. Serve warm with whipped cream or vanilla ice cream.

Regent Alumni Association Cookbook

One of the top paleontological (fossil) museums is at the University of Nebraska-Lincoln. Two of the nation's richest fossil beds are at Agate Fossil Beds National Monument and Ashfall Fossil Beds State Historical Park. The world's largest elephant fossil was found in Nebraska.

Tornadoes

In this whimsical dessert, funnel clouds of pecan meringue touch down on dots of whipped cream and pools of brilliantly colored fruit sauce. It's not Oz, but it's close.

3/4 cup pecan pieces	2 cups fresh or frozen
5 large egg whites	raspberries, blackberries, or
1/4 teaspoon cream of tartar	strawberries
1 cup sugar	Sugar to taste
1 teaspoon vanilla extract	1 cup heavy cream, whipped

Preheat the oven to 300°. Grind the pecans to a fine paste in the bowl of a food processor. In a separate bowl, beat the egg whites and cream of tartar until soft peaks form. Gradually beat in the sugar and vanilla extract until stiff peaks form. Fold in the pecans. Fit a pastry bag with a #4 star tip and spoon in the meringue batter. Line 2 baking sheets with parchment paper. Pipe 24 (2-inch) mounds of meringue onto the parchment to form inverted funnel shapes. Bake for about 10 minutes, then turn down the heat to 100° and leave the meringues to dry out for 1-2 hours, or until crisp. Store in airtight containers or serve immediately.

Purée the fruit in a food processor and add sugar to taste. Place 3 teaspoonfuls of whipped cream randomly on each dessert plate. Spoon about 3 tablespoons of the fruit sauce around the whipped cream. Place the pointed end of each meringue in a dot of whipped cream and serve. Makes 2 dozen (serves 6-8).

Pure Prairie

Foolproof Meringue

3 egg whites	1/2 (7-ounce) jar Kraft
Dash of salt	Marshmallow Creme

Beat egg whites and salt until soft peaks form. Gradually add marshmallow creme. Beat until stiff peaks form. Spread over pie filling; seal to edge of crust. Bake at 350° for 12-15 minutes. Cool.

I Love Recipes

Death by Chocolate

1 (2-layer) package chocolate cake mix
2 (4-ounce) packages chocolate mousse mix
4 large Heath candy bars, crushed
16 ounces whipped topping

Prepare and bake cake mix using package directions. Crumble into small pieces. Prepare chocolate mousse mix using package directions. Reserve a small amount of the crushed candy. Add remaining candy and whipped topping to mousse; mix well. Alternate layers of cake pieces and mousse mixture in 9x13-inch dish until all ingredients are used, ending with mousse. Sprinkle with reserved candy. Chill until serving time. Yields 12 servings.

Y Cook?

Almond Hershey Dessert

32 graham crackers, crushed
1/2 cup melted butter
32 marshmallows
1 cup milk
1 teaspoon vanilla
1 1/2 large almond Hershey bars
Dash salt
1 square baking chocolate
1 pint cream, whipped

Combine crushed graham crackers and melted butter. Mix well and pat half of crumbs in bottom of 9x13-inch pan. Save other half of crumbs for top. Melt marshmallows in double boiler with milk and vanilla. Remove from heat and add Hershey bars, salt, and chocolate. When cool, add whipped cream. Pour into pan and place remaining crumbs on top. Chill at least a few hours before servings. Serve with whipped cream.

Feed My Lambs

Moon Cake

1 cup water
1/2 cup butter or margarine
1 cup flour
4 eggs
1 (8-ounce) package cream
   cheese, softened

2 small boxes vanilla instant
   pudding, prepared
Cool Whip
Chocolate fudge ice cream
   topping
Chopped nuts

Bring water and butter to boil. Add flour all at once and stir rapidly until mixture forms a ball. Remove from heat and cool a little. Add eggs, one at a time, until shiny. Spread into ungreased 11x15-inch jellyroll pan. Bake at 400° for 30 minutes (watch!) Cool—*Do not prick surface!* Beat cream cheese until creamy. Slowly blend pudding into beaten cream cheese. Spread on cooled crust and refrigerate for 20 minutes. Top with Cool Whip. Drizzle with chocolate fudge sauce (ice cream topping) and sprinkle with chopped nuts (slivered almonds are good).

Heavenly Delights

Fruit Pizza

1 roll refrigerator sugar
   cookie dough
1/4 cup sugar
1 tablespoon cornstarch
2 tablespoons lemon juice
1/4 cup orange juice
1/4 cup water
1 (8-ounce) package cream
   cheese, softened

4 ounces whipped topping
1 pint strawberries
2 peaches, sliced
1 pint blueberries
6 slices pineapple, cut into
   pieces

Slice cookie dough 1/4-inch thick. Press into greased pizza pan. Bake at 350° for 8-10 minutes or until golden brown. Cool. Mix sugar and cornstarch in saucepan. Stir in lemon juice, orange juice, and water. Cook until thickened, stirring constantly. Cool.

Blend cream cheese and whipped topping in bowl. Spread on cooled crust. Arrange fruit over cream cheese layer. Spread with orange glaze (1 cup powdered sugar mixed with 2-3 teaspoons of orange juice). Yields 12 servings.

Y Cook?

Pumpkin Pie Squares

CRUST:

1/2 cup all-purpose flour
1/2 cup stone ground whole
    wheat flour
1/2 cup quick cooking rolled oats

1/2 cup brown sugar, packed
1/2 cup butter or margarine

Combine flours, oats, and brown sugar. Cut in butter. Press in ungreased 9x13-inch cake pan. Bake 15 minutes.

FILLING:

2 cups (1-pound can)
    pumpkin
1 (12-ounce) can evaporated
    milk
2 eggs, beaten

3/4 cup sugar
1 teaspoon cinnamon
1/2 teaspoon salt
1/2 teaspoon ginger
1/4 teaspoon cloves

Combine ingredients together well. Pour over crust and bake another 20 minutes.

TOPPING:

1/2 cup chopped pecans
1/2 cup brown sugar

2 tablespoons butter or
    margarine

Combine until crumbly and sprinkle over pumpkin filling. Return to oven and bake 15-20 minutes or until filling is set. Cool and serve plain or with whipped topping.

Whole Wheat Cookery

Cherry Cha-Cha

18 crushed graham crackers
3 tablespoons sugar
1/3 cup melted butter
1 cup whipping cream

4 cups miniature
    marshmallows
1 can cherry pie filling

Mix first 3 ingredients and pat in bottom of 9x13-inch pan. Bake for 10 minutes at 325°. Cool. Whip cream; add 4 cups marshmallows and cherry pie filling. Pour over crust. Top with a few graham cracker crumbs. Refrigerate.

Kelvin Homemakers 50th Anniversary Cookbook

Mile High Strawberry Dessert

1 cup flour
1/2 cup butter
1/4 cup brown sugar
1/2 cup chopped walnuts
1/2 cup sugar

1 (10-ounce) package
   strawberries, halved
1 1/2 teaspoons lemon juice
2 egg whites
1 (8-ounce) container Cool Whip

Combine the first 4 ingredients and pour into 9x13-inch baking pan. Bake at 350° for about 15-18 minutes or until lightly browned. Crumble with a fork. Blend together the sugar, strawberries, lemon juice, and egg whites in a large bowl. Beat with an electric mixer for 20 minutes. Fold in the Cool Whip. Sprinkle about 1/2 the crumb mixture in a 9x13-inch pan. Spread the strawberry mixture over the crumbs and top with remaining crumbs. Freeze. Do not thaw before serving.

Yesterday and Today Friendly Circle Cookbook

Strawberry Dessert

3/4 cup margarine
2 cups graham cracker crumbs,
   (32 squares), or crushed
   pretzels
3 tablespoons sugar
2 (3-ounce) packages
   strawberry Jell-O
2 cups boiling water

1 (16-ounce) package whole
   frozen strawberries
1 (8-ounce) package cream
   cheese
1 cup sugar
1 (9-ounce) carton Cool
   Whip

Melt margarine and add graham cracker crumbs with 3 tablespoons sugar. Press in bottom of 9x13-inch pan. Bake at 400° for 5-6 minutes. Cool. While crust is cooling, dissolve Jell-O in boiling water. Add frozen strawberries, sliced. Beat cream cheese with one cup sugar until light and fluffy. Fold in Cool Whip. Spread on top of crust. Place Jell-O and strawberries over cream cheese mixture. Place in refrigerator until set.

90th Anniversary Trinity Lutheran Church Cookbook

Kansas Mud

1 (8-ounce) package cream
  cheese, softened
1 cup powdered sugar
1/2 cup margarine, softened
2 (3-ounce) packages vanilla
  pudding

3 cups milk
1 teaspoon vanilla
1 large carton Cool Whip
1 large package Oreo cookies,
  crushed

Cream together cream cheese, powdered sugar, and margarine. Mix pudding, milk, and vanilla together then add to above mixture. Fold in Cool Whip. Fold in crushed Oreo cookies, reserving some cookie crumbs to add to top. Line flower pot with foil, add dessert, top with reserved cookie crumbs (dirt), and add artificial sunflower.

125 Years of Cookin' with the Lord

Jack o' Lantern Compote

1 cup port
1 cup cider vinegar
1/2 cup (1 stick) butter
1 medium onion, chopped
3/4 cup dried red tart cherries
3/4 cup dried apricots,
  snipped into pieces

3/4 cup chopped dates
1/3 cup honey
2 tart apples, cored, peeled, and
  chopped
1 small pumpkin, seeds
  removed and lid reserved

In a saucepan, boil the port and cider vinegar together until reduced by half, about 10 minutes. In a skillet melt the butter over medium heat and sauté the onion until translucent, about 4 minutes. Add the dried fruit, honey, and apples to the skillet and stir to blend. Pack the cavity of the pumpkin with this mixture, then pour the port-cider vinegar mixture over the filling. Put the lid back on the pumpkin and bake in a 350° oven for 45-60 minutes, or until the compote is bubbling and the pumpkin is tender. To serve, spoon out both pumpkin flesh and compote into glass dishes.

Pure Prairie

Drei-Frucht Kompott
(Three Fruit Compote)

Serve for dessert or brunch. So easy.

1 can sour pitted cherries
1 (10-ounce) package frozen
  raspberries, thawed
1 package frozen strawberries,
  thawed

1½ tablespoons cornstarch
1 tablespoon lemon juice
1 teaspoon pure vanilla
Heavy cream

Strain juice from fruit, reserving juice. In small saucepan, blend cornstarch with a little of the juices, then add all the juices. Heat until juices are clear and thickened. Add lemon juice and vanilla. Carefully fold in fruit, and refrigerate. Serve in sherbet glasses with cream.

If It Tastes Good, Who Cares? I

Velvety Lime Squares

A pretty and refreshing spring dessert.

1 (3-ounce) can flaked
  coconut
2 cups vanilla wafer crumbs
2 tablespoons butter, melted
2 tablespoons granulated sugar
2 (3-ounce) packages lime
  gelatin
2 cups boiling water

1 (6-ounce) can frozen limeade
  concentrate
3 pints vanilla ice cream,
  softened
⅛ teaspoon salt
Few drops green food
  coloring
Pecans for garnish (optional)

Carefully toast ½ cup coconut in 375° oven until lightly browned, about 5 minutes. Set aside. Combine remaining coconut, vanilla wafer crumbs, butter, and granulated sugar, and lightly press into a 7x11x1½-inch pan. Bake at 375° for 6-7 minutes. Cool.

Dissolve gelatin in boiling water. Add limeade, ice cream, salt and food coloring, and stir until dissolved. Pour into baked crust. Top with reserved toasted coconut and garnish with pecans, if you wish. Cover tightly and freeze until firm. Remove from freezer 20 minutes before cutting into squares.

In the Kitchen with Kate

Pistachio Dessert

45 Ritz crackers, crushed
1 stick margarine, softened
2 boxes instant pistachio
   pudding

1½ cups milk
1 quart vanilla ice cream, softened
Cool Whip (8 ounces)
Milk chocolate for garnish

Mix cracker crumbs and softened margarine. Press into greased 9x13-inch pan. Bake 12-15 minutes at 325°. Cool. In bowl mix pudding and milk; stir until blended, then add ice cream and stir until smooth. Spread on crust; freeze. Spread layer of Cool Whip over pudding mixture. Sprinkle grated chocolate on top.

Wyndmere Community Alumni Cookbook

Krunch Kone Koffee Pie

10 sugar ice cream cones,
   ground fine
¼ cup margarine, melted
½ cup hot fudge sauce
1 quart vanilla ice cream

1½ tablespoons instant coffee
1 teaspoon hot water
1 (8-ounce) tub whipped
   topping
½ chocolate bar, grated

Grind ice cream cones and combine with melted margarine. Press into 9-inch pie plate to form crust. Place in freezer. Microwave hot fudge sauce until pourable. Pour into prepared crust and return to freezer. Put ice cream in a medium bowl. Add instant coffee that has been stirred into hot water. Beat until blended and pour on top of fudge sauce. Return to freezer until solid. Top with whipped topping and grated chocolate bar. Freeze. Let set at room temperature for 5 minutes before serving.

Cooking with Iola

Buster Bar Dessert

1 small package Oreo cookies	1 small jar fudge sauce
1/4 cup butter	1 small jar peanuts
1/2 gallon ice cream	1 (8-ounce) tub Cool Whip

Crush Oreo cookies (in food processor) and add butter. Layer all but one cup of cookie crumb mixture in 9x13-inch pan. Pour softened ice cream over cookies. Freeze until hard. Pour fudge sauce over ice cream. Press peanuts into fudge sauce. Top with Cool Whip and then put rest of crushed cookies on top. Freeze until firm.

Home at the Range III

Pumpkin Cookie Dessert

Wonderful combination of flavors with ginger cookies.

1 1/2 cups ginger cookie crumbs	1/4 cup sugar
	1/3 cup melted margarine

Mix the cookie crumbs and sugar; blend in the melted margarine. Press the crumbs into bottom of 9x9-inch pan. Chill thoroughly in refrigerator.

FILLING:

1 cup canned pumpkin	1 quart vanilla ice cream,
1/2 cup sugar	softened
1/2 teaspoon cinnamon	1/2 of 8-ounce tub whipped
1/2 teaspoon salt (scant)	topping
1/2 cup pecans, chopped	

Combine pumpkin, sugar, cinnamon, salt, and pecans, saving a few nuts for top. In a chilled bowl, fold the mixture into the ice cream. Mix until smooth; then pour into chilled crust. Freeze. When frozen, spread on a layer of whipped topping and reserved pecans. Keep in freezer. Topping and pecan garnish may be added at serving time.

Pumpkin, Winter Squash and Carrot Cookbook

Rainbow Dessert

½ cup butter or margarine
½ cup brown sugar
3 cups crushed vanilla wafers
2 cups whipping cream
1 teaspoon vanilla

3 tablespoons sugar
1 cup chopped walnuts
1 pint lemon sherbet
1 pint raspberry sherbet
1 pint lime sherbet

Melt butter; add brown sugar, and crushed vanilla wafers. Pat mixture into bottom of 9x13-inch pan. In a bowl, whip cream; add vanilla, sugar, and ½ of the nuts. Spoon ½ of the whipped cream mixture over crust. Then add sherbet (which has been thawed, until soft), by spoonfuls, alternating colors. Add remaining whipped cream mixture over top. Sprinkle with remaining nuts. Freeze. Serves 12.

Lakota Lutheran Church Centennial Cookbook

Raspberry Rapture Ice Cream

1 quart half-and-half cream
2 eggs, beaten
1 (3-ounce) package raspberry
  gelatin
½ cup boiling water
12 ounces frozen raspberries,
  thawed

1 (3¾-ounce) package vanilla
  instant pudding mix
¾ cup sugar
1 cup whipping cream
1 tablespoon vanilla

Heat cream and eggs in a saucepan, stirring constantly until the temperature reaches 165°. Let mixture cool to room temperature, stirring occasionally. Dissolve gelatin in the boiling water. Purée the thawed raspberries in a blender. Slowly pour the gelatin mixture into the puréed berries while the blender is running. Combine pudding mix and sugar in a small bowl. Mix the half-and-half mixture, raspberry mixture, pudding mixture, whipping cream, and vanilla in a large bowl. Pour into cylinder of ice cream freezer. Freeze according to manufacturer's instructions. Makes 2 quarts.

Treasures of the Great Midwest

Butter Brickle Ice Cream Pie

The caramel sauce can be made up to three days in advance and refrigerated . . . if you trust yourself to have this sweet treat in your house that long!

1¹/₂ cups pecans, coarsely
   chopped (save 8 whole
   pecans for garnish)
2 egg whites
¹/₄ cup sugar

¹/₄ teaspoon salt
1 quart butter brickle ice cream
   (or butter pecan or butter
   crunch), softened

Lightly toast all the pecans in a 350° oven for 5-8 minutes. Cool on a paper towel before using. Beat egg whites until frothy. Gradually add sugar and salt and beat until stiff. Fold in cooled chopped nuts and spread meringue in bottom and up side of well-buttered 9-inch pie pan. Prick bottom and sides with fork to eliminate bubbles. Bake at 350° for 15-20 minutes. Watch closely. Cool completely. Spread ice cream over crust. Cover with foil and freeze. To serve, cut into wedges, top with sauce and one whole pecan. Serves 8.

CARAMEL SAUCE:
1 cup firmly packed brown
   sugar
¹/₂ cup half-and-half or
   evaporated milk

¹/₄ cup light corn syrup
2 tablespoons butter or
   margarine
1 tablespoon vanilla

Combine all ingredients except vanilla. Bring to a boil over medium heat, stirring occasionally. Boil about 4 minutes, stirring occasionally. Remove from heat, stir in vanilla, and let cool 30 minutes. Store in refrigerator.

Presentations

Mexican Ice Cream

Men love this.

1 cup coffee ice cream	¹/₄ cup amaretto
3 cups vanilla ice cream	¹/₄ cup Kahlua
¹/₄ cup heavy cream	

Soften ice cream. Blend all ingredients until smooth. Serve immediately, or freeze several hours.

If It Tastes Good, Who Cares? I

Tin Can Ice Cream

1 (1-pound) can with lid	¹/₂ teaspoon vanilla
1 (3-pound) can with lid	1 cup cream
³/₄ cup ice cream salt	¹/₃ cup sugar
1 egg	Pinch salt
³/₄ cup milk	

Fill large can half full of ice and ice cream salt. Mix egg, milk, vanilla, cream, sugar and salt in smaller can and put lid on. Place in larger can with lid and roll around about 10 minutes or until frozen.

Sisters Two II

Leavenworth is the oldest city in Kansas, founded in 1854, and has the oldest continuously garrisoned military installation west of the Mississippi, Fort Leavenworth. George Custer, Douglas MacArthur, George S. Patton, and Colin Powell all served there.

CATALOG of CONTRIBUTING COOKBOOKS

Fort Leavenworth officer's quarters. Leavenworth, Kansas.

CATALOG
of
CONTRIBUTING COOKBOOKS

All recipes in this book have been selected from the cookbooks shown on the following pages. Individuals who wish to obtain a copy of any particular book may do so by sending a check or money order to the address listed by each cookbook (not Quail Ridge Press). Please note the postage and handling charges that are required. State residents add tax only when requested. Prices and addresses are subject to change, and books may sell out and become unavailable. Retailers are invited to call or write to same address for discount information.

ALL ABOUT BAR-B-Q KANSAS CITY STYLE

Rich Davis and Shifra Stein
Pig Out Publications
4245 Walnut
Kansas City, MO 64111

E-Mail Kadler@unicom.net
816-531-3119 / Fax 816-531-6113

Kansas City-style recipes for the grill and smoker. Guide to the best BBQ restaurants, too. Over 100 recipes. 144 pages, 7x9 paperback.

$ 14.95 Retail price
$ 3.00 Postage and handling
Make check payable to Pig Out Publications / Visa and MC accepted
ISBN 0-925175-11-0

AMANA LUTHERAN 125th ANNIVERSARY COOKBOOK

Amana Lutheran Church Women
c/o Thelma Larson
601 3rd Street
Scandia, KS 66966

785-335-2339

Recipes that capture seven generations of Scandinavian heritage, along with recipes that utilize modern cooking techniques and ingredients, all blend together in this unique cookbook to commemorate our church's 125th anniversary. The impressive stained glass windows of the Amana Lutheran Church building provide resplendent category dividers for the 850 recipes included.

$ 15.00 Retail price
$ 3.00 Postage and handling
Make check payable to Amana Lutheran Church Women

THE BEST LITTLE COOKBOOK IN THE WEST

by Loaun Werner Vaad
104 S. Main
Chamberlain, SD 57325

605-734-5135

Humorous illustrations add to the "cowboy connoisseur" theme of this 224-page book. The recipes and chuckles are dedicated to all those pioneer spirits that won, or tried to win, the West!

$ 12.95 Retail price   Visa, MC, AmEx accepted
$ .78 Tax for South Dakota residents
$ 2.50 Postage and handling
Make check payable to Buffalo Grass Trading Co.
ISBN 0-9652586-2-9

BLEW CENTENNIAL BON-APPETIT

Blew Family
c/o Vernelle Sammons
655 H Street
Phillipsburg, KS 67661   785-543-5059

Our Kansas Heritage gave each of us memories of "livin', lovin' and good eatin'." For five generations our Blew family reunion, held yearly, has passed all of these treasures on to the next generation. From Grandma's Milk Toast to Karen Blew's Cucumber and Bacon Dip, we have great memories.

$ 10.00 Retail price
$ 2.50 Postage and handling
Make check payable to Blew Reunion

CENTERVILLE COMMUNITY CENTENNIAL COOKBOOK

1897-1997
Centennial Cookbook

Centerville Community Church
Centerville, Kansas

Centerville Community Church
P. O. Box 35
Centerville, KS 66014   913-898-2981

This was put together by the community to celebrate the 100th anniversary of the Centerville Community Church. All ages gave recipes and we included several from people who have been gone 50 years or more. Their recipes are still timely and tasty. The book includes 93 pages and over 300 recipes.

$ 8.00 Retail price
$ 2.00 Postage and handling
Make check payable to Centerville Community Church

A CENTURY IN HIS FOOTSTEPS

A Century In His Footsteps
1891-1991

Mullen United Methodist Church
c/o Judy A. Ridenour
HC 1 Box 22
Mullen, NE 69152-9311   308-546-2626

A Century in His Footsteps 1891-1991 contains 1136 recipes on 342 pages. The centennial goal was to obtain recipes and their history from all who had worshiped in the Mullen United Methodist Church. Tab dividers depict the history of the church buildings, organizations, ministers, and special events, making it a unique cookbook.

$ 12.00 Retail price
$ .54 Tax for Nebraska residents
$ 2.95 Postage and handling
Make check payable to Judy A. Ridenour

A COOKING AFFAIRE I

by Jan Bertoglio and JoLe Hudson
Butcher Block Press, Inc.
P. O. Box 6
Medicine Lodge, KS 67104   316-886-3358

This beautifully illustrated cookbook is a heritage of classics. The book contains 414 pages with 2,500 tried and proven recipes for a beginner or gourmet cook. Variety of sections include brunches, picnics, working person, children, entertaining, Christmas, lite-eating, garden, Boys Club, Italian, Mexican, helpful hints and many more. Wonderful for gifts!

$ 24.95 Retail price
$ 1.60 Tax for Kansas residents
$ 4.50 Postage and handling
Make check payable to Butcher Block Press, Inc.

A COOKING AFFAIRE II

by Jan Bertoglio and JoLe Hudson
Butcher Block Press, Inc.
P. O. Box 6
Medicine Lodge, KS 67104   316-886-3358

Second in the series, this beautifully illustrated cookbook is a heritage of classics. The book contains 430 pages with 2,500 tried and proven recipes for a beginner or gourmet cook. Variety of sections include brunches, picnics, working person, children, entertaining, Christmas, lite-eating, garden, Boys Club, Italian, Mexican, helpful hints and many more. Wonderful for gifts! Book III is now available for $19.95.

$ 24.95 Retail price each book
$ 1.60 Tax for Kansas residents
$ 4.50 Postage and handling
Make check payable to Butcher Block Press, Inc.

COOKING WITH IOLA

by Iola Egle
1610 Centennial Drive
McCook, NE 69001   308-345-3303

Over 400 select family recipes—many have won prizes. Spiral bound.

$ 8.00 Retail price
$ 2.00 Postage and handling
Make check payable to Iola Egle

COOKIN' WITH FARMERS UNION FRIENDS

Cookin' with
Farmers Union
Friends

North Dakota Farmers Union Youth Group
c/o Deb Berger
2531 37th Avenue SW   E-Mail: dberger@westriv.com
Center, ND 58530   701-794-8862

North Dakota Farmers Union
Youth Group

A wide range of over 1000 recipes within 350 pages. The production of this book was a state-wide project. It goes towards funding projects for our youth groups. A great selection for your cookbook collection.

$ 10.00 Retail price
$ 2.50 Postage and handling
Make check payable to Oliver County F.U Youth Group
ISBN 0-688-0700-0 / 0-9614367-1-9

EASTMAN FAMILY COOKBOOK

EASTMAN FAMILY COOKBOOK

c/o Thelma Eastman
Rt 2 Box 260
Winfield, KS 67156

The *Eastman Family Cookbook* was published to preserve the recipes the family enjoys. We have put together a nice variety of recipes, some old, some new, by Eastman ancestors and descendants. We feel sharing recipes promotes good home cooking. 172 pages. 525 recipes.

$ 7.50 Retail price
$ .44 Tax for Kansas residents
$ 2.50 Postage and handling
Make check payable to Thelma Eastman

EASY LIVIN' LOW-CALORIE MICROWAVE COOKING

by Karen Kangas Dwyer
1420 S. 126 Street
Omaha, NE 68144

Over 250 recipes from a former home economics teacher. Easy to prepare, convenient, and healthy food that tastes good. Low-calorie (under 250 calories each) and low-fat (plus low-salt options) such as Micro Stir-fry Vegetables, Blender Red Raspberry Cheesecake, Meatless Lasagna Rolls, etc.

$ 14.95 Retail price
$ .90 Tax for Nebraska residents
$ 3.50 Postage and handling
Make check payable to K. Dwyer
ISBN 0-312-03821-6

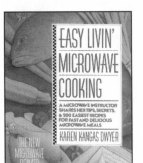

EASY LIVIN' MICROWAVE COOKING: THE NEW PRIMER

by Karen Kangas Dwyer
1420 S. 126 Street
Omaha, NE 68144

A home economist and microwave instructor shares her tips, secrets, and 200 easiest recipes for fast and delicious microwave meals. You'll find Meat Loaf for One or Two, Orange Roughy Amandine, Juicy Baked Chicken and Mushrooms, and Apple Crisp, just to name a few.

$ 11.00 Retail Price
$ .66 Tax for Nebraska residents
$ 3.50 Postage and handling
Make check payable to K. Dwyer
ISBN 0-312-02910-1

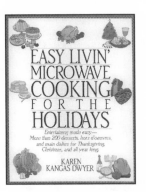

EASY LIVIN' MICROWAVE COOKING FOR THE HOLIDAYS

by Karen Kangas Dwyer
1420 S. 126 Street
Omaha, NE 68144

Over 200 recipes from a former home economics teacher. Easy to prepare, attractive, and delicious for any holiday, especially Christmas. Included are recipes such as English Toffee, Old Fashioned Peanut Brittle (9 minutes), Chocolate Almond Candy Pizza and Holiday-Glazed Ham.

$ 12.00 Retail price
$ .72 Tax for Nebraska residents
$ 3.50 Postage and handling
Make check payable to Karen Kangas Dwyer
ISBN 0-312-03480-6

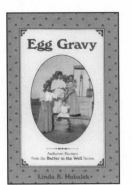

EGG GRAVY: AUTHENTIC RECIPES FROM THE BUTTER IN THE WELL SERIES

by Linda K. Hubalek/Butterfield Books, Inc.
P. O. Box 407   E-Mail: www.bookkansas.com
Lindsborg, KS 67456-0407   800-790-2665 / Fax 785-227-2017

This third volume in the Butter in the Well series offers a telling look at prairie life, when families depended on recipes for everything from salves to soaps, candles to cough syrup. Everyone who has ever treasured a family recipe will enjoy this collection of recipes and wisdom.

$ 9.95 Retail price
$ .83 Tax for Kansas residents
$ 3.00 Postage and handling .50 each add'l book
Make check payable to Book Kansas!
ISBN 1-886652-02-3

FAVORITE RECIPES OF RAINBOW VALLEY LUTHERAN CHURCH

Women of the ELCA
Rt. 2 Box 43
Alamo, ND 58830   701-528-4102 or 701-568-3844

This cookbook contains recipes from former to present members of our church. We are a small rural parish, mostly of Norwegian heritage. 174 pages; over 400 recipes.

$ 10.00 Retail price
$ 2.00 Postage and handling
Make check payable to R.V. Women of the ELCA

FEED MY LAMBS: SECOND HELPING

Central United Methodist Church
201 S. 5th Street
Milbank, SD 57252   605-432-4766 / Fax 605-432-6064

This sturdy three-ring binder cookbook has over 400 church supper tested recipes from mothers and daughters who consider "feeding my lambs" a serious calling. Also includes cooking tips, calorie counter, measurements, substitutions, microwave hints. Basic quantities for 25, 50, 100 people. Includes an herb and spice chart.

$ 9.00 Retail price
$ 3.00 Postage and handling
Make check payable to Love in Action SS Class

THE GIVE MOM A REST (SHE'S ON VACATION) COOKBOOK

by Rita Hewson
RR 1 Box 88A
Larned, KS 67550   316-285-2553

Do you need a vacation from cooking? This unique cookbook features quick and easy recipes that can be made at home or in a camper. Busy families and those just learning to cook will love how these recipes make life easier.

$ 7.95 Retail price
$ .47 Tax for Kansas residents
$ 2.00 Postage and handling
Make check payable to Mom's Publishing
ISBN 0-9659390-0-6

THE HAGEN FAMILY COOKBOOK

by Marilee Nelson
9790 107th Ave. NW
Noonan, ND 58765-9554   701-925-5795

This book has 120-pages with 400 tried-and-true family favorites. Including such Norwegian favorites as lefse, fattigmand, krumkake, rommegrot, etc. Also included are 24 pages of helpful hints, cooking tips, etc. This is not only a cookbook but a fun book to read!

$ 8.00 Retail price
$ 2.00 Postage and handling
Make check payable to Marilee Nelson

HALL'S POTATO HARVEST COOKBOOK

c/o Joann Hall Swenson
4865 Island View Drive
Mound, MN 55364   612-472-0765

Hall's Potato Harvest Cookbook includes 200 plus recipes compiled by the potato-growing Hall family from the Red River Valley of North Dakota. The cookbook is designed for people in today's fast-paced world who still want to be great cooks! You'll find the recipes to be creative, easy to prepare, healthful and time-tested by family members who know potatoes.

$ 8.00 Retail price
$ 2.00 Postage and handling
Make check payable to Hall's Potato Harvest Cookbook
ISBN 0-9639369-0-5

HEART OF THE HOME RECIPES

Ogden Publications, Inc.
Capper Press
1503 S.W. 42nd Street   E-Mail: lauriec@cjnetworks.com
Topeka, KS 66609   800-678-4883 / Fax 785-274-4305

Midwest classics that feature more than 300 practical, family-tested recipes each from the "Heart of the Home" section in Capper's– some from the '70s, '60s, '50s, the days of World War II rationing and back through the Great Depression.

$ 6.95 Retail price   MC, Visa, Discover accepted
$ .42 Tax for Kansas residents
$ 2.00 Postage and handling
Make check payable to Capper's Book Service
ISBN 0-941678-01-6

HEAVENLY DELIGHTS

Sacred Heart Altar Society
Rt. 1 Box 117
Nelson, NE 68961   402-225-4292

Heavenly Delights is a collection of 550 favorite recipes for all age groups, from our children to our grandparents with their Bohemian and German ancestry. If you enjoy home cooking, you'll enjoy this cookbook from our small rural community in south central Nebraska.

$ 8.00 Retail price
$ 2.00 Postage and handling
Make check payable to Sacred Heart Altar Society

HEAVENLY RECIPES

Milnor Lutheran Church WELCA
P. O. Box 355
Milnor, ND 58060   701-427-9301

Heavenly Recipes contains heavenly bodies as well as heavenly recipes. There are 248 pages with 631 unique and valuable recipes along with many of the familiar favorites.

$ 7.00 Retail price
$ 2.00 Postage and handling
Make check payable to Milnor WELCA

HOME AT THE RANGE
VOLUME I

Chapter EX. P E. O.
℅ Alberta Aherns
315 Cherry Avenue
Oakley, KS 67748   913-672-3754 or 672-4456

First of four great cookbooks from rural western Kansas. These recipes have been well established by friends, relatives, church groups, and the most critical group—husbands and family. 220 pages, 644 recipes.

$ 12.00 Retail price (3 or more books $10.00 each plus $5.00 postage)
$ 3.50 Postage and handling
Make check payable to Chapter EX. P. E. O.

HOME AT THE RANGE
VOLUME II

Chapter EX. P E. O.
℅ Alberta Aherns
315 Cherry Avenue
Oakley, KS 67748   913-672-3754 or 672-4456

Second of four great cookbooks from rural western Kansas. Includes Farm Style Biscuits, Cherry Pineapple Dessert, Frosted Banana Cookies, and more delicious favorites. 194 pages, 525 recipes.

$ 12.00 Retail price (3 or more books $10.00 each plus $5.00 postage)
$ 3.50 Postage and handling
Make check payable to Chapter EX. P. E. O.

HOME AT THE RANGE
VOLUME III

Chapter EX. P E. O.
℅ Alberta Aherns
315 Cherry Avenue
Oakley, KS 67748   913-672-3754 or 672-4456

Third of four great cookbooks from rural western Kansas. Includes Tiny Christmas Cheese Cakes, Pumpkin Brread, Italian Beef, Monkey Bread, and oodles of other favorite recipes. 252 pages, 644 recipes.

$ 12.00 Retail price (3 or more books $10.00 each plus $5.00 postage)
$ 3.50 Postage and handling
Make check payable to Chapter EX. P. E. O.

HOME AT THE RANGE
VOLUMES IV

Chapter EX. P E. O.
℅ Alberta Aherns
315 Cherry Avenue
Oakley, KS 67748   913-672-3754 or 672-4456

Latest in the series of four great cookbooks from rural western Kansas. Includes Night Before Coffee Cake, Cheesy Hot French Bread, Snow White Chocolate Fudge, and more from great Kansas cooks. 294 pages, 851 recipes.

$ 12.00 Retail price (3 or more books $10.00 each plus $5.00 postage)
$ 3.50 Postage and handling
Make check payable to Chapter EX. P. E. O.

HOMEMADE MEMORIES

by Dorothy Schraedler
RR 2 Box 8267
Timken, KS 67575   785-355-2391 / Fax 785-355-2290

This book was compiled with one purpose—to preserve old family recipes and favorites of the author's family. Most of the 116 pages have recipes that are simple, with ingredients found in most kitchens.

$ 4.50 Retail price
$ .25 Tax for Kansas residents
$ 1.50 Postage and handling
Make check payable to Dorothy Schraeder

IF IT TASTES GOOD, WHO CARES? I

by Pam Girard/Spiritseekers Publishing
217 East Owens   E-Mail: ScottG@Btigate.com
Bismarck, ND 58501   701-255-3114 / Fax 701-255-3129

Pam Girard's first cookbook is a compilation of recipes tested by students in her classes on quick and easy cooking. It includes not only her students' and friends' favorites, but also ideas on How to Save Time in the Kitchen, Recipes that Freeze, and Family Lore.

$ 12.95 Retail price
$ .80 Tax for North Dakota residents
$ 2.00 Postage and handling
Make check payable to Pam Girard
ISBN 0-9630419-32

IF IT TASTES GOOD, WHO CARES? II

by Pam Girard/Spiritseekers Publishing
217 East Owens   E-Mail: ScottG@Btigate.com
Bismarck, ND 58501   701-255-3114 / Fax 701-255-3129

This sequel to Pam Girard's first cookbook includes more favorites tested in her classes on easy cooking. They are practical, easy to make and use readily available ingredients. Also included are simplified versions of recipes collected during her travels around the world.

$ 12.95 Retail price
$ .80 Tax for North Dakota residents
$ 2.00 Postage and handling
Make check payable to Pam Girard
ISBN 0-9630419-40

I LOVE RECIPES

Kay J. Andera
P. O. Box 286   E-Mail: lealaw@easnet.net
Chamberlain, SD 57325   605-734-6737 / Fax 605-734-6882

I Love Recipes is a cookbook that has been printed and re-printed to share over 400 recipes from family and friends from the heart of South Dakota. Spiral bound; 259 pages; great for "Bear" collectors, too.

$ 12.00 Retail price   MC/Visa accepted
$ .72 Tax for South Dakota residents
Make check payable to *I Love Recipes*

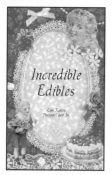

INCREDIBLE EDIBLES

Lake Region Heritage Corporation, Inc.
P. O. Box 245
Devils Lake, ND 58301-0245

E-Mail: jschiele@stellarnet.com
701-662-3701 / Fax 701-662-2810

Over 150 pages crammed with some fantastic mid-west food fixin's. Separate sections encompass all categories including this & that! Decorated throughout in a Victorian style, this cookbook, featuring some heirloom recipes, is a feast for the eye as well as the palate.

$ 10.00 Retail price
$ .65 Tax for North Dakota residents
$ 2.50 Postage and handling
Make check payable to Lake Region Heritage Center, Inc. or LRHC

IN THE KITCHEN WITH KATE

Ogden Publications, Inc.
Capper Press
1503 S.W. 42nd Street
Topeka, KS 66609

E-Mail: lauriec@cjnetworks.com
800-678-4883 / Fax 785-274-4305

The newest "Heart of the Home" cookbook includes recipes for breads, savory main dishes, desserts, cakes and cookies that please! Inspiring culinary poems, helpful charts and space for your own special cook's notes.

$ 6.95 Retail price   MC, Visa, Discover accepted
$ .42 Tax for Kansas residents
$ 2.00 Postage and handling
Make check payable to Capper's Book Service
ISBN 0-941678-49-0

IOLA'S GOURMET RECIPES IN RHAPSODY

by Iola Egle
1610 Centennial Drive
McCook, NE 69001

308-345-3303

Gourmet Recipes in Rhapsody are favorite party and holiday celebration recipes plus a chapter on choice popcorn recipes that have won awards. Hardcover ringbound.

$ 11.95 Retail price
$ 2.00 Postage and handling

THE JOY OF SHARING

Scottsbluff Cosmopolitans
2414 Avenue G
Scottsbluff, NE 69361

308-632-3192

Our cookbook is filled with 300 delicious recipes from members of the community, friends, family and Scottsbluff Cosmopolitans. Our cookbook also includes a diabetic section.

$ 7.50 Retail price
$ .49 Tax for Nebraska residents
$ 2.00 Postage and handling
Make check payable to Scottsbluff Cosmopolitans

THE KANSAS CITY BARBEQUE SOCIETY COOKBOOK

11514 Hickman Mills Drive
Kansas City, MO 64134

E-Mail: 75457.312@compuserve.com
800-963-5227 / Fax 816-765-5860

This 224-page, hardcover (concealed wire binding) book has not only recipes, but getting started, resource guide, nutritional analysis from the members of the world's largest organization of barbecue and grilling enthusiasts. A national award winner—Tabasco Community Cookbook Awards.

$ 19.95 Retail price   MC/Visa/Amex accepted
$ 4.00 Postage and handling
Make check payable to Kansas City Barbeque Society
ISBN 0-9649176-0-2

THE KEARNEY 125th ANNIVERSARY COMMUNITY COOKBOOK

Cookbooks by Morris Press
3212 E Hwy 30
Kearney, NE 68847

800-445-6621 / 308-236-6710

Over 550 favorite recipes, memories and anecdotes from past and present citizens fill the pages of this special keepsake cookbook honoring Kearney, Nebraska's 125th birthday. With seven traditional recipe categories, several pictures of local historical landmarks and a special history section, this book is sure to please your palate and warm your heart!

$ 10.95 Retail price   MC and Visa accepted
$ 2.00 Postage and handling
Make check payable to Cookbooks by Morris Press

KELVIN HOMEMAKERS 50th ANNIVERSARY COOKBOOK

c/o Lola Knox
RR 1 Box 27
Dunseith, ND 58329

701-263-4308

Our club members are all farm wives, living in the beautiful Turtle Mountains of North Dakota. We want to serve good nutritious meals that can be prepared as quickly as possible. Our 86-page cookbook contains approximately 328 of the best basic down-home recipes ever compiled.

$ 6.00 Retail price
$ .30 Tax for North Dakota residents
$ 1.70 Postage and handling
Make check payable to Kelvin Homemakers

LAKOTA LUTHERAN CHURCH CENTENNIAL COOKBOOK

c/o Maxine Holm
P. O. Box 562
Lakota, ND 58344-0562

701-247-2716

Our book contains 746 tasty recipes and 269 pages. Some recipes are old standbys and others are new, using current products. Our pride in our heritage can be found in the pages of the Ethnic Section, featuring flatbread and lefse. The Scandinavian artwork was created by one of our members.

$ 10.00 Retail price
$ 3.00 Postage and handling
Make check payable to L.L.C. Centennial Fund

LICENSE TO COOK KANSAS STYLE

Penfield Press
215 Brown Street
Iowa City, IA 52245-5842   800-728-9998

License to Cook Kansas Style features delicious recipes using flour since wheat is the major crop of Kansas. Focus is on the Swedish immigrant women who homesteaded across Kansas, as well as modern recipes for the on-the-go cook. 3 ½ x 5 ½, 160 pages, a little jewel.

$ 6.95 Retail price including postage (2 for $12; 3 for $18)
$ .42 Tax for Kansas residents
Make check payable to Penfield Press
ISBN 0-941016-96-X

MEASURE FOR PLEASURE

Bethany College Auxiliary
P. O. Box 215
Lindsborg, KS 67456-0215   785-227-2302 / Fax 785-227-3740

From the town that has been described as being "more Swedish than Stockholm" and Bethany College come recipes reflecting that Swedish heritage. Festivals such as Svensk Hyllningsfest, Messiah Festival, Millfest, Midsummers' Day Festival, Broadway R.F.D, Heritage Christmas and Lucia Festival highlight the many foods represented in the 308-page spiral-bound, illustrated book.

$ 11.50 Retail price
$ 2.50 Postage and handling
Make check payable to Bethany College Auxiliary

MORE HEART OF THE HOME RECIPES

Odgen Publications, Inc.
Capper Press
1503 S.W. 42nd Street   E-Mail: lauriec@cjnetworks.com
Topeka, KS 66609   800-678-4883 / Fax 785-274-4305

More of those wonderful recipes from years past, reflecting World War II days as well as the Great Depression. All recipes are practical and family tested. Sure to be a favorite.

$ 6.95 Retail price   MC, Visa, Discover accepted
$ .42 Tax for Kansas residents
$ 2.00 Postage and handling
Make check payable to Capper's Book Service
ISBN 0-941678-04-0

THE MORMON TRAIL COOKBOOK

Cookbooks by Morris Press
3212 E Hwy 30
Kearney, NE 68847   800-445-6621 / 308-236-6710

This historical cookbook highlights the endeavors, struggles and cooking traditions of the Mormon pioneers as they made the journey from Illinois to the Salt Lake Valley of Utah. Filled with 367 old-fashioned and modern recipes and a historical account of the trail, *The Mormon Trail Cookbook* is an excellent keepsake for cooks and history enthusiasts alike.

$ 10.95 Retail price
$ 2.00 Postage and handling
Make check payable to Cookbooks by Morris Press
ISBN 1-57502-476-4

90th ANNIVERSARY TRINITY LUTHERAN CHURCH COOKBOOK

Trinity Ladies Fellowship
c/o LaVina Juergensen
2215 Tyler Street
Great Bend, KS 67530   316-793-5707

This cookbook is a collection of tried-and-true recipes handed down through family and friends, compiled by members of Trinity Lutheran Church. There are 178 pages of recipes divided into 8 categories plus many pages of helpful hints and information.

$ 5.00 Retail price
$ 2.00 Postage and handling
Make check payable to Trinity Ladies Fellowship

NORMAN LUTHERAN CHURCH 125th ANNIVERSARY COOKBOOK

Norman Lutheran Church WELCA
Box 96
Kindred, ND 58051   701-428-3225

This 200-page cookbook has 500 favorite recipes of past and present congregation members. The color cover picture reflects the beautiful setting among the tall oaks on the banks of the Sheyenne River, which has been home to this congregation for 125 years. Norman Lutheran Church is the oldest existing Lutheran Church in the state of North Dakota, and has produced 125 years of outstanding cooks.

$ 8.00 Retail price
$ 2.00 Postage and handling
Make check payable to Norman WELCA

NORTH DAKOTA AMERICAN MOTHERS, INC. COOKBOOK

North Dakota American Mothers
c/o Maybelle Opland
5315 170th St. SW
Des Lacs, ND 58733

Recipes were submitted by North Dakota Mothers of the Year, Merit Mothers and family members. These are their favorites and the ingredients may be found in any supermarket. An excellent addition to your cookbook collection.

$ 10.00 Retail price
$ 3.00 Postage and handling
Make check payable to North Dakota American Mothers, Inc.

NORTH DAKOTA...WHERE FOOD IS LOVE

by Marcella Richman
P. O. Box 107   E-Mail: MarceWhRdg@aol.com
Tower City, ND 58071   701-749-2687

A great gift for anyone who loves to cook. 450 tasty recipes from common ingredients, spiral-bound to lie flat. 200 pages. An essay explaining why "Food is Love" in North Dakota.

$ 10.95 Retail price
$ .55 Tax for North Dakota residents
$ 2.00 Postage and handling
Make check payable to North Dakota Cookbook
ISBN 0-9642215-00

125 YEARS OF COOKIN' WITH THE LORD

Trinity Lutheran Church (ELCA)
731 SW Buchanan Street
Topeka, KS 66606-1426   785-233-0767

In celebration of Trinity's 125th anniversary, our youth compiled
the flavors of our Midwestern and Scandinavian heritage. The
attractive glossy hardcover cookbook has over 390 recipes, old
time favorites, heart-healthy and diabetic friendly. The proceeds
from this cookbook help support the youth ministry in our central
city church.

$ 7.00 Retail price
$ 2.00 Postage and handling
Make check payable to Trinity Lutheran Church: Hi-Times

THE OREGON TRAIL COOKBOOK

Cookbooks by Morris Press
3212 E Hwy 30
Kearney, NE 68847   800-445-6621 / 308-236-6710

The Oregon Trail Cookbook lets readers celebrate the traditions of the
people who settled the West. This 220-page cookbook includes 372
authentic and updated recipes, an extensive Oregon Trail history
section and excerpts from the diaries of those who forged the trail.
A perfect gift, *The Oregon Trail Cookbook* will be used, read and
treasured for years to come.

$ 10.95 Retail price   MC and Visa accepted
$ 2.00 Postage and handling
Make check payable to Cookbooks by Morris Press
ISBN 0-9631249-3-5

OUR DAILY BREAD

Our Class
c/o Pat Fellers
Box 698
Ashland, KS 67831   316-635-4448

A collection of over 800 recipes (257 pages) from the best cooks in
the 115-year history of the Ashland United Methodist Church in
this community. The hard cover features a special stained glass
window of the church, and the dividers for food sections feature
the various churches that now comprise the Ashland United Methodist Church. The three-ring binder offers easy use.

$ 13.00 Retail price
$ 3.00 Postage and handling
Make check payable to OUR Class

OUR HERITAGE: A COLLECTION FROM RUTLAND, NORTH DAKOTA

Rutland Community Club
P. O. Box 67   E-Mail: Kathybrakke@hotmail.com
Rutland, ND 58067   701-724-3467

A North Dakota centennial cookbook, consisting of 230 ring-bound
pages with many pioneer and ethnic recipes from the area. Includes pioneer pictures, remedies, and some descriptions of the
recipe origins. Very attractive in antique brown-tone printing.

$ 10.00 Retail price
$ .50 Tax for North Dakota residents
$ 3.00 Postage and handling
Make check payable to Rutland Community Club

PIONEER DAUGHTERS OF TOWNER COOKBOOK

Pioneer Daughters of Towner
c/o Harriet Evensvold
P. O. Box 5
Towner, ND 58788-0005   701-537-5785

Our cookbook is unique as it is a tribute to the pioneers who settled in the part of the territory (prior to statehood on 11/2/1889) now known as the state of North Dakota. Blue 3-ring vinyl cover folds back to stand for easy reading and kitchen use.

$ 12.00 Retail price
$ .60 Tax for North Dakota residents
$ 3.00 Postage and handling
Make check payable to Pioneer Daughters of Towner

PRESENTATIONS... A COLLECTION OF CULINARY FAVORITES

Friends of Lied, Lied Center for Performing Arts
P. O. Box 880151   E-Mail: gmcnair@unlinfo.unl.edu
Lincoln, NE 68588-0151   402-472-4712 / Fax 402-472-4730

Presentations... is a cookbook to turn to for encore culinary performances. Proceeds from this creative compilation benefit the programs and performances of the University of Nebraska—Lincoln's Lied Center for Performing Arts. This book features more than 325 twice-tested recipes, imaginative party menus designed to share the tastes of our Nebraska home.

$ 19.95 Retail price   MC and VISA accepted
$ 4.95 Postage and handling
Make check payable to Friends of Lied
ISBN 0-9636502-0-3

PUMPKIN, WINTER SQUASH AND CARROT COOKBOOK

Community Cookbooks/Jane Winge, Editor
P.O. Box 11
Litchville, ND 58461   701-762-3642

Glowing orange pumpkins, winter squash and carrots are worth their weight in gold . . . in both nutrition and good taste. Here's a treasure chest of 500 ways to use these versatile vegetables. Desserts and pies, main courses and soups, salads and veggies, pickles and preserves and low-cal/low-cholesterol. Tasting bee tested.

$ 9.95 Retail price
$ .55 Tax for North Dakota residents
$ 2.05 Postage and handling
Make check payable to Community Cookbooks
ISBN 0-9632860-1-3

PURE PRAIRIE

by Judith Fertig
Pig Out Publications
4245 Walnut   E-Mail: kadler@unicom.net
Kansas City, MO 64111   816-531-3119 / Fax 816-531-6113

Delicious home-style cooking with a 90's twist. The author shares stories in side-bars, too. 144 pages, 7x9 paperback.

$ 15.95 Retail price   MC and Visa accepted
$ 3.00 Postage and handling
Make check payable to Pig Out Publications
ISBN 1-878686-16-X

QUE QUEENS: EASY GRILLING AND SIMPLE SMOKING

by Karen Adler and Judith Fertig
Pig Out Publications
4245 Walnut   E-Mail: kadler@unicom.net
Kansas City, MO 64111   816-531-3119 / Fax 816-531-6113

Upscale collection of grilled and smoked fare in menu format. Lots of vegetable recipes for on the grill, too. 96 pages, 7x8½ paperback.

$ $9.95 Retail price
$ 3.00 Postage and handling
Make check payable to Pig Out Publications / Visa and MC accepted
ISBN 0-925175-26-9

RAINBOW'S ROUNDUP OF RECIPES

Rainbow Bible Ranch
14676 Lonetree   E-Mail: lonetree@rapidnet.com
Sturgis, SD 57785-8995   605-923-2367

Rainbow's Roundup of Recipes is a collection of recipes from fine cooks that have been associated with the ranch over the past 15 years. Rainbow Bible Ranch is a unique Christian camping experience for youths (ages 6-18), as it is located on a real working ranch in Western South Dakota.

$ 7.00 Retail price
$ .28 Tax for South Dakota residents
$ 2.00 Postage and handling
Make check payable to Rainbow Bible Ranch

READERS' FAVORITE RECIPES

Odgen Publications, Inc.
Capper Press
1503 S.W. 42nd Street   E-Mail: lauriec@cjnetworks.com
Topeka, KS 66609   800-678-4883 / Fax 785-274-4305

You'll find helpful tips, useful charts and space for your own special cook's notes. With its wide variety of dishes—from quick-and-easy to elegant—it offers eleven chapters with more than 330 recipes.

$ 6.95 Retail price   MC, Visa, Discover accepted
$ .42 Tax for Kansas residents
$ 2.00 Postage and handling
Make check payable to Grit Book Service
ISBN 0-941678-48-2

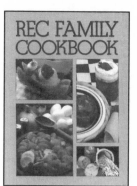

REC FAMILY COOKBOOK

North Dakota REC/RTC Magazine
REC Family Cookbook (BOB)
P. O. Box 727
Mandan, ND 58554

This 302-page, 6x9-inch book contains more than 450 kitchen-tested recipes, reprinted from the North Dakota REC/RTC Magazine. This attractive, top-quality book includes a hard, spiral-bound cover; tabbed divider pages; nutrient analysis of most recipes; photos of many foods in the book, and a thorough index.

$ 9.95 Retail price
$ .72 Tax for North Dakota residents
$ 2.00 Postage and handling
Make check payable to NDAREC

RECIPES & REMEMBRANCES

Buffalo Lake Lutheran Church WMF
44778 125th Street
Eden, SD 57232-6216
605-698-7843

This inspired cookbook commemorates the centennial of a small, rural South Dakota church by members past and present. Selections are diverse, eclectic, and personal, from old Norwegian delicacies to French farmhouse chicken. Over 300 recipes are included in the beautiful padded three-ring binder, plus stories of by-gone days.

$ 12.00 Retail price
$ 3.00 Postage and handling
Make check payable to Buffalo Lake WMF

RECIPES & REMEMBRANCES

Covenant Women of Courtland Kansas
P. O. Box 20
Courtland, KS 66939   785-374-4227 / Fax 785-374-4256

Recipes & Remembrances was compiled by the Covenant Women of Courtland, Kansas. The recipes are from members and friends. The secrets of many kitchens are here for you to enjoy. The book contains 158 pages with over 400 recipes.

$ 10.00 Retail price
$ .60 Tax for Kansas residents
$ 2.00 Postage and handling
Make check payable to Courtland Covenant Women

RECIPES FROM THE HEART

Epsilon Omega Sorority
c/o Sandra Sanders
9143 Road 56
Dalton, NE 69131   308-377-2231

The members of Epsilon Omega Chapter of Beta Sigma Phi have published some of our favorite recipes which have been very well tested and are truly recipes from our heart. With the proceeds from this book, we plan to continue to give back to our community all that it has given us.

$ 8.50 Retail price
$ .43 Tax for Nebraska residents
$ 2.50 Postage and handling
Make check payable to Epsilon Omega Sorority

RECIPES FROM THE HEART: 100 YEARS OF RECIPES AND FOLKLORE

by Pattie Sanders
3108 10th Street
Great Bend, KS 67530   316-792-4403

Recipes from as far back as 100 years are interspersed with folklore for your enjoyment. For more than 10 years Pattie gathered these recipes to share with others. Most recipes are economical as well as fast and easy.

$ 14.95 Retail price
$ .88 Tax for Kansas residents
$ 2.00 Postage and handling
Make check payable to Pattie Sanders

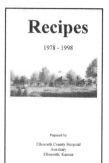

RECIPES: 1978 - 1998

Ellsworth County Hospital Auxiliary c/o Diane O'Connor
305 East 10th Street
Ellsworth, KS 67439
E-Mail: dmoc@ellsworth.net
785-472-5481

Includes 20 years of favorite recipes from the best cooks in Ellsworth County. This easy-to-use 216-page book features larger than usual type, all recipes complete on one page, and generous white space for documenting personal modifications. Proceeds from cookbook sales are used to support the needs of Ellsworth County Hospital.

$ 10.00 Retail price
$ 1.50 Postage and handling
Make check payable to Ellsworth County Hospital Auxiliary

RECIPES WORTH SHARING

by Janet Majure
Breadbasket Publishing Co.
Lawrence, KS 66044
E-Mail: bbasket@sunflower.com
785-749-0949 / Fax 785-841-0969

Recipes Worth Sharing assembles a rich collection of the best recipes that cooks have shared across five years in *The Kansas City Star's* popular "Come Into My Kitchen" column. Author Janet Majure, who wrote the weekly food column, includes 194 tried-and-true recipes, comments from contributors and detailed instructions.

$ 14.95 Retail price
$ 1.03 Tax for Kansas residents
$ 3.00 Postage and handling
Make check payable to Breadbasket Publishing
ISBN 0-9656695-0-5

RED RIVER VALLEY POTATO GROWERS AUXILIARY COOKBOOK

R.R.V.P.G. Auxiliary
P.O. Box 301
East Grand Forks, MN 56721

We are so proud of our all-potato cookbook with good down-home cooking recipes from our area farm women and auxiliary. You won't believe all the ways you can prepare potatoes. Our book has 300 pages of recipes and helpful hints. The book has a washable cover that doubles as an easel for easy reading.

$ 10.00 Retail price
$ 2.00 Postage and handling
Make check payable to RRVPG Auxiliary

REGENT ALUMNI ASSOCIATION COOKBOOK

Regent Alumni Association
P. O. Box 192
Regent, ND 58650
E-Mail: cherberh@regent.ctctel
701-563-4321

The *Regent Alumni Association Cookbook* is indexed and contains over 800 recipes. The recipes in this 300-page cookbook were contributed by Regent Public School Alumni. These recipes all contain ingredients most people would have on hand. It has a section on household hints.

$ 10.00 Retail price
$ 1.75 Postage and handling
Make check payable to Regent Alumni Association

RITZY RHUBARB SECRETS COOKBOOK

Community Cookbooks/Jane Winge, Editor
P. O. Box 11
Litchville, ND 58461   701-762-3642

How many rhubarb recipes? 214! You're kidding! And each was tasting bee tested? Yes! Cooks are rediscovering the tart, delicious possibilities of rhubarb . . . from muffins and punch to chutney and ice cream. Pies and sauces? Of course! Just imagine, you'll have all your favorite recipes in one place!

$ 9.95 Retail price
$ .55 Tax for North Dakota residents
$ 2.05 Postage and handling
Make check payable to Community Cookbooks
ISBN 0-9632860-0-5

SAVOR THE INNS OF KANSAS

Recipes from Kansas Bed & Breakfasts Cookbook and Directory
Winters Publishing
P. O. Box 501
Greensburg, IN 47240   800-457-3230 / Fax 812-663-4948

A 112-page cookbook and directory with complete information about member inns of Kansas B & B Association. Includes breakfast recipes and a variety of other tasty treats, from Cherry-Almond Coffee Cake to Homemade Vegetable Soup, Mexican Crazy Crust to Lemon Squares. You will enjoy many tried-and-true favorites.

$ 9.95 Retail price   MC and Visa accepted
$ 2.00 Postage and handling
Make check payable to Winters Publishing
ISBN 0-9625329-9-1

SHARING GOD'S BOUNTY

Recipes from the Tri-Parish
First Lutheran Church c/o Geri Carlson
1254 22nd Road
Clay Center, KS 67432   785-632-2087

Recipes from the tri-parish churches, including First Lutheran in Clay Center, St Paul's in Linn, and Zion Lutheran near Clyde, Kansas make up this unique collection. Some of these recipes are from a cookbook published in 1912 by women of First Lutheran. Many ethnic recipes of Swedish origin are included.

$ 10.00 Retail price
$ 3.00 Postage and handling
Make check payable to First Lutheran Church

SHARING OUR "BEARY" BEST VOLUME II

Teddy Bear Day Care
40502 125th Street
Groton, SD 57445   605-397-8646

The cookbook was created as a fund-raiser for our center. Children and staff were invited to share favorite recipes from home, so they are almost all "kid-tested" and easy. Our cookbook includes approximately 400 recipes on 122 pages, plus cooking hints and guides.

$ 8.00 Retail price
$ 1.50 Postage and handling
Make check payable to Kim Weber

SILVER CELEBRATION COOKBOOK

Peace Lutheran Church
716 N. Plum Street
Newton, KS 67114   316-283-4754

Often as members of Peace Lutheran Church gather to do Our
Lord's work, our activities center around a meal. Our 186-page,
over 300-recipe cookbook is a collection of some of our favorite
recipes. Funds raised through the sale of books will be used to
further our work in God's Kingdom.

$ 8.50 Retail price
$ 2.00 Postage and handling
Make check payable to WELCA

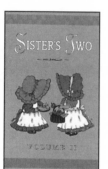

SISTER'S TWO: VOLUME II

by Nancy Barth and Sue Hergert
RR 1 Box 240
Ashland, KS 67831   580-735-2685

Sisters Two Volume II was created by two sisters who wanted to
preserve and share their families' favorite recipes. This volume
has 362 pages, 1026 recipes and lots of helpful hints. Over 90
relatives and friends contributed their favorite recipes to make this
a wonderful cookbook to have.

$ 16.00 Retail price
$ .96 Tax for Kansas residents
$ 3.00 Postage and handling
Make check payable to Sister's Two

SOUTH DAKOTA SUNRISE—A COLLECTION OF BREAKFAST RECIPES

Bed & Breakfast Innkeepers of South Dakota
Winters Publishing
P. O. Box 501
Greensburg, IN 47240   800-457-3230 / Fax 812-663-4948

This sensational 96-page cookbook features many tempting recipes. With everything from Dakota Omelet to Pumpkin Waffles,
Bunkhouse Biscuits to Skillet Breakfast Casserole, some of the
finest B&B's in the state have included recipes for their favorite
dishes. Complete inn listings to help plan your stay.

$ 10.95 Retail price   MC and Visa accepted
$ 2.00 Postage and handling
Make check payable to Winters Publishing
ISBN 1-883651-08-5

ST. JOSEPH'S TABLE

St. Joseph's Catholic Church
844 5th Street
Spearfish, SD 57783   605-642-2306 / Fax 605-642-1024

A collection of recipes by St. Joseph's Catholic Church consisting
of 150 pages and approximately 500 recipes. This cookbook contains quick and easy recipes submitted by our parishioners from
low-fat and delicious to sinfully fattening and delicious.

$ 8.00 Retail price
$ 2.00 Postage and handling
Make check payable to St. Joseph's Catholic Church

TASTE OF COFFEYVILLE

Coffeyville Cultural Arts Council, Inc.
P. O. Box 487
Coffeyville, KS 67337

E-Mail: khbccac@horizon.hit
316-251-0088

The book is dedicated to the many good cooks who contributed approximately 800 recipes. Some recipes are new and some are treasured family keepsakes enjoyed many times by those who have handed them down through their children. The cookbook also contains historical facts and pictures about Coffeyville.

$ 14.95 Retail price
$ 3.00 Postage and handling
Make check payable to Coffeyville Cultural Arts Council, Inc.

TASTE THE GOOD LIFE! NEBRASKA COOKBOOK

Cookbooks by Morris Press
3212 E Hwy 30
Kearney, NE 68847

800-445-6621 / 308-236-6710

Taste the Good Life is filled with 365 praise-worthy recipes from the heart of the Midwest. It's all here, from Honey Mustard Glazed Steaks to wild game dishes. A special section includes old-fashioned recipes, dating back over 100 years. Experience the serene beauty of Nebraska through the artwork included in this unique cookbook!

$ 10.95 Retail price   MC and Visa accepted
$ 2.00 Postage and handling
Make check payable to Cookbooks by Morris Press
ISBN 0-9631249-0-0

A TASTE OF PRAIRIE LIFE

by Loaun Werner Vaad
104 S. Main
Chamberlain, SD 57325

605-734-5135

An eye-catching comb bound book with full color cover featuring the pasque flower. The 224-page book features recipes, remedies and reminiscings of the people of the northern plains.

$ 12.95 Retail price   Visa, MC, AmEx accepted
$ .78 Tax for South Dakota residents
$ 2.50 Postage and handling
Make check payable to Buffalo Grass Trading Co.
ISBN 0-9652586-3-7

TO TAYLA WITH TLC

RCRH Medical Imaging Department
P. O. Box 6000
Attn: Cardiac Cath Lab
Rapid City, SD 57701

605-341-8996 / Fax 605-341-8983

This cookbook was created by staff of the Medical Imaging Department of Rapid City Regional Hospital to benefit Tayla Peterson, infant daughter of Kristin, our co-worker. At three months of age, Tayla underwent a liver transplant. The book contains 350 favorite family recipes and includes a special children's section. 190 pages.

$ 10.00 Retail price
$ .60 Tax for South Dakota residents
$ 1.00 Postage and handling
Make check payable to Tayla Peterson Fund

TREASURES OF THE GREAT MIDWEST

Junior League of Wyandotte & Johnson Counties
P. O. Box 17-1487
Kansas City, KS 66117-0487   913-371-2303

A collection of over 250 exquisite recipes for home cooking from some of the finest kitchens in the Midwest. This elegant collection introduces each of the twelve chapters with a full-color photograph and narration to accompany the lead recipe. From Grandma's favorites to modern gourmet fare, you will find recipes perfect for every occasion. 248 pages, 9x12 hardbound.

$ 24.95 Retail price
$ 1.72 Tax for Kansas residents
$ 2.50 Postage and handling
Make check payable to Junior League of Wyandotte & Johnson Counties
ISBN 0-9606412-1-1

TRIED & TRUE II

Spring Creek WELCA c/o Karen Freed
HC 2 Box 72
Watford City, ND 58854   701-842-2265

Tried & True II contains 300 recipes that are a combination of family and potluck favorites and best recipes from the original *Tried & True*. It's a collection from membership of Spring Creek Lutheran who worship in an "underground" church building that is rooted in a prairie hilltop in western North Dakota.

$ 6.00 Retail price
$ 2.50 Postage and handling
Make check payable to Spring Creek WELCA

WE LOVE COUNTRY COOKIN':
MAR-DON'S FAMILY FAVORITES

by Marlene Grager and Donna Young
171 54th Avenue SE
Sykeston, ND 58486   701-984-2413

Mar-Don's Family Favorites is the result of two North Dakota farm wives' dream to share the recipes that have been family favorites. In addition to the common categories, special sections include: Crockpot; Kid's Kookin; Old Favorites; Norwegian and German Specialties. 198 pages with over 600 recipes for good ole country cookin', with most ingredients found in your kitchen.

$ 10.00 Retail price
$ .50 Tax for North Dakota residents
$ 1.75 Postage and handling
Make check payable to Mar-Don's Country Catering

WHOLE WHEAT COOKERY:
TREASURES FROM THE WHEAT BIN

by Howard and Anna Ruth Beck
HowAnn Enterprises
205 South Weavery
Hesston, KS 67062   316-327-4530

To add value to our wheat crop, we made and delivered stone ground flour, cracked wheat cereal, and KWIK Mix (the whole wheat all-purpose mix) to grocery stores. To educate people in the use of wheat in their diets, we published *Whole Wheat Cookery*. The cookbook includes over 300 recipes.

$ 12.95 Retail price
$ .76 Tax for Kansas residents
Make check payable to HowAnn Enterprises
ISBN 0-9617875-0-3

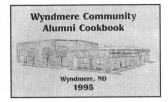

Wyndmere Community
Alumni Cookbook

Wyndmere, ND
1995

WYNDMERE COMMUNITY ALUMNI COOKBOOK

Wyndmere Community Center
P. O. Box 188
Wyndmere, ND 58081

A wide variety of recipes from young and old. 600+ recipes; 270 pages; 12 sections; index in each section. Recipes include quick and easy ideas plus many of Grandma's favorites. Pictures of community throughout book. Laminated cover, spiral binding. A fun book!

$ 10.00 Retail price
$ 3.50 Postage and handling
Make check payable to Wyndmere Community Center

Y COOK?

YWCA Fargo-Moorhead
3100 12th Avenue N
Fargo, ND 58102   701-232-2547/Fax 701-232-2590

Proceeds from the sale of *Y Cook?* go to the YWCS Endowment Fund which helps women to overcome the obstacles of poverty, family violence and discrimination in order to cope with the challenge of our world. The recipes are all favorites. 160 pages.

$ 5.00 Retail price
$ 3.00 Postage and handling
Make check payable to YWCA-FM
ISBN 0-87197-401-0

Y WINNERS: COOKBOOK OF CHAMPIONS

Fargo/Moorhead Family YMCA
c/o Merrie Sue Holtan
16 N. Terrace   E-Mail: MSHoltan@Gloria.cord.edu
Fargo, ND 58102   701-232-2528 / Fax 218-299-4256

The *Cookbook of Champions* has 180 pages divided into an athlete's seasons—Training Diet, Pre-event, Post-event and Off Season. Written for athletes and all concerned about nutrition, the book includes motivational sayings and nutritional tips for peak performance.

$ 10.00 Retail price
$ .06 Tax for North Dakota residents
$ 2.50 Postage and handling
Make check payable to FMY Gator Swim Team
ISBN 0-911007-34-2

YEARS AND YEARS OF GOODWILL COOKING

Goodwill Circle of New Hope Lutheran Church
7732 7th Avenue N
Upham, ND 58789-9481   701-768-2522

Years and Years of Goodwill Cooking reflects both the basic cooking of this Scandinavian/German area and the varied cuisine perfected by more recent generations. There is much fellowship to be had from 600 family-tested recipes; over 232 pages.

$ 6.00 Retail price
$ 2.00 Postage and handling
Make check payable to Goodwill Circle

YESTERDAY AND TODAY FRIENDLY CIRCLE COOKBOOK

Beulah Congregation Church
106-10th Street NE
Beulah, ND 58523

E-Mail: geider@Westriv.com
701-873-4779

We started our cookbook as a fun project. Our church, established in 1914, had never published a book. We have nearly 900 recipes from over 90% of our congregation in this 325-page book. Our ethnic section, mainly German, is a great hit.

$ 8.00 Retail price
$ 2.00 Postage and handling
Make check payable to Friendly Circle, Congregational Church

INDEX

Custer State Park, South Dakota

INDEX

Preserving America's Food Heritage

BEST OF THE BEST COOKBOOK SERIES

Best of the Best from
ALABAMA
288 pages, $16.95

Best of the Best from
ARKANSAS
288 pages, $16.95

Best of the Best from
COLORADO
288 pages, $16.95

Best of the Best from
FLORIDA
288 pages, $16.95

Best of the Best from
GEORGIA
336 pages, $16.95

Best of the Best from the
GREAT PLAINS
288 pages, $16.95

Best of the Best from
ILLINOIS
288 pages, $16.95

Best of the Best from
INDIANA
288 pages, $16.95

Best of the Best from
IOWA
288 pages, $16.95

Best of the Best from
KENTUCKY
288 pages, $16.95

Best of the Best from
LOUISIANA
288 pages, $16.95

Best of the Best from
LOUISIANA II
288 pages, $16.95

Best of the Best from
MICHIGAN
288 pages, $16.95

Best of the Best from
MINNESOTA
288 pages, $16.95

Best of the Best from
MISSISSIPPI
288 pages, $16.95

Best of the Best from
MISSOURI
304 pages, $16.95

Best of the Best from
NEW ENGLAND
368 pages, $16.95

Best of the Best from
NEW MEXICO
288 pages, $16.95

Best of the Best from
NORTH CAROLINA
288 pages, $16.95

Best of the Best from
OHIO
352 pages, $16.95

Best of the Best from
OKLAHOMA
288 pages, $16.95

Best of the Best from
PENNSYLVANIA
320 pages, $16.95

Best of the Best from
SOUTH CAROLINA
288 pages, $16.95

Best of the Best from
TENNESSEE
288 pages, $16.95

Best of the Best from
TEXAS
352 pages, $16.95

Best of the Best from
TEXAS II
352 pages, $16.95

Best of the Best from
VIRGINIA
320 pages, $16.95

Best of the Best from
WISCONSIN
288 pages, $16.95

Cookbooks listed above have been completed as of January 1, 2000.

Special discount offers available!
(See previous page for details.)

To order by credit card, call toll-free **1-800-343-1583** or send check or money order to:
QUAIL RIDGE PRESS • P. O. Box 123 • Brandon, MS 39043
Visit our website at **www.quailridge.com** to order online!

- -

ⓠ Order form

Send completed form and payment to:
QUAIL RIDGE PRESS • P. O. Box 123 • Brandon, MS 39043

❑ Check enclosed

Charge to: ❑ Visa ❑ MasterCard
❑ Discover ❑ American Express

Card #_____

Expiration Date _____

Signature _____

Name _____

Address _____

City/State/Zip_____

Phone # _____

Qty.	Title of Book (State)	Total

Subtotal	_____
7% Tax for MS residents	_____
Postage ($3.00 any number of books)	+ 3.00
Total	_____